8th

Government

&

Not-For-Profit

Accounting

For the US CPA Exam

목차

Chapter 08 | Ratio Analysis

서문 · Preface

Government & Not-For-Profit Accounting for the US CPA exam 의 특징입니다.

● WHO?

미국 공인회계사 시험을 응시하는 수험생을 대상으로 한 교재이다. 미국 공인회계사 시험 4과목 중 하나인 'Financial Accounting & Reporting (FAR)' 과목에서 중요한 부분을 차지하고 있는 정부, 비영리단체 및 파트너십의 회계처리와 기업회계의 연결재무제표 작성의 영역을 대비하기 위한 교재이다.

● WHAT?

미국공인회계사 시험의 추세 및 난이도에 맞게 구성된 내용으로 장마다 미국 공인회계사 시험에 출제되는 'Task-Based Simulation' 유형의 문제를 대비하기 위한 다양한 문제를 수록하였다.

● SMART

미국공인회계사 오랜 강의 경력의 경험과 노하우를 압축한 교재이다. 본 교재와 강의로 공부한 수험생들의 재무회계의 합격률이 최근 70%를 넘고 있으며 점수도 90점 이상을 넘는 고득점을 많이 받고 있다. 스마트한 교재와 강의로 스마트한 합격을 기원한다.

● CHAPTER

학습의 난이도에 맞추어 본서의 순서는 구성되었다. 정부회계, 비영리회계 및 파트너십회계에 대해서 학습한 후 연결재무제표작성, 상장기업의 재무제표 및 재무제표분석에 대해서 학습하게 될 것이다.

● ADVANCED

회계는 어려운 것! 하지만 이해하면 세상이 쉬워진다!

폴 부르제 (Paul Bourget)
"One must live the way one thinks or end up thinking the way one has lived."
"생각하는 대로 살지 않으면, 사는 대로 생각하게 된다."

공인회계사 / 미국공인회계사 / 미국재무분석사(CFA)
김용석.

CBT Introduction

I. CBT 과목구성

미국 공인회계사 시험은 2004년도에 PBT에서 CBT로 변경이 되었으며, 2017년에는 TBS(Task-Based Simulation)의 비중을 높인 새로운 방식으로 변경되었다. 2023년에 시험제도는 새롭게 변경이 되어 2024년 1월 1일 이후의 시험은 아래의 표와 같다.

Section	Section time	MCQ	TBS
AUD-Core	4 hours	50%(78)	50%(7)
FAR-Core	4 hours	50%(50)	50%(7)
REG-Core	4 hours	50%(72)	50%(8)
BAR-Discipline	4 hours	50%(50)	50%(7)
ISC-Discipline	4 hours	60%(82)	40%(6)
TCP-Discipline	4 hours	50%(68)	50%(7)

MCQ : Multiple Choices Questions
TBS: Task-Based Simulation

The CPA licensure model requires all candidates to pass three Core exam sections and one Discipline exam section of a candidate's choosing.

The Core exam sections assess the knowledge and skills that all newly licensed CPAs (nlCPAs) need in their role to protect the public interest. The three Core exam sections, each four hours long, are: Auditing and Attestation(AUD), Financial Accounting and Reporting (FAR) and Taxation and Regulation(REG).

The Discipline exam sections assess the knowledge and skills in the respective Discipline domain applicable to nlCPAs in their role to protect the public interest.The three Discipline exam sections, each four hours long, are: Business Analysis and Reporting (BAR), Information Systems and Controls (ISC) and Tax Compliance and Planning (TCP).

	Content Area
Area I	Financial Reporting (30~40%)
Area II	Select Balance Sheet Accounts (30~40%)
Area III	Select Transactions (25~35%)

● FAR 과목에서 다루는 내용은 다음과 같다.

(1) FASB GAAP에 의한 기업회계처리 및 재무제표

(2) GASB GAAP에 의한 정부회계처리 및 재무제표

(3) FASB GAAP에 의한 비영리회계처리 및 재무제표

(4) SEC Regulatory Reporting : 10-Q, 10-K

(5) AICPA에 의한 비상장기업 회계처리 및 재무제표

● Area I (Financial Reporting)에서 다루는 내용은 다음과 같다.

• General-purpose financial reporting and ratios and performance metrics applicable to for-profit entities and not-for-profit entities prepared under the FASB Accounting Standards Codification.

• Disclosures specific to public companies including earnings per share prepared under the FASB Accounting Standards Codification and the interim, annual and periodic filing requirements for U.S. registrants in accordance with the rules of the U.S. SEC.

- Financial statements prepared under special purpose frameworks as described in AU-C Section 800 of the Codification of Statements on Auditing Standards.

- State and local government concepts including measurement focus, basis of accounting and determining the appropriate funds to record activities in accordance with the GASB Codification of Governmental Accounting and Financial Reporting Standards.

- Area II (Select Balance Sheet Accounts)에서 다루는 내용은 다음과 같다.

  - Cash and cash equivalents.

  - Trade receivables.

  - Inventory.

  - Property, plant and equipment.

  - Investments, including financial assets at fair value, financial assets at amortized cost and equity method investments.

  - Intangible assets, with a focus on finite-lived intangible assets.

  - Payables and accrued liabilities.

  - Long-term debt, including notes and bonds payable and debt covenant calculations.

  - Equity transactions, specifically focusing on equity issuance, stock dividends, stock splits and treasury stock.

- Area III (Select Transactions)에서 다루는 내용은 다음과 같다.

  - Accounting changes and error corrections.

  - Contingencies and commitments.

  - Revenue recognition, specifically focusing on recalling and applying the five-step model and accounting for contributions received by not-for-profit entities.

  - Accounting for income taxes.

  - Fair value measurement concepts and classification within the fair value hierarchy.

  - Leases, specifically focusing on recalling and applying lessee accounting requirements.

  - Subsequent events.

Government & Not-For-Profit Accounting For the **US CPA** Exam

Governmental Accounting

Governmental Accounting

01 Introduction

1 정부회계의 의의

회계는 자본시장의 발달과 함께 투자 및 신용 의사결정에 유용한 정보를 제공하는 것으로 발전하고 있다. 회계는 회계실체에 따라 기업회계와 정부회계로 구분되는데 기업회계가 주주와 채권자의 경제적 의사결정을 위한 정보제공을 목적으로 한다면 정부회계는 정부(국가 또는 지방자치단체)의 경제적, 정치적 및 사회적 의사결정을 위한 다양한 이해관계자들에게 정보를 제공하는 것을 목적으로 한다.

정부회계는 중앙정부나 지방자치단체와 같은 정부조직의 재정활동에 대한 회계를 말한다. 정부조직의 재정활동은 국방, 치안, 교육과 같은 서비스를 제공하기 위하여 조세를 부과하거나 채권 등을 발행하여 재원을 조달하는 사용하는 활동을 말한다. 정부회계가 기업회계와 다른 특징은 다음과 같다.

(1) 비영리

정부조직은 민간기업과 달리 영리추구를 목적으로 하지 않고 공공서비스를 제공하는 것을 목적으로 한다. 정부는 기업처럼 수익이 비용을 초과하는 순이익을 보인다고 해서 정부의 기능을 잘 수행했다고 할 수 없다.

(2) 소유권

민간기업의 주인인 주주는 기업을 팔거나 해산할 수 있지만 정부의 주인인 국민은 정부를 팔거나 해산할 수 없다.

(3) 법령

정부의 서비스는 공권력에 의해 집행되기 때문에 법령에 의해서 강한 통제를 받는다. 정부 서비스를 위한 지출은 예산에 의하여 통제된다.

2 정부회계의 정보이용자

(1) Council

민간기업은 기업의 소유주인 주주가 재무제표를 가장 활발하게 이용하며, 정부회계는 국민을 대표하는 의회가 가장 중요한 정보이용자가 된다. 정부의 수탁책임과 서비스 활동의 효율적인 이행여부 등이 가장 중요한 정보인 것이다.

(2) Investors and creditors

정부에서 채권을 발행하여 사업을 추진하는 경우, 이를 취득하는 투자자는 해당 정부의 재무상태에 대한 정보를 필요로 한다.

(3) Citizenry (taxpayers and voters)

납세자는 자신이 납부한 세금이 정당하고 효율적으로 사용되는지에 대한 정보를 필요로 하며 유권자는 자신이 선출한 공직자가 임무를 유능하게 수행하는 지에 대한 정보를 필요로 한다.

(4) Legislative and oversight bodies

정부기관 중 상급기관은 자신이 감독하는 하급기관에 대한 재무적 정보를 필요로 한다. 특히 중앙정부는 지방자치단체에게 지원하는 국고보조금의 사용에 대한 정보를 필요로 한다.

3 미국 정부회계의 의의

　미국 기업회계는 1930년내의 미국 대공황을 계기로 발전되었다면 미국의 정부회계는 1970년에 지방정부 중에서 재정규모가 가장 큰 뉴욕시의 파산위기를 계기로 발전하게 되었다. 1973년에 NCGA(National Council on Governmental Accounting)에서 정부의 재무제표에 대한 회계기준 (GAAP)을 제정하였고 1984년부터는 미국 GASB (Governmental Accounting Standard Board)에서 회계기준(GAAP)을 제정하고 있다. 특히, GASB Statement No. 34는 미국 정부회계 역사상 가장 획기적인 내용으로, 정부도 기업과 마찬가지로 재무정보를 발생주의를 적용하여 엄격하게 보고하는 것을 강조하고 있다.

　정부회계기준위원회(GASB)는 미국의 주정부 및 지방정부의 회계기준을 제정하고 있으며 미국의 기업, 정부 및 비영리단체의 회계기준을 제정하는 기관을 요약하면 다음과 같다. 단, 연방정부 회계는 본서의 범위에서 제외한다.

Corporation		FASB
State and local government		GASB
NFP	Private	FASB
	Public	GASB

　미국정부가 적용하여야 할 회계기준의 체계순서는 다음과 같다.

GAAP hierarchy for all state and local governmental entities

Category A	GASB Statement(GASBS)
Category B	GASB technical bulletins GASB Implementation Guides Literature of the AICPA cleared by the GASB

※ GASB Interpretation : 2016년도부터 폐지

4 정부의 기초지식

(1) 대한민국 조세의 분류

1) 과세주체
- 국세 : 국가가 부과하는 세금
- 지방세 : 지방자치단체가 부과하는 세금

2) 세수의 용도가 정해져 있는가?
- 보통세 : 일반경비에 충당하는 세금
- 목적세 : 특정경비에 충당하는 세금

3) 납세의무자가 누구인가?
- 직접세 : 납세의무자와 세금부담자가 동일한 세금
- 간접세 : 납세의무자와 세금부담자가 다른 세금

	과세주체	세수용도	납세의무자
부가가치세	국세	보통세	간접세
종합소득세	국세	보통세	직접세
법인세	국세	보통세	직접세
취득세 및 등록면허세	지방세	보통세	직접세
재산세	지방세	보통세	직접세
교육세	국세	목적세	직접세
상속세 및 증여세	국세	보통세	직접세

(2) 미국 정부의 종류

미국 정부는 행정, 입법 및 사법권의 분리에 따라 다음 3가지로 구분된다.

1) Federal government (연방정부)
2) State government (주정부)
3) Local government (지방정부)

미국은 50개의 주(states)와 1개의 특별구(District of Columbia)로 이루어져 있으며, State 아래 단위의 행정구역은 County로 3,000개 이상이 있다.

(3) 정부의 수익구조

정부의 수익은 비교환수익과 교환수익으로 분류 된다.

1) Non-exchange transaction (비교환수익)

직접적인 반대급부 없이 발생하는 수익   ex) tax, penalty, grant, donation

2) Exchange transaction (교환수익)

정부가 재화용역을 공급하고 대가를 받은 수익   ex) user charge

(4) 미국 조세의 분류

Federal (연방세)	State (주세)	Local (지방세)
- Individual income tax - Corporate income tax - Estate & gift tax - FICA & Medicare tax	- Sales tax - Individual income tax - Corporate income tax	- Property tax - Sales tax - Consumption tax - Individual income tax - Corporate income tax

※ Sales tax는 재화의 판매에 수반되는 조세로서 한국의 부가가치세와 유사하며 보통 5%~9%의 범위 내에서 State마다 세율이 다르다.

(5) 정부회계의 보고실체

정부회계의 보고 실체는 일반목적정부(General government)와 특별목적정부(Special government)로 나누어 다음과 같이 분류한다.

General government	Special government
1) State 2) County 3) Sub-county 　① Municipality : City, Borough, Village 　② Township : Town, Township	1) School district 2) Special district

5 정부회계와 기업회계의 차이점

(1) Fund accounting

펀드회계란 정부의 자원을 펀드별로 구분하여 회계처리 및 재무보고를 하여야 한다.

(2) Modified accrual accounting

정부 펀드 중 일부는 발생주의가 아닌 수정발생주의로 회계처리를 하여 재무제표를 작성하여야 한다.

(3) Budgetary accounting

예산회계는 정부가 예산수립을 하여 그 내용을 회계처리 하여 보고하는 과정이다.

(4) Two-types financial statements

정부는 펀드 재무제표와 통합 재무제표의 두 종류 재무제표를 작성하여야 한다.

6 Accounting cycle

정부회계는 기업회계와 마찬가지로 다음과 같은 회계순환과정을 가진다.

---

1. Analyze each transaction
2. Journalizing
3. Posting : Transferring journal entries to the ledger account.
4. Unadjusted trial balance (수정전 시산표 작성)
5. Adjusting entries (수정분개)
6. Adjusted Trial balance (수정후 시산표 작성)
7. Financial statement (재무제표의 작성)
8. Closing Entries (마감분개)

정부회계는 기업회계와 마찬가지로 총 계정원장(general ledger)의 기록을 위하여 통제계정(control accounts)을 사용한다.

A control account is a summary account in the general ledger. This account contains aggregated totals for transactions that are individually stored in subsidiary-level ledger accounts.

A/R subsidiary-level ledger	General ledger
Customer 1 : $200 Customer 2: 100 Customer 3: 150	A/R Control : $450

Revenue subsidiary-level ledger	General ledger
Taxes : $200 Fines : 100 Grant : 150	Revenue Control : $450

※ Closing Entries

마감분개는 수익과 비용 계정을 제거하여 자본에 기록하는 과정이다.

Permanent or real account: assets, liabilities and equity

Temporary or nominal account: revenues and expenses

	Dr	Cr
Revenue-control	100	
Expense-control		90
Retained earnings (plug)		10

ex) 수익 100, 비용 90의 마감분개는 다음과 같다.

▶ 정부회계는 Fund Balance 또는 Net Position에 마감한다.

7 GASB Concepts Statement

(1) Financial reporting objectives

Governmental financial reporting should provide information to assist users in assessing accountability and making economic, social, and political decisions.

(2) Accountability

재산의 관리를 위탁받은 경영자나 정부조직이 수탁책임(stewardship)을 회계정보로 보고 하는 것을 회계보고책임(accountability)이라고 한다.

(3) Interperiod equity

Financial reporting should provide information to determine whether current—year revenues were sufficient to pay for current—year services.

기간 간의 형평성은 한 해의 세입이 그 해의 서비스제공을 위한 지출을 감당하기에 충분한 지에 대한 여부와 그해의 납세자가 제공받은 서비스의 원가가 장래의 납세자에 게 떠넘겨졌 는지에 대한 여부에 대한 정보이다.

(4) Fiscal accountability

Financial reporting should demonstrate whether resources were obtained and used in accordance with the entity's legally adopted budget.

적법성은 정부가 자원을 조달하고 지출한 내용이 예산에 따라 적법하게 이루에 겼는지를 나타내며, 법규나 계약의 내용과 합치되는지를 나타낸다.

(5) Operation accountability

Financial reporting should provide information to assist users in assessing the service efforts, costs, and accomplishments of the governmental entity.

운영의 효율성은 정부가 제공한 서비스의 원가가 얼마이며 각 부서가 업무를 얼마나 효율 적으로 수행했는지를 판단할 수 있는 정부를 제공하는 것을 말한다.

(6) Basic characteristics of financial information

1) Understandability

Information in financial reports should be expressed as simply as possible

2) Reliability

Information in financial reports should be verifiable and free from bias and should faithfully represent what it purports to represent.

3) Relevance

Information is relevant if it is capable of making a difference in a user's assessment of a problem, condition, or event.

4) Timeliness

If financial reports are to be useful, they must be issued soon enough after the reported events to affect decisions.

5) Consistency

Financial reports should be consistent over time.

6) Comparability

Financial reports should be comparable. This does not imply that similarly designated governments perform the same functions.

(7) Elements of Financial statements

1) Assets

Assets are resources with present service capacity that the government presently con-trols.

2) Liabilities

Liabilities are present obligations to sacrifice resources that the government has little or no discretion to avoid.

3) Deferred outflow of resources

A deferred outflow of resources is a consumption of net assets by the government that is applicable to a future reporting period.

4) Deferred inflow of resources

A deferred inflow of resources is an acquisition of net assets by the government that is applicable to a future reporting period.

5) Net position

Net position is the residual of all other elements presented in a statement of finan-cial position.

> Assets + Deferred outflow of resources
> = Liabilities + Deferred inflow of resources + Net position

6) Outflow of resources

An outflow of resources is a consumption of net assets by the government that is ap-plicable to the reporting period.

7) Inflow of resources

An inflow of resources is an acquisition of net assets by the government that is appli-cable to the reporting period.

> Inflow of resources − Outflow of resources = Changes in Net position

Example-1

In the government-wide financial statement, the statement of net position, deferred outflows of resources are presented

a. As a part of liabilities.
b. As a part of equity.
c. In a separate section following assets.
d. In a separate section following liabilities.

정답 : c

Deferred outflows of resources는 자산과 별도로 표시한다.

Example-2

At the end of the fiscal year, a state government reported capital assets of $20 million, accumulated depreciation of $5 million, current assets of $2 million, liabilities of $7 million, deferred inflows of resources of $3 million and deferred outflows of resources of $1 million. What amount should the government report as the total net position in its government-wide financial statements?

정답

Assets = 20 − 5 + 2 = 17
Net position = 17 + 1 − (7 + 3) = $8 million

02 ⟩ Fund accounting

1 Definition

미국 정부회계에서 가장 중요한 개념이 펀드회계이다. 펀드회계는 자원의 사용목적과 제약에 따라 각각의 펀드를 설정하며, 설정된 각각의 펀드를 회계실체로 하여 수입과 지출 등의 회계처리를 별도로 하는 시스템이다. 각 펀드는 각 단위회계실체로서 자체적으로 복식부기 형태의 독립적인 장부체계를 갖는다.

> Fund is a sum of money or other resources segregated for the purpose of carrying on specific activities. Fund is an independent fiscal and accounting entity and each fund is self—balancing and is a separate entity having its own financial statements.

2 Types of funds

미국 주 및 지방 정부의 경우 펀드를 크게 정부형 펀드, 사업형 펀드, 수탁형 펀드로 구분하여 각 유형별 펀드는 다음과 같이 세분류한다.

Governmental fund	General fund (GF) Special revenue fund (SRF) Capital project fund (CPF) Debt service fund (DSF) Permanent fund (PF)
Proprietary fund	Enterprise fund (EF) Internal service fund (ISF)
Fiduciary fund	Pension trust fund (PTF) Investment trust fund (ITF) Private-purpose trust fund (PPTF) Custodial Fund (CF)

3 Governmental fund

Account for activities that provide public with services financed by taxes.

정부형 펀드는 주로 조세수입과 정부활동을 위한 세출을 기록하기 위한 펀드를 말하며, 다음의 다섯 종류의 펀드로 구성된다.

(1) General Fund (GF)

한국의 일반예산에 해당되는 펀드로 다른 펀드에서 특별히 규정하지 않는 모든 자금의 변동을 기록하고 관리하는 펀드이다.

- Accounts for ordinary operations which are financed from taxes and all transactions not accounted for in some other fund are accounted for in this fund
- Example: police department, fire department

(2) Capital Projects Fund (CPF)

정부형 자원 중에서 유형 자산의 취득 또는 건설목적으로 특정되어 있는 자원을 보고하는 펀드로서 다음과 같은 특징이 있다.

- Capital projects funds are used to account for and report financial resources that are restricted, committed, or assigned to expenditure for capital outlays, including the acquisition or construction of capital facilities and other capital assets.
- Capital projects funds exclude those types of capital-related outflows financed by proprietary funds or fiduciary funds
- Example : Bond proceeds for construction of new City Hall Building

(3) Debt Service Fund (DSF)

정부형 자원 중에서 지방채의 원금과 이자상환의 목적으로 특정되어 있는 자원을 보고하는 펀드로서 다음과 같은 특징이 있다.

- Debt service funds are used to account for and report financial resources that are restricted, committed, or assigned to expenditure for principal and interest on all general obligation debt. Financial resources that are being accumulated for principal and interest maturing in future years also should be reported in debt service funds.

- Debt service funds should be used to report resources if legally mandated.
- Example : Tax dedicated to servicing general obligation bonds

(4) Special Revenue Fund (SRF)

정부형 자원 중에서 capital project와 debt service 목적을 제외한 목적이 특정되어 있는 자원을 보고하는 펀드로서 다음과 같은 특징이 있다.

- Special revenue funds are used to account for and report the proceeds of specific revenue sources that are restricted or committed to expenditure for specified purposes other than debt service or capital projects.
- Earmarked taxes (목적세)
  ① Motor-fuel tax
  ② Hotel tax used to promote tourist

(5) Permanent fund (PF)

정부형 자원 중에서 원금은 그대로 유지하고 투자수익으로만 사용이 특정되어 있는 자원을 보고하는 펀드로서 다음과 같은 특징이 있다.

- Permanent funds should be used to account for and report resources that are restricted to the extent that only earnings, and not principal, may be used for purposes that support the reporting government's programs—that is, for the benefit of the government or its citizenry.
- Permanent funds do not include private-purpose trust funds, which should be used to report situations in which the government is required to use the principal or earnings for the benefit of individuals, private organizations, or other governments.
- Example : Citizen's gifts for maintenance of city's cemetery

4 Proprietary fund

Account for business—type activities that derive their revenue from user charge

사업형 펀드는 정부가 민간기업과 같은 사업을 하는 데 따르는 펀드로서 다음의 두 가지 종류의 펀드로 구성된다.

(1) Enterprise Funds (EF)

정부가 시민에게 민간기업과 같은 재화를 판매하거나 용역을 제공하는 데 따르는 자금을 관리하기 위한 펀드로서, 상수도나 하수도, 지하철 같은 서비스를 제공하는 데 필요한 자금을 관리하는 것이다.

- Account for the operation of governmental facilities and services that are intended to be primarily from user charges.
- Examples : water and sewer utilities, transportation systems, lottery

(2) Internal Service Funds (ISF)

한 정부기관이 다른 정부기관에 민간기업과 같은 서비스를 유상으로 제공하는 데 따르는 자금을 관리하기 위한 펀드로서, 예를 들면 한 정부기관에서 자동차를 구입한 후 이를 다른 정부기관에게 임차하는 서비스를 제공하는 데 필요한 자금을 관리하는 것이다.

- Account for goods and services provided to other departments within governmental unit on a cost reimbursement fee basis.
- Examples : Motor pool, EDP processing , Self insurance

5 Fiduciary funds (신탁형 펀드)

> The assets associated with the activity have one or more of the following characteristics:
> (1) The assets are administered through a trust in which the government itself is not a beneficiary (Trust)
> (2) The assets are for the benefit of individuals and the government does not have administrative involvement with the assets (Agent)

신탁형 펀드는 정부가 다른 수혜자를 위하여 자산을 관리하는 펀드로서 다음의 네 가지 종류의 펀드로 구성된다.

(1) Pension Trust Funds (PTF)

공무원 연금을 관리하는 펀드로서 다음과 같은 특징이 있다.

- Used to report fiduciary activities for pension plans and other post-employment benefit (OPEB) plans that are administered through trusts.
- Examples : Public Employees Retirement Systems (PERS)

(2) Investment Trust Funds (ITF)

타 정부기관의 투자업무를 대행하는 펀드로서 다음과 같은 특징이 있다.

- Used to report fiduciary activities from the external portion of investment pools that are held in a trust
- Examples : Investment pools for all cities within its borders.

(3) Private-purpose Trust Funds (PPTF)

pension trust와 investment trust를 제외한 trustee의 업무를 보고하는 펀드이다.

- Used to report all fiduciary activities that are not required to be reported in PTF or ITF and are held in a trust.
- May be non-expendable or expendable
- Non-expendable : The principal is intact and cannot be used

(4) Custodial funds (CF)

정부가 단기간 자산을 맡아 이를 다른 기관이나 민간부문에 분배하는 펀드이다.

- Used to report fiduciary activities that are not required to be reported in PTF, ITF, or PPTF.
- Examples : Property tax collections for other cities
  ⇨ replace an agency fund with a custodial fund (2019)

6 Financial Reporting (GASBS 34)

정부재무보고서의 양식은 다음과 같다.

---

(1) Management's discussion and analysis (MD &A)

(2) Government−wide F/S

(3) Fund F/S
   1) Governmental funds
   2) Proprietary funds
   3) Fiduciary funds

(4) Notes to F/S

(5) Required Supplementary Information (other than MD&A)

※ (1)과 (5)는 재무보고서의 필수사항이지만 재무제표는 아니다.

7 Measurement focus

펀드는 자원의 측정목적에 따라 spending과 capital maintenance로 분류된다.

(1) Spending

1) Financial resource

   기업회계의 운전자본과 유사한 개념으로 지출 가능한 자원을 의미하며 재무상태표에 fixed asset과 long-term debt은 보고하지 않는다.

2) 재무상태표의 자본을 "Fund balance"라고 한다.

3) 수익과 지출을 "Modified Accrual basis"로 측정한다.

4) Governmental funds (5개)가 여기에 해당된다.

(2) Capital maintenance

1) Economic resource

   기업회계의 자산 및 부채와 동일하며 정부의 모든 자원을 측정한 것으로 재무상태표에 fixed asset과 long-term debt를 보고한다.

2) 재무상태표의 자본을 "Net position"이라고 한다.

3) 수익과 비용을 "Accrual basis"로 측정한다.

4) Proprietary funds (2개) & fiduciary funds(4개)가 여기에 해당된다.

5) Government-wide F/S가 여기에 해당된다.

	Governmental	Proprietary	Fiduciary	G-wide F/S
Focus	Spending	Capital maintenance		
Resource	Financial resource	Economic resource		
Accounting	Modified Accrual basis	Accrual basis		

8 Financial statements

펀드별 재무제표와 통합 재무제표의 종류는 다음과 같다.

Governmental funds	1) Balance Sheet 2) Statement of Revenue, Expenditures and Changes in Fund Balances
Proprietary funds	1) Statement of Net Position 2) Statement of Revenue, Expenses and Changes in Net Position 3) Statement of Cash Flow
Fiduciary funds	1) Statement of Fiduciary Net Position 2) Statement of Changes in Fiduciary Net Position
Government-wide F/S	1) Statement of Net Position 2) Statement of Activities

※ 재무제표의 구체적인 사례는 부록을 참고한다.

03 ▶ Modified accrual accounting

1 Financial statements

수정발생주의를 사용하는 정부형 펀드의 재무제표를 요약하면 다음과 같다.

(1) Governmental Fund Balance Sheet

> ① Assets (current assets)   xxx
> ② Deferred outflows of resources   xxx
> ③ Liabilities (current liabilities)   xxx
> ④ Deferred inflows of resources   xxx
> ⑤ Fund Balance   xxx

(2) Statement of Revenue, Expenditures and Changes in Fund Balances

> ① Revenues   xxx
> ② Expenditures   (xxx)
> ③ Other Financing Sources   xxx
>   Other Financing Uses   (xxx)
> ④ Special Items   xxx
> ⑤ Changes in Fund Balance   xxx

2 Modified accrual accounting

	Modified accrual accounting	Accrual accounting
Revenue	Measurable and Available	Earned and Realized
Expense/ Expenditure*	Measurable and Incurred	Matching

* 수정발생주의에서는 expense가 아닌 expenditure로 용어를 사용한다.
  수정발생주의는 재무적 자원을 이용하여 지출 가능한 자원을 측정하는 회계처리 방법으로 지출은 발생 즉시 인식하며 수익은 지출에 사용가능한 시점에 인식한다.

3 Capital assets

수정발생주의는 유형 자산의 취득시점에서 "expenditure"로 인식하고 감가상각을 하지 않으며 매각시의 매각대금은 "special items"로 회계처리한다.

Example-3

20X1년 1월 1일 내용연수 5년인 유형 자산을 $100에 취득하여 20X2년 1월1일에 $90에 처분하였다.

	Modified accrual	Accrual basis

1/1/20X1	Dr) Expenditure 100
	    Cr) Cash 100
		Dr) Capital assets 100
		    Cr) Cash 100

12/31/20X1	No entry	Dr) Expense 20 Cr) Accumulated Depreciation 20

1/1/20X2	Dr) Cash 90
	    Cr) Special items 90
		Dr) Cash 90
		    Accumulated Depreciation 20
		    Cr) Capital assets 100
		       Special items 10

4 Bond payable

수정발생주의는 지방채권 발행시점에서 "other financing sources (OFS)"로 인식하고 이자와 원금의 상환시에는 "expenditure"로 회계처리한다. 지방채의 회계처리를 거래별로 수정발생주의와 발생주의를 비교하면 다음과 같다.

   ※ General Obligation Bonds(GOB) : 정부형 활동을 지원하기 위하여 발행한 채권

      Revenue Bonds(RB) : 사업형 활동을 지원하기 위하여 발행한 채권

Example-4

20X1년 1월 1일 지방채를 $100에 액면 발행하였고 20X1년 12월31일에 이자 $10와 원금 $20를 상환하였다.

	Modified accrual	Accrual basis

1/1/20X1	Dr) Cash 100
	   Cr) OFS 100
		Dr) Cash 100
		   Cr) Bond payable 100

12/31/20X1	Dr) Expenditure 10
	   Cr) Cash 10
		Dr) Expense 10
		   Cr) Cash 10

	Dr) Expenditure 20
	   Cr) Cash 20
		Dr) Bond payable 20
		   Cr) Cash 20

※ 수정발생주의에서는 이자지급시기와 재무제표 작성시점이 불일치하여도 기간귀속에 따른 accrual을 하지 않는다.

5   Interfund transaction

펀드간의 자원의 이전은 각 펀드별로 회계처리를 하여야 하며 자원이 유입된 펀드는 "other financing sources (OFS)"로 인식하고 자원이 유출된 펀드는 "other financing uses (OFU)"로 인식한다.

Example-5

general fund에서 capital project fund로 $100의 현금이 이전되었다.

General Fund	Capital Project Fund

Dr) Transfer-out (OFU)   100
   Cr) Cash   100
	Dr) Cash 100
	   Cr) Transfer-in (OFS) 100

6 Inflow of resources

수정발생주의는 자원의 유입을 다음 항목으로 분류하여 보고한다.

Revenue	Other Financing Sources	Special items
- Tax - Grant - Fines - User charge	- Proceeds from LT Debt - Operating transfer-in	- Proceeds from sale of capital assets

※ Long-term debt : General obligation bond, Lease liability, Bond anticipation payable

7 Outflow of resources

수정발생주의는 자원의 유출을 다음 항목으로 분류하여 보고한다.

Expenditures	Other Financing Uses
- Operating activities - Acquisition of capital asset - Payment of interest and principal for LT Debt	- Operating transfer-out

04 ▶ Accrual accounting

1 Proprietary Funds

(1) Statement of Net Position

> ① Assets (all assets)
> ② Deferred outflows of resources
> ③ Liabilities (all liabilities)
> ④ Deferred inflows of resources
> ⑤ Net Position

(2) Statement of Revenues, Expenses and Changes in Net Position

> ① Operating revenues
> ② Operating expenses
> ③ Non-operating revenues (expenses)
> ④ Operating Transfer in (out)
> ⑤ Change in net position

(3) Statement of Cash Flows

> ① Cash Flows from Operating Activities
> ② Cash Flows from Noncapital Financing Activities
> ③ Cash Flows from Capital and Related Financing Activities
> ④ Cash Flows from Investing Activities
> ⑤ Change in Cash and Cash Equivalents

2 Fiduciary Funds

(1) Statement of Fiduciary Net Position

① Assets (all assets)
② Deferred outflows of resources
③ Liabilities (all liabilities)
④ Deferred inflows of resources
⑤ Net Position

(2) Statement of Changes in Fiduciary Net Position

① Additions
② Deductions
③ Change in net position

3 Government—wide Financial Statements

(1) Statement of Net Position

① Assets (all assets)
② Deferred outflows of resources
③ Liabilities (all liabilities)
④ Deferred inflows of resources
⑤ Net Position

(2) Statement of Activities

① Expenses
② Program Revenues
③ General Revenues
④ Change in net position

Example-6

01. Central County received proceeds from various towns and cities for capital projects financed by the county's long-term debt. A special tax was assessed by each local government, and a portion of the tax was properly restricted to repay the long-term debt of the county's capital projects. Central County should account for the restricted portion of the special tax in which of the following funds?

      A. Debt service fund   B. Enterprise fund
      C. Internal service fund   D. Capital projects fund

02. The following financial resources were among those received by Seco City during Year 1:
For acquisition of major capital facilities : $6,000,000
To create a nonexpendable trust to support a public cemetary : $2,000,000
With respect to the foregoing resources, what amount should be recorded in special revenue funds?

03. Receipts from a special tax levy to retire and pay interest on general obligation bonds should be recorded in which fund?
    A. Special revenue.   B. Capital projects.   C. General.   D. Debt service.

04. A city received a $9,000,000 federal grant to finance the construction of a homeless shelter. In which fund should the proceeds be recorded?
    A. Special revenue.   B. Permanent.   C. General.   D. Capital project.

05. Kew City received a $15,000,000 federal grant to finance the construction of a substance abuse rehabilitation center. The proceeds of this grant should be accounted for in the:

      A. Fiduciary funds.   B. Special revenue funds.
      C. General fund.   D. Capital projects funds.

06. In what fund type should the proceeds from special assessment bonds issued to finance construction of sidewalks in a new subdivision be reported?
      A. Capital projects fund.   B. Custodial fund.
      C. Special revenue fund.   D. Enterprise fund.

07. Stone Corp. donated investments to Pine City and stipulated that the income from the investments be used to acquire art for the city's museum. Which of the following funds should be used to account for the investments?
      A. Permanent fund.   B. Endowment fund.
      C. Special revenue fund.   D. Private purpose trust fund.

Example-6

08. Bay Creek's municipal motor pool maintains all city-owned vehicles and charges the various departments for the cost of rendering those services. In which of the following funds should Bay account for the cost of such maintenance?

    A. General fund.   B. Special assessment fund.

    C. Special revenue fund.   D. Internal service fund.

09. King City Council will be establishing a library fund. Library fees are expected to cover 55% of the library's annual resource requirements. King has decided that an annual determination of net income is desirable in order to maintain management control and accountability over the library. What type of fund should King establish in order to meet their measurement objectives?

    A. Special revenue fund.   B. Enterprise fund.

    C. Internal service fund.   D. General fund.

10. Kenn City obtained a municipal landfill and passed a local ordinance that required the city to operate the landfill so that the costs of operating the landfill, as well as the capital costs, are to be recovered with charges to customers. Which of the following funds should Kenn City use to report the activities of the landfill?

    A. Enterprise.   B. Internal service.   C. Special revenue.   D. Permanent.

11. Old Town added a water and sewer department to its municipal services. The department provided the services to the residents of Old Town and issued quarterly billings to customers. In which of the following types of funds would this activity be recorded?

    A. Special revenue   B. Enterprise   C. Permanent   D. Capital projects

12. The town of Hill operates municipal electric and water utilities. In which of the following funds should the operations of the utilities be accounted for?

    A. Enterprise fund.   B. Special revenue fund.

    C. Custodial fund.   D. Internal service fund.

13. Taxes collected and held by Franklin County for a separate school district would be accounted for in which fund?

    A. Custodial   B. Internal service   C. Special revenue   D. Trust

Government & Not-For-Profit Accounting For the US CPA Exam

Chapter 02

Not-for-Profit Accounting

Volume
8

Chapter 2

Not-for-Profit Accounting

01 ▶ Introduction

1 Not-for-profit entity

(1) Definition

비영리 조직은 다음 항목의 특징을 모두 가지고 있으며 이러한 점이 영리조직인 기업과는 구별된다.

1) Contributions of significant amounts of resources from resource providers

2) Operating purposes other than to provide goods or services at a profit

3) Absence of ownership interests like those of business entities.

(2) Major resources of NFPO

1) Contribution (=gifts, donation)

2) User charge

3) Investment income including dividend and interest

4) Government grants

2 Types of NFPO

(1) Universities and colleges

(2) Health care organizations

Hospitals, Nursing homes, Hospices

(3) Voluntary health and welfare organizations (VHWO)

United Way, Red Cross, the American Heart Association, Girl Scouts, YMCA

A NFPO that is formed for the purpose of performing voluntary services for various segments of society and that is tax exempt (organized for the benefit of the public), supported by the public, and operated on a not-for-profit basis.

(4) Other NFP organizations

Labor unions, Religious organization, Political parties, Foundations, Fraternal organizations, Museums, Libraries, Performing arts, AICPA

3 GAAP for NFPO

Private NFPO	Public NFPO
FASB	GASB

02 >> Financial statements for private NFPO

1 Financial statements for private NFPO (ASC 958)

(1) Financial statements for private NFPO

> 1) Statement of Financial Position
> 2) Statement of Activity
> 3) Statement of Cash Flows
> 4) Notes

(2) Comparative financial statements

FASB encourages but does not require comparative financial statements.

(3) Accrual basis

Accrual basis is required for private and public NFPO.

(4) Fund accounting

Fund accounting is not required for private NFPO but required for public NFPO.

2 Statement of financial position

(1) Format

<table>
<thead>
<tr><th colspan="3" align="center">Not-for-Profit Entity A
Statements of Financial Position
June 30 20X1 and 20X0
(in thousands)</th></tr>
<tr><th>Assets:</th><th>20X1</th><th>20X0</th></tr>
</thead>
<tbody>
<tr><td>Cash and cash equivalents</td><td>$4,575</td><td>$4,960</td></tr>
<tr><td>Accounts and interest receivable</td><td>2,130</td><td>1,670</td></tr>
<tr><td>Inventories and prepaid expenses</td><td>610</td><td>1,000</td></tr>
<tr><td>Contributions receivable</td><td>3,025</td><td>2,700</td></tr>
<tr><td>Shortterm investments</td><td>1,400</td><td>1,000</td></tr>
<tr><td>Assets restricted to investment in land, buildings, and equipment</td><td>5,210</td><td>4,560</td></tr>
<tr><td>Land, buildings, and equipment</td><td>61,700</td><td>63,590</td></tr>
<tr><td>Long-term investments</td><td>218,070</td><td>203,500</td></tr>
<tr><td>Total Assets</td><td>$296,720</td><td>$282,980</td></tr>
<tr><td colspan="3"></td></tr>
<tr><td>Liabilities and net assets:</td><td></td><td></td></tr>
<tr><td>Liabilities:</td><td></td><td></td></tr>
<tr><td>Accounts payable</td><td>$2,570</td><td>$1,050</td></tr>
<tr><td>Refundable advance</td><td></td><td>650</td></tr>
<tr><td>Grants payable</td><td>875</td><td>1,300</td></tr>
<tr><td>Notes payable</td><td></td><td>1,140</td></tr>
<tr><td>Annuity trust obligations</td><td>1,685</td><td>1,700</td></tr>
<tr><td>Long-term debt</td><td>5,500</td><td>6,500</td></tr>
<tr><td>Total liability</td><td>10,630</td><td>12,340</td></tr>
<tr><td colspan="3"></td></tr>
<tr><td>Net assets:</td><td></td><td></td></tr>
<tr><td>Without donor restrictions</td><td>92,600</td><td>84,570</td></tr>
<tr><td>With donor restrictions</td><td>193,490</td><td>186,070</td></tr>
<tr><td>Total net assets</td><td>286,090</td><td>270,640</td></tr>
<tr><td>Total liabilities and net assets</td><td>$296,720</td><td>$282,980</td></tr>
</tbody>
</table>

(2) Asset and liability

재무상태표의 자산과 부채는 기업회계와 동일하게 유동성(liquidity) 배열을 한다.

1) Assets and liabilities based on their relative liquidity

2) Cash and cash equivalents of donor-restricted endowment funds held temporarily until suitable long-term investment opportunities are identified are included in the classification long-term investments.

3) Cash and contributions receivable restricted by donors to investment in PPE are not included with the line items cash and cash equivalents or contributions receivable. Rather, those items are reported as assets restricted to investment in PPE and are sequenced closer to PPE.

4) Assets and liabilities may be arrayed by their relationship to net asset classes, classified as current and noncurrent, or arranged in other ways.

(3) Net assets

1) Classify and report net assets in two groups—net assets with donor restrictions and net assets without donor restrictions—based on the existence or absence of donor-imposed restrictions.

2) Net assets must be classified according to donor-imposed stipulations.

⇒ Internally designated funds for a specific purpose are considered unrestricted

(4) Net assets with donor restrictions

Purpose restriction	Support of particular operating activities
	Acquisition of long-lived assets
Time restriction	Use in a specified future period
Endowment	Principal must remain intact

3 Statement of activities

(1) Format-A

Not-for-Profit Entity A
Statement of Activities
Year Ended June 30, 20X1(in thousands)

Changes in net assets without donor restrictions:	
Revenues and gains:	
Contributions of cash and other financial assets	$ 6,790
Contributions of nonfinancial assets	1,850
Fees	5,200
Investment return, net	6,650
Gain on sale of equipment	200
Other	150
Total revenues and gains without donor restrictions	20,840
Net assets released from restrictions	
Satisfaction of program restrictions	8,990
Satisfactions of equipment acquisition restrictions	1,500
Expiration of time restrictions	1,250
Appropriation from donor endowment and subsequent satisfaction of any related donor restrictions	7,500
Total net assets released from restrictions	19,240
Total revenues, gains, and other support without donor restrictions	40,080
Expenses and losses:	
Salaries and benefits	15,115
Grants to other organizations	4,750
Supplies and travel	3,155
Services and professional fees	2,840
Office and occupancy	2,528
Depreciation	3,200
Interest	382
Total expenses	31,970
Fire loss on building	80
Total expenses and losses	32,050
Increase in net assets without donor restrictions	8,030
Changes in net assets with donor restrictions:	
Contributions of cash and other financial assets	7,430
Contributions of nonfinancial assets	960
Investment return, net	18,300
Actuarial loss on annuity trust obligations	(30)
Net assets released from restrictions	(19,240)
Increase in net assets with donor restriction	7,420
Increase in total net assets	15,450
Net assets at beginning of year	270,640
Net assets at end of year	$ 286,090

(2) Format-B

Format B (a multicolumn format) is as follows.

Not-for-Profit Entity A
Statement of Activities
Year Ended June 30, 20X1
(in thousands)

	Without Donor Restrictions	With Donor Restrictions	Total
Revenues, gains, and other support:			
~~Contributions~~	$ ~~8,640~~	$ ~~8,390~~	$ ~~17,030~~
Contributions of cash and other financial assets	$ 6,790	$ 7,430	$ 14,220
Contributions of nonfinancial assets	1,850	960	2,810
Fees	5,200		5,200
Investment return, net	6,650	18,300	24,950
Gain on sale of equipment	200		200
Other	150		150
Net assets released from restrictions (Note D):			
Satisfaction of program restrictions	8,990	(8,990)	
Satisfaction of equipment acquisition restrictions	1,500	(1,500)	
Expiration of time restrictions	1,250	(1,250)	
Appropriation from donor endowment and subsequent satisfaction of any related donor restrictions	7,500	(7,500)	
Total net assets released from restrictions	19,240	(19,240)	-
Total revenues, gains, and other support	40,080	7,450	47,530
Expenses and losses:			
Program A	13,296		13,296
Program B	8,649		8,649
Program C	5,837		5,837
Management and general	2,038		2,038
Fundraising	2,150		2,150
Total expenses (Note F)	31,970		31,970
Fire loss on building	80		80
Actuarial loss on annuity trust obligations		30	30
Total expenses and losses	32,050	30	32,080
Change in net assets	8,030	7,420	15,450
Net assets at beginning of year	84,570	186,070	270,640
Net assets at end of year	$ 92,600	$ 193,490	$ 286,090

Note: See paragraph 958-205-55-21 for the notes to financial statements.

(3) Format-C

Not-for-Profit Entity A
Statement of Revenue. Expenses. and
Other changes in Net Assets without Donor Restrictions
Year Ended June 30. 20X1(in thousands)

Revenues and gains without donor restrictions:	
Contributions of cash and other financial assets	$ 6,790
Contributions of nonfinancial assets	1,850
Fees	5,200
Investment return, net	6,650
Gain on sale of equipment	200
Other	150
Total revenues and gains without donor restrictions	20,840
Net assets released from restrictions	
Satisfaction of program restrictions	8,990
Satisfaction of equipment acquisition restrictions	1,500
Expiration of time restrictions	1,250
Appropriation from donor endowment and subsequent satisfaction of any related donor restrictions	7,500
Total net assets released from restrictions	19,240
Total revenues, gains, and other support without donor restrictions	40,080
Expenses and losses:	
Program A	13,296
Program B	8,649
Program C	5,837
Management and general	2,038
Fundraising	2,150
Total expenses	31,970
Fire loss on building	80
Total expenses and losses without donor restrictions	32,050
Increase in net assets without donor restrictions	$ 8,030

Not-for-Profit Entity A
Statement of Changes in Net Assets
Year Ended June 30. 20X1(in thousands)

Net assets without donor restrictions:	
Total revenues and gains	$ 20,840
Net assets released from restrictions	19,240
Total expenses and losses	(32,050)
Increase in net assets without donor restrictions	8,030
Net assets with donor restrictions:	
Contributions of cash and other financial assets	7,430
Contributions of nonfinancial assets	960
Investment return, net	18,300
Actuarial loss on annuity trust obligations	(30)
Net assets released from restrictions	(19,240)
Increase in net assets with donor restrictions	7,420
Increase in net assets	15,450
Net assets at beginning of year	270,640
Net assets at end of year	$ 286,090

(4) Summary

		Without	With	Total
Revenues & gains	Contribution	xxx	xxx	xxx
	User charges	xxx		xxx
	Investment returns	xxx	xxx	xxx
	Gain on sale of PPE	xxx		
	Reclassifications	xxx	(xxx)	
Expenses & losses	Program services	(xxx)		(xxx)
	Supporting activities	(xxx)		(xxx)
Changes in net assets		xxx	xxx	xxx

(5) Contributions

In the absence of a donor's explicit stipulation or circumstances surrounding the receipt of the contribution that make clear the donor's implicit restriction on use, contributions are reported as without donor restrictions revenues or gains. Donor-restricted contributions are reported as with donor restrictions revenues or gains.

An NFP should present contributed non-financial assets as a separate line item in the statement of activities, apart from contributions of cash and other financial assets.

(6) User charge

Fees from rendering services are without donor restrictions.

(7) Investment returns

Gains and losses on investments and dividends, interest, and other investment income should be reported in the period earned as increases in without donor restrictions net assets unless the use of the assets received is limited by donor-imposed restrictions. Donor-restricted investment income should be reported as an increase in with donor restrictions net assets.

explicit donor stipulations (O)	with donor restrictions net assets
explicit donor stipulations (X)	without donor restrictions net assets

Report investment return net of external and direct internal investment expenses and no longer require disclosure of those netted expenses.

(8) Endowment

일정금액을 투자만 하고 사용할 수 없는 기부금으로 아래와 같이 분류한다.

Regular endowment	기부자가 영구적 투자를 요구한 기부금 ⇨ with donor restrictions net assets
Term endowment	기부자가 한시적 투자를 요구한 기부금 ⇨ with donor restrictions net assets
Quasi-endowment	내부적으로 장기투자를 결정한 자원 ⇨ without donor restrictions net assets

(9) Reclassifications of net assets

1) Reclassifications shall be made if any of the following events occur:

a. The NFP fulfills the purposes for which the net assets were restricted.

b. Donor-imposed restrictions expire with the passage of time

2) If two or more temporary restrictions are imposed on a contribution, the effect of the expiration of those restrictions should be recognized in the period in which the last remaining restriction has expired.

A gift of a term endowment that is to be invested for five years has two temporary restrictions—a purpose restriction (to be invested) and a time restriction (for a period of five years). After five years of investing, the purpose restriction will be met and the time restriction will lapse. In Year 5, when that term endowment becomes unrestricted, a reclassification shall be reported to reflect the decrease in with donor restrictions net assets and the increase in without donor restrictions net assets.

3) If an expense is incurred for a purpose for which both without donor restrictions net assets and with donor restrictions net assets are available, a donor-imposed restriction is fulfilled to the extent of the expense incurred

4) Simultaneous Release Option

An NFP may elect a policy to report donor-restricted contributions whose restrictions are met in the same reporting period as the revenue is recognized as support within net assets without donor restrictions.

5) PPE Reclassification

There may be circumstances in which a donor restriction might extend beyond the point at which the PPE is placed in service. For example, a donor might specify that a donation restricted for the acquisition of PPE must continue to be used for a specified period of time. In such circumstances, the restriction would expire over the period of time that the asset is to be used.

(10) Reporting expenses

1) Expenses should be deducted from without donor restrictions column only.

2) Expenses should be reported by functional classification

비용의 기능별 분류는 사용목적에 따른 분류이며 다음 두 가지로 분류한다.

- program activities
- supporting activities

3) Combined costs (fund raising + programs) should be allocated.

(11) Program Activities

The activities that fulfill the purposes or mission for which the NFPO exists.

1) Universities - education, research

2) Hospitals - patient care, education

3) Union - labor negotiations, training

4) Day Care - Child care

(12) Supporting Activities

Supporting activities are all activities of a NFPO other than program services.

1) Management and general activities

2) Fundraising activities

3) Membership development activities

(13) Membership development activities

Membership development activities include soliciting for prospective members and membership dues, membership relations, and similar activities.

(14) Fundraising activities

Activities undertaken to induce potential donors to contribute resources.

- Publicizing and conducting fundraising campaigns
- Maintaining donor mailing lists
- Conducting special fundraising events
- Preparing and distributing fundraising manuals, instructions, and other materials
- Conducting other activities involved with soliciting contributions

(15) Management and general activities

Activities that are not identifiable with a single program, fundraising activity, or membership-development activity.

- Oversight
- Business management
- General record-keeping
- Budgeting
- Financing, including unallocated interest costs
- Soliciting funds other than contributions and membership dues
- Making announcements concerning appointments
- Producing and disseminating the annual report
- All other management and administration except for direct conduct of program services

(16) Disclosure

Reporting expenses by nature and function is useful in associating expenses with service efforts and accomplishments of NFPs.

All NFPs should report information about all expenses in one location

1) on the face of the statement of activities, or

2) as a schedule in the notes to financial statements, or

3) in a separate financial statement.

	Program Activities				Supporting Activities			
	A	B	C	Programs Subtotal	Management and General	Fund–Raising	Supporting Subtotal	Total Expenses
Salaries and benefits	$ 7,400	$ 3,900	$ 1,725	$ 13,025	$ 1,130	$ 960	$ 2,090	$ 15,115
Grants to other organizations	2,075	750	1,925	4,750				4,750
Supplies and travel	890	1,013	499	2,402	213	540	753	3,155
Services and professional fees	160	1,490	600	2,250	200	390	590	2,840
Office and occupancy	1,160	600	450	2,210	218	100	318	2,528
Depreciation	1,440	800	570	2,810	250	140	390	3,200
Interest	171	96	68	335	27	20	47	382
Total expenses	$ 13,296	$ 8,649	$ 5,837	$ 27,782	$ 2,038	$ 2,150	$ 4,188	$ 31,970

Example-1

A NFP received a cash donation of $10,000 to be used at the board of directors' discretion in 20X1. The board of directors stipulated that $10,000 would be used to create an endowment.

20X1	Cash	10,000	
	Contribution-without donor restrictions		10,000

⇒ 20X1 : change in without donor restrictions net assets   +10,000

Example-2

A NFP received a cash donation of $20,000 in 20X1 from donor specifying that the amount would be used in 20X2.

20X1	Cash	20,000	
	Contribution-with donor restrictions		20,000
20X2	Reclassification-with donor restrictions	20,000	
	Reclassification-without donor restrictions		20,000

⇒ 20X1 : change in with donor restrictions net assets   +20,000
20X2 : change in with donor restrictions net assets   −20,000
         change in without donor restrictions net assets   +20,000

Example-3

A donor gave $100,000 for the purpose of creating as a regular endowment in 20X1. During 20X2, the NFP purchased investments of $100,000

20X1	Cash	100,000	
	Contribution-with donor restrictions		100,000
20X1	Long-term Investment	100,000	
	Cash		100,000

⇒ 20X1 : change in with donor restrictions net assets   +100,000

    20X2 : change in with donor restrictions net assets   no effect

☞ 영구제한 기부금은 재분류조정 하지 않는다.

Example-4

During 20X1, a NFP received a cash donation of $150,000 restricted by donor to the acquisition of equipment. The equipment of $90,000 was purchased in 20X2.

20X1	Cash (Assets restricted to investment in PPE)	150,000	
	Contribution-with donor restrictions		150,000
20X2	Equipment	90,000	
	Cash (Assets restricted to investment in PPE)		90,000
	Reclassification-with donor restrictions	90,000	
	Reclassification-without donor restrictions		90,000

⇒ 20X1 : change in with donor restrictions net assets   +150,000

    20X2 : change in with donor restrictions net assets   −90,000

          change in without donor restrictions net assets   +90,000

Example-5

During 20X1, a NFP received a cash donation of $150,000 restricted by donor to be used for research. The donation of $90,000 was used for research in 20X2.

20X1	Cash	150,000	
	Contribution-with donor restrictions		150,000
20X2	Program-research expense	90,000	
	Cash		90,000
	Reclassification-with donor restrictions	90,000	
	Reclassification-without donor restrictions		90,000

⇒ 20X1 : change in with donor restrictions net assets   +150,000

   20X2 : change in with donor restrictions net assets   −90,000

         change in without donor restrictions net assets   0

4 Statement of cash flows

(1) Format-direct method

Not-for-Profit Entity A
Statement of Cash Flows
Year Ended June 30, 20X1(in thousands)

Cash flows from operating activities:	
Cash received from service recipients	$ 5,020
Cash received from contributors	8,030
Cash collected on promises to give	2,615
Interest and dividends received	8,570
Miscellaneous receipts	150
Cash paid to employees and retirees	(13,400)
Cash paid to suppliers	(5,658)
Interest paid	(382)
Grants paid	(5,175)
Net Cash used by operating activities	(230)
Cash flows from investing activities:	
Purchase of equipment	(1,500)
Proceeds on sale of equipment	200
Insurance proceeds from fire loss on building	250
Proceeds from sale of investments	76,100
Purchase of investments	(75,000)
Net cash provided by investing activities	50
Cash flows from financing activities:	
Proceeds from contributions restricted for:	
Investment in perpetual endowment	200
Investment in term endowment	70
Investment in land, buildings, and equipment	1,210
Investment subject to annuity trust agreements	200
	1,680
Other financing activities:	
Interest and dividends restricted for reinvestment	300
Payments of annuity trust obligations	(145)
Payments on notes payable	(1,140)
Payments on long-term debt	(1,000)
	(1,985)
Net cash used by financing activities	(305)
Net decrease in cash, cash equivalents, and restricted cash	(485)
Cash, cash equivalents, and restricted cash at beginning of year	5,120
Cash, cash equivalents, and restricted cash at end of year	$ 4,635
Supplemental data for noncash investing and financing activities:	
Gifts of equipment	$ 140
Gift of paid-up life insurance, cash surrender value	80

(2) Format–indirect method

Not-for-Profit Entity A
Statement of Cash Flows
Year Ended June 30. 20X1(in thousands)

Cash flows from operating activities:	
Change in net assets	$ 15,450
Adjustments to reconcile change in net assets to net cash used by operating activities:	
Depreciation	3,200
Fire loss	80
Actuarial loss on annuity trust obligations	30
Gain on sale of equipment	(200)
Increase in accounts and interest receivable	(460)
Decrease in inventories and prepaid expenses	390
Increase in contributions receivable	(325)
Increase in accounts payable	1,520
Decrease in refund receivable	(650)
Decrease in grant payable	(425)
Contributions restricted for long–term investment	(2,740)
Realized and unrealized gains on investments	(15,800)
Interest and dividends restricted for reinvestment	(300)
Net cash used by operating activities	(230)
Cash flows from investing activities:	
Purchase of equipment	(1,500)
Proceeds on sale of equipment	200
Insurance proceeds from fire loss on building	250
Proceeds from sale of investments	76,100
Purchase of investments	(75,000)
Net cash provided by investing activities	50
Cash flows from financing activities:	
Proceeds from contributions restricted for:	
Investment in perpetual endowment	200
Investment in term endowment	70
Investment in land, buildings, and equipment	1,210
Investment subject to annuity trust agreements	200
	1,680
Other financing activities:	
Interest and dividends restricted for reinvestment	300
Payments of annuity trust obligations	(145)
Payments on notes payable	(1,140)
Payments on long–term debt	(1,000)
	(1,985)
Net cash used by financing activities	(305)
Net decrease in cash, cash equivalents, and restricted cash	(485)
Cash, cash equivalents, and restricted cash at beginning of year	5,120
Cash, cash equivalents, and restricted cash at end of year	$ 4,635
Supplemental data for noncash investing and financing activities:	
Gifts of equipment	$ 140
Gift of paid–up life insurance, cash surrender value	80
interest paid	382

(3) General

1) 기부금 및 투자수익을 제외하고는 기업의 현금흐름표와 동일

2) Either the direct or indirect method may be used

3) An NFP may choose either method of reporting cash flows from operating activities.

If the direct method is used, a reconciliation to the indirect method is not required.

(4) Contributions and investment income

Restricted for long-term purpose (O)	Cash flows from financing activities (CFF) ① regular endowment ② term endowment ③ restricted for acquisition of long-lived assets ④ restricted for long-term time restriction
Restricted for long-term purpose (X)	Cash flows from operating activities (CFO) ① quasi endowment ② unrestricted ③ restricted for operating activities ④ restricted for short-term time restriction ⑤ Contribution for agent transaction ⑥ Conditional contribution

(5) Reconciliation adjustments

1) from the change in total net assets to CFO

2) 조정사항은 다음 항목을 제외하고는 기업회계와 동일하다.

   ① contributions restricted for long-term purpose   (−)

   ② dividend and interest restricted for long-term purpose   (−)

Example-6

A NFP received a cash donation of $10,000 to be used at the board of directors' discretion in 20X1. The board of directors stipulated that $10,000 would be used to create an endowment.

20X1	Cash flows from operating activities (CFO) + 10,000

Example-7

A NFP received a cash donation of $20,000 in 20X1 from donor specifying that the amount would be used in 20X2.

20X1	Cash flows from operating activities (CFO) + 20,000

Example-8

A donor gave $100,000 for the purpose of creating as a regular endowment in 20X1. During 20X2, the NFP purchased investments of $100,000

20X1	Cash flows from financing activities (CFF) + 100,000
20X1	Cash flows from investing activities (CFI) - 100,000

Example-9

During 20X1, a NFP received a cash donation of $150,000 restricted by donor to the acquisition of equipment. The equipment of $90,000 was purchased in 20X2.

| 20X1 | Cash flows from financing activities (CFF) +150,000 |
| 20X2 | Cash flows from investing activities (CFI) -90,000 |

Example-10

During 20X1, a NFP received a cash donation of $150,000 restricted by donor to be used for research. The donation of $90,000 was used for research in 20X2.

| 20X1 | Cash flows from operating activities (CFO) +150,000 |
| 20X2 | Cash flows from operating activities (CFO) -90,000 |

(6) Cash, Cash Equivalents, and Restricted Cash

Transfers among cash, cash equivalents, and restricted cash included in assets restricted to investment in PPE are not reported as cash flow activities in the statement of cash flows.

Assets restricted to investment in PPE on the statement of financial position include restricted cash received with a donor-imposed restriction that limits use of that cash to long-term purposes.

	6 / 30 / 20X1
Cash and cash equivalents	$ 4,575
Restricted cash included in assets restricted to investment in land, buildings, and equipment	60
Total cash, cash equivalents, and restricted cash shown in the statement of cash flows	$ 4,635

03 ▶ Contributions

1 Contributions

(1) Definition

> An unconditional transfer of cash or other assets, as well as unconditional promises to give, to an entity or a reduction, settlement, or cancellation of its liabilities in a voluntary non-reciprocal transfer by another entity acting other than as an owner.

1) Exchange transactions

reciprocal transfers in which each party receives and sacrifices approximately commensurate value.

2) Investments by owners and distributions to owners

non-reciprocal transfers between an entity and its owners

3) Taxes, fines, and thefts

not voluntary non-reciprocal transfers

4) Conditional transfer

조건 기부는 기부수익으로 인식하지 않는다.

- 다음의 거래는 기부로 보지 않는다.

> ① Exchange transactions in which each party receives and sacrifices commensurate value. However, if an entity voluntarily transfers assets to another in exchange for assets of substantially lower value, the contribution received that is inherent in that transaction.
> ② Transfers of assets in which the entity acts as an agent, trustee, or intermediary, rather than as a donor or donee.
> ③ Tax exemptions or tax incentives
> ④ Transfers of assets from government entities to business entities.
> ⑤ Transfers of assets that are part of an existing exchange transaction between a recipient and an identified customer.

Example-11

During 20X1, a NFP received $10,000 and gave inventories, which generally price $2,000. The NFP received on other benefits.

Dr) Cash   10,000

    Cr) Exchange revenue   2,000

        Contribution-without donor restrictions   8,000

Example-12

Student L is enrolled at University A. Student L's total tuition charged for the semester is $30,000. Student L received a grant in the amount of $2,000 to use toward the tuition fee, which is paid directly by the grantor to University A.

⇨ Payment relating to an existing exchange transaction

Example-13

Patient R is a patient at Hospital B. The total amount due for services rendered is $10,000. Patient R has Medicare, and it covers $8,000 of the services, which is paid directly by the government to Hospital B. Hospital B bills Patient R for $2,000.

⇨ Payment relating to an existing exchange transaction

Example-14

The local government provided funding to NFP C to perform a research study on the benefits of a longer school year. The agreement requires NFP C to plan the study, perform the research, and summarize and submit the research to the local government. The local government retains all rights to the study.

⇨ Exchange transactions

Example-15

The local government provided funding to NFP C to perform a research study on the benefits of a longer school year. The agreement requires NFP C to plan the study, perform the research, and summarize and submit the research to the local government. The local government retains all rights to the study.

⇨ Exchange transaction
a procurement arrangement in which commensurate value is being exchanged between two parties.

Example-16

University D applied for and was awarded a grant from the federal government. University D must follow the rules and regulations established by the Office of Management and Budget of the federal government and the federal awarding agency. University D is required to incur qualifying expenses to be entitled to the assets. Any unspent money during the grant period is forfeited, and University D is required to return any advanced funding that does not have related qualifying expenses. University D also is required to submit a summary of research findings to the federal government, but University D retains the rights to the findings and has permission to publish the findings if it desires.

⇨ Contribution
The federal government does not receive direct commensurate value in exchange for the assets provided to University D because University D retains all rights to the research and findings.

(2) Initial measurement

Contributions received shall be measured at their fair values

(3) Donor-imposed restriction

A restriction results either from a donor's explicit stipulation or from circumstances surrounding the receipt of the contribution that make clear the donor's implicit restriction on use.

(4) Donor-imposed condition

1) Condition

A donor-imposed condition must have both:

a. One or more barriers that must be overcome before a recipient is entitled to the assets transferred or promised

b. A right of return to the contributor for assets transferred or a right of release of the promisor from its obligation to transfer assets.

For a donor-imposed condition to exist, it must be determinable from the agreement that a recipient is only entitled to the transferred assets if it has overcome the barrier.

2) A transfer of assets that is a conditional contribution should be accounted for as a refundable advance until the conditions have been substantially met or explicitly waived by the donor.

조건 기부는 조건이 충족되지 않으면 자산을 돌려주기 때문에 조건을 충족하는 시점까지는 수익으로 인식할 수 없다. 조건이 실질적으로 충족이 되기 전에는 부채로 인식하고 실질적으로 충족되면 기부수익으로 인식한다.

자산 이전	Assets	xxx
	Refundable advance (L)	xxx
조건 만족	Refundable advance (L)	xxx
	Contribution-???	xxx

ex a promise to contribute cash if a like amount of new gifts is raised from others within 30 days and a provision that the cash will not be transferred if the gifts are not raised impose a condition.

3) Donation with both donor-imposed restrictions and conditions

조건이 실질적으로 충족이 되기 전에는 부채로 인식하고 실질적으로 충족되면 제한수익으로 인식한다.

4) If it is difficult to determine whether conditions or restrictions

조건기부로 가정하여 부채로 인식한다.

5) Indicates a barrier

> The existence of measurable performance−related barriers or other barriers that may indicate a condition include:
> ① Specified levels of service
> (e.g., the provision of a specific number of meals at a facility).
> ② Specific outputs or outcomes
> (e.g., the construction of a building to an exact architectural design, the achievement of specific program objectives, or the conditioning of revenue on incurring specific eligible expenses).
> ③ Matching
> (e.g., revenue conditioned on the collection or accumulation of community match).
> ④ Outside event
> (e.g., the satisfaction of a contingency outside the control of the not−for−profit receiving the contribution).

6) Administrative and trivial stipulations

Administrative and trivial stipulations is not indicative of a barrier. Administrative and trivial stipulations could include routine reporting such as a requirement to provide (a) an annual report or (b) a report that summarizes the recipient's performance to demonstrate the underlying actions that were taken to meet the barrier(s) specified in the agreement.

Example-17

NFP DD is a hospital that received an upfront cash contribution from an individual to perform research on Alzheimer's disease during NFP DD's next fiscal year. The agreement does not include a right of return or a barrier that must be overcome to be entitled to the funds.

⇨ This contribution is not conditional because it does not include a right of return.

Example-18

NFP J operates as a homeless shelter that provides individuals with temporary accommodations, meals, and counseling. NFP J receives an upfront grant of $75,000 from the city for its meals program. The grant requires NFP J to use the assets to provide at least 5,000 meals to the homeless. The grant contains a right of return for meals not served.

⇨ This grant is conditional because it contains a measurable performance–related barrier (to provide 5,000 meals) and a right of return.

Example-19

Foundation A gives NFP D a grant in the amount of $400,000 to provide specific career training to disabled veterans. The grant requires NFP D to provide training to at least 8,000 disabled veterans during the next fiscal year (2,000 during each quarter), with specific minimum targets that must be met each quarter. Foundation A specifies a right of release from the obligation in the agreement that it will only give NFP D $100,000 each quarter if NFP D demonstrates that those services have been provided to at least 2,000 disabled veterans during the quarter.

⇨ This grant is conditional because Foundation A requires NFP D to achieve a specific level of service that would be considered a measurable performance-related barrier.

Example-20

Foundation B receives a grant proposal from an animal rescue facility, NFP F, which requests a 2-year grant in the amount of $500,000 upfront to be used to expand its operations. The agreement indicates that NFP F must expand its facility by at least 5,000 square feet to accommodate additional animals by the end of the 2 years. The grant contains a right of return if the minimum expansion target is not achieved.

⇨ This grant is conditional.
The grant includes a measurable barrier (5,000 additional square feet) that must be achieved by NFP to be entitled to the assets and a right of return for unmet requirements.

Example-21

NFP H is a recreational organization that provides various sports programs to children that live in the community. NFP H receives an upfront grant in the amount of $40,000 from a foundation to be used toward its tennis program. Consistent with NFP H's grant proposal, the agreement includes specific guidelines for which NFP H could use the assets (for example, to hire 10 tennis instructors or to provide a summer camp for 9 weeks) but does not specify that NFP H's entitlement to the $40,000 is dependent upon NFP H meeting any of the specific indicated guidelines in the agreement. The grant contains a right of return for funds not spent on the tennis program.

⇨ This grant is not conditional.
Because the agreement does not specify that entitlement to the transferred assets are dependent upon meeting any of the guidelines, the agreement does not contain a barrier to overcome.

Example-22

NFP G is a university that is conducting a capital campaign to build a new building to house its school of mathematics and to make capital improvements to existing buildings on campus, including a new heating system and an upgraded telephone and computer network. NFP G receives an upfront grant in the amount of $10,000 from a foundation as part of its capital campaign. The agreement contains a right of return requiring that the assets be reimbursed to the resource provider if the assets are not used for the purposes outlined in the capital campaign solicitation materials. The resource provider does not include any specifications in the agreement about how the building should be constructed or on how other improvements should be made.

⇨ This grant is not conditional.
The resource provider does not include any specifications about how the building should be constructed, and the agreement only indicates that NFP G must use the grant for the purpose outlined in the capital campaign materials.

Example-23

NFP B is a hospital that has a research program. NFP B receives a $300,000 grant from the federal awarding agency to fund thyroid cancer research. The terms of the grant specify that NFP B must incur certain qualifying expenses (or costs) in compliance with rules and regulations established by the Office of Management and Budget and the federal awarding agency. The grant is paid on a cost-reimbursement basis by NFP B initiating drawdowns of the grant assets. Any unused assets are forfeited, and any unallowed costs that have been drawn down by NFP B are required to be refunded.

⇨ This grant is conditional.
The requirement to spend the assets on qualifying expenses is a barrier to entitlement.
The grant also includes a release from the promisor's obligation for unused assets.

Example-24

NFP E is a public charity that performs research on various diseases and allergies, including gluten-related allergies, as part of its overall mission. It receives a $100,000 grant from a foundation to perform research on gluten-related allergies over the next year. The grant agreement includes a right of return as part of the foundation's standard wording and a requirement that at the end of the grant period a report must be filed with the foundation that explains how the assets were spent.

⇨ This grant is not conditional.

The reporting requirement alone is not a barrier because it is an administrative requirement and not related to the purpose of the agreement, which is the actual research.

Example-25

NFP I is a museum that receives a grant from an individual donor to build a new wing on the existing museum building. The agreement contains a $1 million multiyear promise to give the money to be used for the new wing on the building. The agreement also includes specific building requirements, including square footage and that the new wing must be environmen- tally friendly with Leadership in Energy and Environmental Design certification. The first installment of the gift will not be paid until NFP I submits architectural designs that meet the building requirements. Additional installments of the grant will be paid in specified increments upon achieving other milestones identified in the grant agreement. If a particular milestone is not achieved, the donor is released from its obligation to make installment payments.

⇨ This agreement is conditional

NFP I is not entitled to the assets until a milestone is met (for example, an architectural plan including square footage and Leadership in Energy and Environmental Design certification).

(5) The process for determining whether a transfer of assets to a recipient is a contribution, an exchange transaction, or another type of transaction and whether a contribution is conditional.

<Step 1>
Is the transaction one in which each party directly received commensurate value?

   Yes → Exchange transaction (ASC 606 수익인식)
   No → Step 2

<Step 2>
Is the payment a transfer of assets that is part of an existing exchange transaction?
   Yes → Exchange transaction (ASC 606 수익인식)
   No → Step 3

<Step 3>
Is the transaction one in which the reporting entity acts as an agent, trustee, or intermediary for another party that may be a donor or donee?

   Yes → Agency transaction (Apply Agency transaction guidance)
   No → Step 4 (Apply contribution guidance)

<Step 4>
In there a donor-imposed condition(a barrier and a right of return must exist)?

  Yes → refundable advance
  No → Step 5 (Apply contribution guidance)

<Step 5>
Are restrictions present?

  Yes → Recognized contribution revenue with donor restrictions.
  No → Recognized contribution revenue without donor restrictions.

2 Promise to give

(1) An unconditional promise to give (pledge)

1) 기부서약은 문서화로 되어야 하며 서약시점의 공정가치로 측정하여 자산과 수익으로 인식한다.

2) 서약시점의 공정가치

    – 1년 이내에 회수되는 경우 : net realizable value

    – 1년 이후에 회수되는 경우 : present value

3) Receipts of unconditional promises to give cash in future years

    ⇒ increase with donor restrictions net assets.

(2) A conditional promise to give

실질적으로 조건을 충족하기 전에는 재무제표에 인식하지 않는다.

(3) A conditional promise to give if the possibility that the condition will not be met is remote

실질적으로 조건을 충족한 것으로 간주하여 자산과 수익으로 인식한다.

(4) Present value

Contributions receivable should be reported net of the discount that arises if measuring a promise to give at present value.

If an unconditional promise to give is measured using present value techniques, a not-for-profit entity (NFP) should report the subsequent accrual of the interest element recognized as an increase in net assets with donor restrictions if the underlying promise to give is donor restricted.

Recipients of unconditional promises to give should disclose all of the following:

1) The amounts of promises receivable in less than one year, in one to five years, and in more than five years

2) The amount of the allowance for uncollectible promises receivable

3) The discount that arises if measuring a promise to give at present value, if that discount is not separately disclosed by reporting it as a deduction from contributions receivable on the face of a statement of financial position.

Example-26

During 20X1, a NFP received unconditional promises to give totaling $6,000. Of this $6,000, $2,000 is not collectible until 20X2. The NFP estimates that 10% of the pledges will be uncollectible.

20X1 pledge	Dr) Contributions receivable	6,000
	Cr) Contribution-with donor restrictions	1,800
	Contribution-without donor restrictions	3,600
	Allowance for uncollectible accounts	600
20X1 collections	Dr) Cash	3,600
	Cr) Contributions receivable	3,600
20X1 write—off	Dr) Allowance for uncollectible accounts	400
	Cr) Contributions receivable	400
20X2 collections	Dr) Cash	1,800
	Cr) Contributions receivable	1,800
	Dr) Reclassification-with donor restrictions	1,800
	Cr) Reclassification-without donor restrictions	1,800
20X2 write—off	Dr) Allowance for uncollectible accounts	200
	Cr) Contributions receivable	200

Present value for initial recognition and measurement of unconditional promises to give cash that are expected to be collected one year or more after the financial statement date.

Assume that a NFP receives a promise to give $100 in five years, that the anticipated future cash flows from the promise are $70 and that the present value of the future cash flows is $50

Dr) Contribution Receivable	70
Cr) Contribution Revenue-with donor restrictions	50
Cr) Discount on Contribution Receivable	20

3 Contributions of services

(1) Recognition

Contributions of services shall be recognized if the services received meet any of the following criteria:

> 1) They create or enhance non-financial assets
> 2) They require specialized skills, are provided by individuals possessing those skills, and would typically need to be purchased if not provided by donation.

위의 수익인식 기준 요건 충족여부에 따라 서비스 기부는 다음과 같이 회계처리한다.

요건 충족 (O)	Dr) Expense xxx Cr) Contribution-without donor restrictions xxx
요건 충족 (X)	No entry

(2) Non-financial assets

재고자산, 유형자산, 무형자산 및 서비스 등

(3) Services requiring specialized skills

accountants, architects, carpenters, doctors, electricians, lawyers, nurses, plumbers, teachers, and craftsmen.

4 Gifts in kind

(1) Recognition

Gifts in kind that can be used or sold shall be measured at fair value.

(2) Contributions of Use of Property, Utilities, or Advertising Time

The use of property, utilities, or advertising time are considered to be forms of contributed assets, rather than contributed services. An NFP would recognize the fair value of the use of property, utilities, or advertising time as both revenue and expense in the period received and used.

(3) Works of Art, Historical Treasures, and Similar Items

Works of art, historical treasures, and similar items that are not part of a collection shall be recognized as assets in financial statements.

An NFP that holds works of art, historical treasures, and similar items that meet the definition of a collection has the following three alternative policies for reporting that collection. Capitalization of selected collections or items is precluded.

1) Capitalization of all collection items
2) Capitalization of all collection items on a prospective basis
3) No capitalization.

Example-27

Foundation D operates from a building it owns. The holding company of a local utility has been contributing electricity on a continuous basis subject to the donor's cancellation.

> 자산기부이며 전기료의 공정가치를 측정하여 수익과 비용으로 인식한다.
> 전기료의 공정가치는 일반 소비자에게 부과되는 요금을 기준으로 한다.

Example-28

A NFPO decides to construct a building on its property. It obtains the necessary architectural plans and specifications and purchases the necessary continuing architectural services, materials, permits, and so forth at a total cost of $400,000. A local construction entity contributes the necessary labor and equipment. An independent appraisal of the building (exclusive of land), obtained for insurance purposes, estimates its fair value at $725,000.

(출처 : ASC−958)

기부수익 조건을 만족하기 때문에 $325,000을 수익으로 인식한다.

Example-29

Hospital J provides short-term inpatient and outpatient care and also provides long-term care for the elderly. As part of the long-term care program, the hospital has organized a program whereby local high school students may contribute a minimum of 10 hours a week, from 3:00 p.m. to 6:00 p.m., to the hospital. These students are assigned various duties, such as visiting and talking with the patients, distributing books and magazines, reading, playing chess, and similar activities. Hospital J does not pay for these services or similar services. The services are accepted as a way of enhancing or supplementing the quality of care and comfort provided to the elderly long-term care patients.

(출처 : ASC−958)

기부수익 조건을 만족하기 않기 때문에 수익으로 인식하지 않는다.

Example-30

College K conducts an annual fund-raising campaign to solicit contributions from its alumni. In prior years, College K recruited unpaid student volunteers to make phone calls to its alumni. This year, a telemarketing entity, whose president is an alumnus of College K, contributed its services to College K for the annual alumni fundraising campaign. The entity normally provides telemarketing services to a variety of clients on a fee basis. College K provided the entity with a list of 10,000 alumni, several copies of a typed appeal to be read over the phone, and blank contribution forms to record pledges received. The entity contacted most of the 10,000 alumni.

(출처: ASC−958)

> 기부수익 조건을 만족하기 않기 때문에 수익으로 인식하지 않는다.

Example-31

Faculty salaries are a major expense of University H. The faculty includes both compensated faculty members (approximately 80 percent) and uncompensated faculty members (approximately 20 percent) who are associated with religious orders and contribute their services to the university. The performance of both compensated and uncompensated faculty members is regularly and similarly evaluated; both must meet the university's standards and both provide services in the same way.

(출처: ASC−958)

> 기부수익 조건을 만족하기 때문에 수익으로 인식한다.

Example-32

Mission A, a religious NFP, receives a building (including the land on which it was constructed) as a gift from a local corporation with the understanding that the building will be used principally as an education and training center for Mission A's members or for any other purpose consistent with Mission A's plans.

⇨ Mission A would recognize the contributed property as an asset and as support and measure that property at its fair value.

Example-33

Charity E receives the free use of 10,000 square feet of prime office space provided by a local entity. The local entity has informed Charity E that it intends to continue providing the space as long as it is available, and although it expects it would be able to give the charity 30 days advance notice, it may discontinue providing the space at any time. The local entity normally rents similar space for $14 to $16 annually per square foot, the going market rate for office space in the area. Charity E decides to accept this gift—the free use of office space—to conduct its daily central administrative activities.

⇨ Charity E would recognize the receipt of the unconditional promise as a receivable and as donor-restricted support at its fair value.

Example-34

In 19X0, Individual notifies Church F that she has remembered the church in her will and provides a written copy of the will. In 19X5, Individual dies. In 19X6, Individual's last will and testament enters probate and the probate court declares the will valid. The executor informs Church F that the will has been declared valid and that it will receive 10% of Individual's estate, after satisfying the estate's liabilities and certain specific bequests. The executor provides an estimate of the estate's assets and liabilities and the expected amount and time for payment of Church F's interest in the estate.

⇨ When the probate court declares the will valid, Church F would recognize a receivable and revenue for an unconditional promise to give at the fair value of its interest in the estate

Example-35

Museum B, which preserves its collections, receives a gift of a valuable painting from a donor. The donor obtained an independent appraisal of the fair value of the painting for tax purposes and furnished a copy to the museum. The museum staff evaluated the painting to determine its authenticity and worthiness for addition to the museum's collection.

(출처: ASC−958)

---

(1) 미술관이 기부받은 그림을 전시품으로 결정한 경우

　1) 미술관의 회계정책이 전시품을 자본화하는 경우

　　⇨ 그림의 공정가치를 수익(PR)과 자산으로 인식한다.

　2) 미술관의 회계정책이 전시품을 자본화하지 않는 경우

　　⇨ 회계처리 하지 않는다.

(2) 미술관이 기부받은 그림을 전시품으로 결정하지 않는 경우

　⇨ 그림의 공정가치를 수익(UR)과 자산으로 인식한다.

---

5 Works of art, historical treasures, and similar items

(1) Collections

Works of art, historical treasures, or similar assets that meet all of the following criteria:

1) They are held for public exhibition, education, or research in furtherance of public service rather than financial gain.

2) They are protected, kept unencumbered, cared for, and preserved.

3) They are subject to an organizational policy that requires the use of proceeds from items that are sold to be for the acquisition of new collections items, the direct care of existing collections, or both.

⇒ Direct care is an investment that enhances the life, usefulness or quality of a museum' collection.

(2) Accounting policy

⇒ 다음 회계처리 중 하나를 회계정책으로 선택할 수 있다.

수익인식 (O)	Dr) Assets xxx Cr) Contribution-with donor restrictions xxx
수익인식 (X)	No entry

(3) No capitalization

전시품을 자본화하지 않는 비영리기관은 다음 사항을 손익계산서에 다른 손익과는 별도로 표시하여야 한다.

1) Costs of collection items purchased

⇒ decrease in the appropriate class of net assets

2) Proceeds from sale of collection items

⇒ increase in the appropriate class of net assets

3) Proceeds from insurance recoveries of lost or destroyed collection items

⇒ increase in the appropriate class of net assets

Organization M
Statement of Activities
For the Year Ended June 30, 20X1

	Without Donor restrictions	With Donor restrictions	Total
Revenues and other support	XXX	XXX	XXX
Gain on sale of art that is not held in a collection	1		1
Net assets released from restrictions	XXX	(XXX)	
Total revenues, gains, and other support	XXX	XX	XXX
Expenses	XXX		XXX
Chance in net assets before changes related to collection items not capitalized	XX	XX	XXX
Change in net assets related to collection items not capitalized:			
Proceeds from sale of collection items	5	10	15
Proceeds from insurance recoveries on destroyed collection items		1	1
Collection items purchased bit not capitalized	(12)	(25)	(37)
	(7)	(14)	(21)
Change in net assets	XX	XX	XXX

(4) Statement of cash flows

Cash flows from purchases, sales, and insurance recoveries of unrecognized, non-capitalized collection items shall be reported as investing activities.

(5) Depreciation

비영리기관은 기업과 마찬가지로 발생주의 회계처리를 하기 때문에 감가상각도 동일한 규정을 적용하며 다음 자산은 내용연수가 비한정이거나 수익비용대응의 원칙에 의하여 감가상각을 하지 않는다.

- Land used as a building site
- Construction-in-progress
- A work of art or historical treasure

6 Agency transactions

Transfer of assets from a donor to a recipient entity on behalf of a beneficiary specified by the donor

<Step 1>

If any of the following conditions are present:

(1) The transfer is subject to the resource provider's unilateral right to redirect the use of the assets to another beneficiary.

(2) The transfer is accompanied by the resource provider's conditional promise to give or is otherwise revocable or repayable.

(3) The resource provider controls the recipient entity and specifies an unaffiliated beneficiary.

A transfer of assets should be accounted for as an asset by the resource provider and as a liability by the recipient entity.

resource provider	recipient entity
Dr) Refundable advance xxx	Dr) Asset xxx
Cr) Asset xxx	Cr) Refundable advance xxx

<Step 2>

Does the resource provider specifies itself or its affiliate as the beneficiary?

   No ⇨   Step 3
   Yes ⇨   Step 4

<Step 3>

(Step 3-1) Did the donor grant variance power to the recipient entity?

   Yes ⇨   (1)
   No ⇨   (2)

(Step 3-2) Are the recipient entity and the specified beneficiary financially interrelated?

   Yes ⇨   (1)
   No ⇨   (2)

(1) The donor granted variance power to the recipient entity

(Variance power: The unilateral power to redirect the use of the transferred assets to another beneficiary.)

resource provider	Dr) Expense xxx Cr) Asset xxx
recipient entity	Dr) Asset xxx Cr) Contribution revenue xxx
specified beneficiary	No entry

(2) The recipient entity and the specified beneficiary are financially interrelated.

resource provider	Dr) Expense xxx Cr) Asset xxx
recipient entity	Dr) Asset xxx Cr) Contribution revenue xxx
specified beneficiary	Dr) Interest in net assets of recipient entity xxx Cr) Change in interest in recipient entity xxx

<Financially interrelated entities>

A recipient entity and a specified beneficiary are financially interrelated entities if the relationship has both of the following characteristics:

  a) One of the entities has the ability to influence the operating and financial decisions of the other.

  b) One of the entities has an ongoing economic interest in the net assets of the other.

(3) Agency transaction

resource provider	Dr) Expense xxx Cr) Asset xxx
recipient entity	Dr) Asset xxx Cr) Payable to specified beneficiary xxx
specified beneficiary	Dr) Receivable xxx Cr) Contribution revenue xxx

\<Step 4\>

If the resource provider specifies itself or its affiliate as the beneficiary.

(1) The transfer is not an equity transaction

resource provider	Dr) Receivable xxx Cr) Asset xxx
recipient entity	Dr) Asset xxx Cr) Payable to resource provider xxx
specified beneficiary	No entry

(2) The transfer is an equity transaction

resource provider	Dr) Interest in net assets of recipient entity xxx Cr) Asset xxx
recipient entity	Dr) Asset xxx Cr) Equity transaction xxx
specified beneficiary	No entry

Example-36

Local Church G transfers cash to Seminary H and instructs Seminary H to use the money to grant a scholarship to Individual, who is a parishioner of Local Church G.

⇨ Seminary H would recognize the cash and a liability to Individual.

Example-37

The governing board of City Botanical Society E decides to raise funds to build an endowment. The governing board signs an agreement to establish a fund at Community Foundation F. Community Foundation F and City Botanical Society E are not financially interrelated entities. City Botanical Society E solicits gifts to the fund. The campaign materials inform donors that the endowment will be owned and held by Community Foundation F. The materials explain that the gifts will be invested and that the return from their investment will be distributed to City Botanical Society E, subject to Community Foundation F's spending policy and to Community Foundation F's right to redirect the return to another beneficiary without the approval of the donor, City Botanical Society E, or any other party if distributions to City Botanical Society E become unnecessary, impossible, or inconsistent with the needs of the community. The donor-response card also clearly describes Community Foundation F's right to redirect the return of the fund. The campaign materials indicate that donors should send their contributions to Community Foundation F using a preaddressed envelope included for that purpose.

⇨ Community Foundation F would recognize the fair value of gifts received as assets and as contribution revenue. The donors explicitly granted variance power by using a donor-response card.

Example-38

Corporation sends dental supplies to University Foundation to be used by students in University's dental clinic. University Foundation's bylaws state that it is organized for the purpose of stimulating voluntary financial support from alumni and other donors for the benefit of University, especially for addressing the long-term academic priorities of University. As with most gifts it receives, University Foundation can choose the timing of the distribution to University and can place additional limitations on the distribution if those limitations are consistent with Corporation's restrictions. University does not control University Foundation.

⇨ University Foundation recognizes the fair value of the dental supplies as an increase in assets and as contribution revenue that increases net assets with donor restrictions because there are donor-imposed restrictions and because University and University Foundation are financially interrelated entities.

Example-39

Individual transfers cash to Arts Foundation and specifies that the money be used to support the expenses of the ballet. Arts Foundation's bylaws state that it is organized for the purpose of stimulating voluntary financial support from donors for the benefit of Community Ballet and Community Theater. At the time Arts Foundation was created, the three NFPs entered into an agreement that specifies that if a donor does not specify the NFP to which the gift should be transferred, the gift will be split equally between Community Ballet and Community Theater. The agreement also specifies that representatives from the three NFPs will meet annually and determine campaign priorities for the next year and the costs of operating Arts Foundation will be equally split between Community Ballet and Community Theater. Arts Foundation is not controlled by Community Ballet, Community Theater, or Individual.

⇨ Arts Foundation would report assets and contribution revenue that increases net assets with donor restrictions because there are donor-imposed restrictions and because Community Ballet and Arts Foundation are financially interrelated entities.

7 Split-Interest Agreement

(1) Split-Interest Agreement

An agreement in which a donor enters into a trust or other arrangement under which a NFP receives benefits that are shared with other beneficiaries.

A typical split-interest agreement has the following two components:

1) A lead interest
  The right to the benefits (cash flows or use) of assets during the term of a split-interest agreement, which generally starts upon the signing of the agreement and terminates at either of the following times:

  a) After a specified number of years (period-certain)
  b) Upon the occurrence of a certain event, commonly either the death of the donor or the death of the lead interest beneficiary (life-contingent).

2) A remainder interest
  The right to receive all or a portion of the assets of a split-interest agreement remaining at the end of the agreement's term.

(2) Revocable Agreements

Assets received by a NFP acting as a trustee should be recognized at fair value when received as assets and as a refundable advance.

Contribution revenue for the assets received should be recognized when the agreement becomes irrevocable or when the assets are distributed to the NFP for its unconditional use, whichever occurs first.

(3) **Irrevocable Agreements**

Under irrevocable split-interest agreements the assets contributed by the donor may be either Held by an NFP or Held by a third party.

(4) Held by an NFP

An NFP should recognize contribution revenue and related assets and liabilities when an irrevocable split-interest agreement is executed.

(5) Held by a third party

If an NFP is the beneficiary of a split-interest agreement held by a third party and has an unconditional right to receive all or a portion of the specified cash flows from the assets held pursuant to that agreement, the NFP should recognize that beneficial interest as an asset and contribution revenue. The contribution should be recognized when the NFP is notified of the split-interest agreement's existence.

04 Investment

1 Scope

Investment의 적용 기준서는 다음과 같다.

(1) ASC 320. Investment-debt and equity securities

(2) ASC 323. Equity method

(3) ASC 810. Consolidation

2 Investment-debt and equity securities (ASC 320)

(1) Initial measurement

measured at its acquisition cost. (including transaction fees)

(2) Subsequent measurement

Equity securities	공정가치를 알 수 있는 경우 ⇒ 공정가치로 측정
	공정가치를 알 수 없는 경우 ⇒ 원가법으로 측정
Debt securities	공정가치로 측정

(3) Investment income, unrealized and realized gains and losses

reported as increases or decreases in without donor restrictions net assets unless their use is restricted by explicit donor stipulations or by law

(4) Statement of cash flows

1) investment income restricted for long-term purpose

⇒ Cash flows from financing activities (CFF)

2) investment income not restricted for long-term purpose

⇒ Cash flows from operating activities (CFO)

05 ▷ Other matters

1 Costs of premiums and sales

(1) Cost of premiums

1) Postcard or calendars that are given to potential donors as part of mass fundraising appeals

   ⇒ 기부수익과 관계없이 발생시점에서 전액 기부모집비용으로 인식한다.

2) Coffee mugs that are given to resource providers to acknowledge receipt of a contribution

   ⇒ 기부수익과 대응하여 기부모집비용으로 인식한다.

(2) Cost of sales

A NFO museum that has a store that is a major or central activity

1) If the store sells merchandise that is related to the its program

   ⇒ the cost of the store's sales would be reported as a program expense

2) If the store sells merchandise that is not related to its program

   ⇒ the cost of the store's sales would be reported as a supporting service

---

Example-40

A NFP may provide a coffee mug to people making a contribution of $50 or more; the mug costs the NFP $1.

> The NFP shall recognize contributions for the total amount contributed and fundraising expense of $1 for each mug provided to donors.

2 Joint activity

(1) Joint activity

An activity that is part of the fundraising function and has elements of one or more other functions.

1) If membership development is in part soliciting membership dues and in part soliciting contributions

⇒ a joint activity

2) If membership development is conducted in conjunction with other activities but does not include soliciting contributions

⇒ not a joint activity

(2) If the criteria of purpose, audience, and content are met

⇒ all costs of the joint activity shall be allocated

(3) If any of the criteria are not met

⇒ all costs of the joint activity shall be reported as fundraising costs

(4) Purpose criterion

The purpose criterion is met if the purpose of the joint activity includes accomplishing program or management and general functions.

(5) Audience criterion

The audience criterion is not met if the audience includes prior donors or is otherwise selected based on its ability or likelihood to contribute.

(6) Content criterion

The content criterion is met if the joint activity supports program or management and general functions, as follows:

1) Program

The joint activity calls for specific action by the recipient that will help accomplish the NFP's mission.

2) Management and general

The joint activity fulfills one or more of the NFP's management and general responsibilities.

Example-41

NFP A's mission is to prevent drug abuse.

NFP A mails informational materials to the parents of all junior high school students explaining the prevalence and dangers of drug abuse. The materials encourage parents to counsel children about the dangers of drug abuse and inform them about how to detect drug abuse. The mailing includes a request for contributions. NFP A conducts other activities informing the public about the dangers of drug abuse and encouraging parents to counsel their children about drug abuse that do not include requests for contributions and that are conducted in different media. NFP A's executive director is involved in the development of the informational materials as well as the request for contributions. The executive director's annual compensation includes a significant bonus if total annual contributions exceed a predetermined amount.

> The purpose, audience, and content criteria are met, and the joint costs should be allocated.

3 Healthcare entities (ASC 954)

(1) Financial statements

영리 및 비영리 의료기관의 재무제표는 다음과 같다.

(1) Balance sheet
(2) Statement of operations
(3) Statement of changes in equity (or net assets)
(4) Statement of cash flows
(5) Notes

(2) Statement of operations

1) Changes in unrestricted net assets

손익계산서는 기부자의 제약이 없는 순자산의 증감만을 보고하며 기부자에 의하여 일시적 또는 영구적 제약이 있는 순자산의 증감은 손익계산서에 보고되지 않으며 순자산 변동표에 보고된다.

2) A performance indicator

비영리의료기관은 손익계산서에 영리의료기관의 계속사업손익과 유사한 개념인 성과지표를 표시하여야 하며 다음 항목들은 성과지표에 포함되지 않는다.

- Equity transfers involving other entities
- Receipt of restricted contributions and investment income*
- Contributions of long-lived assets
- Net assets released from donor restrictions related to long-lived assets
- Items that are required to be reported in other comprehensive income
- Discontinued operations and extraordinary items
- Unrealized gains and losses on investments on other than trading securities

* 손익계산서에도 보고되지 않는다.

3) 수익은 서비스의 형태에 따라 다음과 같이 표시한다.

Patient service revenue (net of contractual allowances and discounts)	$ 60,000
Provision for bad debts	(9600)
Net patient service revenue less provision for bad debts	50,400
Premium revenue	23,000
Other operating revenue	14,000
Total revenue	$ 87,400

(3) Patient service revenue

1) Charity care → Gross revenue shall not include charity care.

2) Contractual adjustments and discounts

The provision for contractual adjustments and discounts are deducted from gross service revenue to determine net service revenue.

※ contractual adjustments

: the difference between established rates and third-party payor payments

※ discounts

: the difference bctween established rates and the amount billable

3) Bad debt

① 수익의 차감으로 표시되는 대손

Bad debts related to receivables from patient service revenue

② 영업비용으로 표시되는 대손

Bad debts related to receivables from revenue other than patient service

(4) Premium revenue

Capitation fee is a fixed amount per individual that is paid periodically (usually monthly) to a provider as compensation for providing comprehensive health care services for the period. Significant revenue earned under capitation arrangements shall be reported separately.

(5) Other revenue

손익계산서의 프리미엄 수익의 아래에 표시하는 기타수익은 다음과 같다.

1) Investment income

2) Fees from educational program

3) Proceeds from sale of cafeteria meals and gift shop

4 Public Colleges and Universities

(1) Introduction

국공립대학의 재무제표는 GASB 35를 적용하며 이에 따라 재무보고목적으로 국공립대학을 다음 세 가지 유형으로 구분하며 이는 GASB 34의 special government의 유형 및 재무제표를 준용한다.

(1) engaged only in business-type activities

(2) engaged only in governmental activities

(3) engaged in business-type and governmental activities

(2) Public universities engaged only in business-type activities

사업형 국공립대학은 다음의 재무보고서를 작성한다.

(1) Management's discussion and analysis (MD&A)
(2) Fund financial statements
   - Statement of net position
   - Statement of revenue, expense & changes in net position
   - Statement of cash flow
(3) Notes
(4) Required supplementary information(RSI) other than MD&A

☞ 영리성 펀드재무제표를 작성하며 GW재무제표를 작성하지 않는다.

(3) Public universities engaged only in governmental activities

정부형 국공립대학은 다음의 재무보고서를 작성한다.

(1) Management's discussion and analysis (MD&A)
(2) GW financial statements
   − Statement of net position
   − Statement of activities
(3) Fund financial statements
   − Balance sheet
   − Statement of revenue, expenditures & changes in fund balance
(4) Notes
(5) Required supplementary information(RSI) other than MD&A

(4) Public universities engaged in governmental activities and business-type activities

정부형 및 사업형 국공립대학은 다음의 재무보고서를 작성한다.

(1) Management's discussion and analysis (MD&A)
(2) GW financial statements
   − Statement of net position
   − Statement of activities
(3) Fund financial statements
   − Balance sheet
   − Statement of revenue, expenditures & changes in fund balance
   − Statement of net position
   − Statement of revenue, expense & changes in net position
   − Statement of cash flow
(4) Notes
(5) Required supplementary information(RSI) other than MD&A

06 ▶ Task-Based Simulation

Problem-1

Indicate how each transaction should be reported by KIM University on (1) the statement of activities and (2) the statement of cash flows prepared for the year ended December 31, Year 2.

1. A donor contributed $100,000 and stipulated that it be invested permanently.

2. Investments of $100,000 were acquired with the cash received from the donor in transaction 1.

3. Interest and dividends of $8,000 were received from the investments acquired in transaction 2. The donor stipulated that the earnings be used for student scholarships in Year 2.

4. Donors contributed $500,000 for the acquisition of equipment.

5. Depreciation expense of $750,000 was recorded for Year 2.

6. $3,000,000 was received, representing tuition for the spring, summer, and fall semesters.

7. $75,000 was received from donors who had pledged that amount in Year 1. The cash will be used to pay for a marketing campaign that aimed at increasing enrollment. The cost was incurred in Year 2 and will be paid in Year 3.

8. $900,000 was paid to faculty for salaries incurred during the Year 2.

9. $25,000 was given to faculty for summer research grants. The grants came from donations made by alumni in Year 1.

10. $40,000 of donations were received from alumni who did not stipulate how their donations were to be used.

[Selection items]

Statement of Activities

A	Increase in changes in without donor restrictions net assets
B	Decrease in changes in without donor restrictions net assets
C	Increase in changes in with donor restrictions net assets
D	Decrease in changes in with donor restrictions net assets
E	Not reported

Statement of Cash Flows (Indirect method)

A	In operating activities as an addition to change in net assets
B	In operating activities as a deduction from change in net assets
C	As an investing activities inflow
D	As an investing activities outflow
E	As a financing activities inflow
F	As a financing activities outflow
G	As supplemental disclosures in its statement of cash flows
H	Not reported

Problem-2

The Good Food for the Hungry Institute is a nongovernmental not-for-profit organization that provides free meals for the destitute in a large metropolitan area.

1. Cash gifts that were received last year, but designated for use in the current year, totaled $20,000.

2. Unrestricted pledges of $65,000 were received. Five percent of pledges typically prove uncollectible. Additional cash contributions during the year totaled $35,000.

3. Donations of food totaled $150,000. The inventory of food on hand decreased by $1,200 during the year.

4. Expenses were incurred as follows: salary of director, $10,000; facility rental, $8,000; purchases of food, $70,000; and supplies, $27,000. Supplies inventory increased by $5,000 during the year.

5. Restricted pledges of $300,000 were received during the year. The pledges are restricted for use in constructing a new kitchen and dining hall. Of the pledges received, 5% is expected to be uncollectible.

• Required •

Prepare journal entries to account for these transactions. Include net asset classifications.

Problem-3

The following information was taken from the accounts and records of the Community Society, a nongovernmental not-for-profit organization. The balances are as of December 31, 20X1, unless otherwise stated:

Unrestricted support—contributions	$3,000,000
Unrestricted support—membership dues	400,000
Unrestricted revenues—investment income	83,000
Temporarily restricted gain on sale of investments	5,000
Expenses—education	300,000
Expenses—research	2,300,000
Expenses—fund-raising	223,000
Expenses—management and general	117,000
Restricted support—contributions	438,000
Restricted revenues—investment income	22,500
Permanently restricted support-contributions	37,000
Without donor restrictions net assets, January 1, 20X1	435,000
With donor restrictions net assets, January 1, 20X1	5,040,000

The unrestricted support from contributions was all received in cash during the year. Additionally, the society received pledges totaling $425,000. The pledges should be collected during 20X2, except for the estimated uncollectible portion of $16,000. The society spent $3,789,000 of restricted resources on construction of a major capital facility during 20X1, and $500,000 of research expenses were for research financed from restricted donations.

· Required ·

Prepare the statement of activities for the Community Society for 20X1.

Problem-4

A private NFP is preparing its Year 1 statement of cash flows using the indirect method. Using the code below, indicate how each item will affect Year 1 statement of cash flows.

A	In operating activities as an addition to change in net assets
B	In operating activities as a deduction from change in net assets
C	As an investing activities inflow
D	As an investing activities outflow
E	As a financing activities inflow
F	As a financing activities outflow
G	As supplemental disclosures in its statement of cash flows
H	Not reported

(1) Depreciation

(2) Amortization of bond discount on long-term debt

(3) Amortization of bond premium on long-term debt

(4) Proceeds from borrowing

(5) Payments on long-term debt

(6) Interest paid

(7) Receipts from sales of property, plant, and equipment

(8) Gain on sale of equipment

(9) Purchase of equipment

(10) Proceeds from sales of investments

(11) Purchase of investments

(12) Realized gain on sale of investments

(13) Unrealized gain on sale of investments

(14) Decrease in accrued payable

(15) Decrease in inventory

(16) Cash contributions without donor restrictions

(17) Cash contributions with donor restrictions with specific requirements relative to the acquisition of property

(18) Cash contributions to establish a perpetual endowment fund whose investment returns must be used for the maintenance of a building owned by the entity.

(19) Net assets released from restrictions

(20) Contributed legal services

(21) Cash contributions restricted by the donor to be used for meals for the children.

(22) Interest and dividends received

(23) Interest and dividends restricted for reinvestment

(24) Proceeds from sale of work of art

(25) Acquisition of works of art

(26) Gifts of equipment

(27) Payments for debt issue costs

Government & Not-For-Profit Accounting For the **US CPA** Exam

Chapter 03

Partnership

Volume
8

Partnership

01 ▷ Partnership accounting

1 Introduction

(1) Definition

"Association of two or more persons to carry on as co-owners a business for profit."

partnership은 주식회사와 더불어 미국의 대표적인 영리조직으로 한국의 합명회사 또는 합자회사와 유사한 조직이다.

(2) Limited life

주식회사가 계속기업을 가정하지만 partnership은 사원을 기준으로 한 인적회사이기 때문에 사원의 사망 또는 퇴사로 청산이 가능하다.

(3) Unlimited liability

주식회사의 주주는 출자금에 대해서만 유한책임을 가지지만 partnership의 일반사원(general partners)은 partnership의 행위에 대하여 연대무한책임을 가진다.

2 Formation

(1) Measurement

1) Assets contributed to the partnership should be recorded at fair value

2) Liabilities assumed by the partnership should be recorded at present value

3) Each partner's net contribution should be credited to his capital account.

partnership의 자본은 납입자본과 잉여금을 구분하지 않고 각 사원별로 자본을 구분하며 capital이라는 계정을 사용한다.

Example-1

Air & Bird form a partnership. Air contributes cash of $20,000, while Bird contributes land with a fair value of $45,000 and the partnership assumes a liability on the land of $15,000.

Dr) Cash	20,000	
Land	45,000	
Cr) Mortgage payable		15,000
Capital-Air		20,000
Capital-Bird		30,000

(2) Owners' equity accounts

1) Capital account
출자, 당기순손익 및 영구적인 인출을 기록하는 계정이다.

2) Drawing account
일반적인 인출을 기록하는 계정이다.

3) Loans to or from partners
출자가 아닌 자금의 대여 및 차입을 기록하는 계정이다.

(3) Unidentifiable assets contributed-bonus method

사원이 출자한 영업권을 인식하지 않고 영업권 사원의 자본을 증가하고 다른 사원의 자본을 감소하여 조정한다.

Example-2

Air & Bird form a partnership. Air contributes cash of $20,000, while Bird contributes land with a fair value of $45,000 and the partnership assumes a liability on the land of $15,000. Air & Bird are given equal capital balances.

Dr) Cash	20,000	
Land	45,000	
Cr) Mortgage payable		15,000
Capital-Air		25,000
Capital-Bird		25,000

(4) Unidentifiable assets contributed–goodwill method

사원이 출자한 영업권을 자산으로 인식하고 영업권 사원의 자본을 증가하며 다른 사원의 자본은 변동하지 않는다.

Example-3

Air & Bird form a partnership. Air contributes cash of $20,000, while Bird contributes land with a fair value of $45,000 and the partnership assumes a liability on the land of $15,000. Air & Bird are given equal capital balances.

Dr) Cash	20,000	
Land	45,000	
Goodwill	10,000	
Cr) Mortgage payable		15,000
Capital-Air		30,000
Capital-Bird		30,000

3 Allocation of profit or loss

(1) Allocation by RUPA(Revised Uniform Partnership Act)

당기순손익은 사원의 출자금에 비례하여 배분하지 않으며 다음 순서대로 배분한다.

Step-1	각 사원별로 급여, 보너스 및 출자금의 이자를 배분한다.
Step-2	잔여금액을 약정된 손익비율을 기준으로 배분한다. (a predetermined agreement about P/L ratio) ⇨ 만일 약정된 손익비율이 없다면 균등 배분한다.

Example-4

The beginning capital balance and P&L ratio is the following respectively.
- Air : $30,000 (50%)
- Bird : $10,000 (30%)
- Cage : $5,000 (20%)

Each partner receives 5% interest on beginning capital balances.

Partner Bird receives a $6,000 salary.

Partner Cage receives a 10% bonus after interest and salaries.

Assuming partnership's income before allocation is $18,250.

	Air	Bird	Cage	Total
Beginning balance	30,000	10,000	5,000	45,000
Interest	1,500	500	250	2,250
Salary	0	6,000	0	6,000
Bonus	0	0	1,000*	1,000
Allocation	4,500**	2,700	1,800	9,000
Ending balance	36,000	19,200	8,050	63,250

* $(18,250 - 2,250 - 6,000) \times 10\% = 1,000$

** $(18,250 - 2,250 - 6,000 - 1,000) \times 50\% = 4,500$

4 Admission of a new partner

(1) Bonus method

사원의 영업권을 인식하지 않고 영업권 사원의 자본을 증가하고 다른 사원의 자본을 감소하여 조정한다.

Example-5

ABC partnership's capital balance and P&L ratio is the following respectively.

Air : $10,000 (40%), Bird : $20,000 (40%), Cage : $30,000 (20%)

Dean was admitted as a partner with 20% interest in capital for $30,000.

The bonus method was used to record the admission.

Dr) Cash   30,000

     Cr) Capital-Dean   18,000

         Capital-Air   4,800

         Capital-Bird   4,800

         Capital-Cage   2,400

---

1) Capital-Dean = (60,000 + 30,000) × 20% = 18,000

2) Bonus = 30,000 − 18,000 = 12,000

3) Allocation of bonus

    ⇨ 기존사원의 자본을 증가 (손익비율에 비례)

       Air 자본의 증가 = 12,000 × 40% = 4,800

       Bird 자본의 증가 = 12,000 × 40% = 4,800

       Cage 자본의 증가 = 12,000 × 20% = 2,400

사원 입사 후의 자본구성은 다음과 같다.

Capital-Air = 10,000 + 4,800 = 14,800

Capital-Bird = 20,000 + 4,800 = 24,800

Capital-Cage = 30,000 + 2,400 = 32,400

Capital-Dean = 18,000

Example-6

ABC partnership's capital balance and P&L ratio is the following respectively.

Air : $10,000 (40%), Bird : $20,000 (40%), Cage : $30,000 (20%)

Dean was admitted as a partner with 20% interest in capital for $10,000.

The bonus method was used to record the admission.

Dr) Cash	10,000	
Capital-Air	1,600	
Capital-Bird	1,600	
Capital-Cage	800	
Cr) Capital-Dean		14,000

1) Capital−Dean = (60,000 + 10,000) × 20% = 14,000
2) Bonus = 14,000 − 10,000 = 4,000
3) Allocation of bonus
   ⇨ 기존사원의 자본을 감소 (손익비율에 비례)
   Air 자본의 감소 = 4,000 × 40% = 1,600
   Bird 자본의 감소 = 4,000 × 40% = 1,600
   Cage 자본의 감소 = 4,000 × 20% = 800

사원 입사 후의 자본구성은 다음과 같다.

Capital−Air = 10,000 − 1,600 = 8,400
Capital−Bird = 20,000 − 1,600 = 18,400
Capital−Cage = 30,000 − 800 = 29,200
Capital−Dean = 14,000

(2) Goodwill method

영업권 사원의 영업권을 자산으로 인식하고 영업권 사원의 자본을 증가하며 다른 사원의 자본은 변동하지 않는다.

Example-7

ABC partnership's capital balance and P&L ratio is the following respectively.
Air : $10,000 (40%), Bird : $20,000 (40%), Cage : $30,000 (20%)
Dean was admitted as a partner with 20% interest in capital for $30,000.
The goodwill method was used to record the admission.

Dr) Cash	30,000	
Cr) Capital-Dean		30,000
Dr) Goodwill	60,000	
Capital-Air		24,000
Capital-Bird		24,000
Capital-Cage		12,000

1) Goodwill = Max [30,000/0.2, 60,000/0.8] − 90,000 = 60,000
2) Allocation of goodwill
⇨ 기존사원의 자본을 증가 (손익비율에 비례)
Air 자본의 증가 = 60,000 × 40% = 24,000
Bird 자본의 증가 = 60,000 × 40% = 24,000
Cage 자본의 증가 = 60,000 × 20% = 12,000

사원 입사 후의 자본구성은 다음과 같다.
Capital−Air = 10,000 + 24,000 = 34,000
Capital−Bird = 20,000 + 24,000 = 44,000
Capital−Cage = 30,000 + 12,000 = 42,000
Capital−Dean = 30,000

Example-8

ABC partnership's capital balance and P&L ratio is the following respectively.

Air : $10,000 (40%), Bird : $20,000 (40%), Cage : $30,000 (20%)

Dean was admitted as a partner with 20% interest in capital for $10,000.

The goodwill method was used to record the admission.

```
Dr) Cash                    10,000
    Cr) Capital-Dean                    10,000


Dr) Goodwill                 5,000
    Capital-Dean                         5,000
```

1) Goodwill = Max [10,000/0.2, 60,000/0.8] − 70,000 = 5,000

2) Allocation of goodwill

 ⇨ 신입사원의 자본을 증가

  Dean 자본의 증가 = 5,000 × 100% = 5,000

사원 입사 후의 자본구성은 다음과 같다.

Capital−Air = 10,000

Capital−Bird = 20,000

Capital−Cage = 30,000

Capital−Dean = 10,000 + 5,000 = 15,000

5 Partner withdrawal

(1) Bonus method

사원의 영업권을 인식하지 않고 남은 사원의 자본을 감소하여 조정한다.

Example-9

ABC partnership's capital balance and P&L ratio is the following respectively.
Air : $10,000 (40%), Bird : $20,000 (40%), Cage : $30,000 (20%)
Air decided to retire from the partnership and received $16,000.
The bonus method was used to record the retirement.

Dr) Capital-Air	10,000	
Capital-Bird	4,000	
Capital-Cage	2,000	
Cr) Cash		16,000

1) Bonus = 16,000 − 10,000 = 6,000
2) Allocation of bonus
   ⇨ 남은사원의 자본을 감소 (손익비율에 비례)
   Bird 자본의 감소 = 6,000 × 40% / 60% = 4,000
   Cage 자본의 감소 = 6,000 × 20% / 60% = 2,000

사원 퇴사 후의 자본구성은 다음과 같다.

Capital−Air = 10,000 − 10,000 = 0
Capital−Bird = 20,000 − 4,000 = 16,000
Capital−Cage = 30,000 − 2,000 = 28,000

(2) Goodwill method

사원 전체의 영업권을 자산으로 인식하고 퇴사사원 및 남은 사원의 자본을 모두 증가한 후 퇴사사원의 자본을 감소한다.

Example-10

ABC partnership's capital balance and P&L ratio is the following respectively.

Air : $10,000 (40%), Bird : $20,000 (40%), Cage : $30,000 (20%)

Air decided to retire from the partnership and received $16,000.

The goodwill method was used to record the retirement.

Dr) Goodwill	15,000	
Capital-Air		6,000
Capital-Bird		6,000
Capital-Cage		3,000
Dr) Capital-Air	16,000	
Cr) Cash		16,000

1) Goodwill = (16,000 − 10,000) / 0.4 = 15,000

2) Allocation of goodwill

⇨ 전 사원의 자본을 증가 (손익비율에 비례)

Air 자본의 증가 = 15,000 × 40% = 6,000

Bird 자본의 증가 = 15,000 × 40% = 6,000

Cage 자본의 증가 = 15,000 × 20% = 3,000

사원 퇴사 후의 자본구성은 다음과 같다.

Capital−Air = 10,000 + 6,000 − 16,000 = 0

Capital−Bird = 20,000 + 6,000 = 26,000

Capital−Cage = 30,000 + 3,000 = 33,000

6 Partnership liquidation

(1) Basic steps

청산의 잔여재산 분배는 다음 순서대로 진행한다.

Step-1	기초시점부터 청산시점까지의 영업 손익을 측정하여 각 사원에게 손익비율을 기준으로 배분한다.
Step-2	비현금자산을 매각하여 발생한 처분손익을 각 사원에게 손익비율을 기준으로 배분한다.
Step-3	현금자산을 채권자에게 먼저 배분하고 남은 현금은 각 사원에게 capital 잔액을 기준으로 배분한다. 이 과정에서 다음 계정은 capital에 가감한다. Loan to a partner ⇨ decrease capital balance Loan from a partner ⇨ increase capital balance Withdrawal ⇨ decrease capital balance

(2) Lump-sum sales approach

비현금재산을 일괄매각한다고 가정하여 잔여재산을 배분하는 접근방법이다.

(3) Installment sales approach

청산일정표를 작성하여 비현금재산의 매각시점마다 손익을 배분하고 각 사원에게 잔여재산을 배분하는 접근방법이다.

Example-11

On January 1, 20X1, Air and Bird decided to liquidate the A&B partnership.
On that date, the partnership condensed balance sheet was as follows:

Cash	15,000	Account payable	10,000
Other assets	90,000	Capital-Air (40%)	50,000
Loan to Bird	5,000	Capital-Bird (60%)	50,000
	$110,000		$110,000

During 20X1, the other assets are sold for $30,000.
The lump-sum sales approach was used to record the liquidation.

[Step-1]
기초에 청산을 결정하기 때문에 영업손익 배분은 없다.

[Step-2]
Loss = 90,000 - 30,000 = 60,000
⇨ 처분손실 배분후의 각 사원의 자본
Capital$-$Air = 50,000 $-$ 60,000 $\times$ 0.4 = 26,000
Capital$-$Bird = 50,000 $-$ 60,000 $\times$ 0.6 = 14,000

[Step-3]
Cash = 15,000 + 30,000 = 45,000
⇨ 현금 45,000의 배분 Creditors = 10,000
Capital$-$Air = 26,000
Capital$-$Bird = 14,000 $-$5,000 =9,000

Example-12

On January 1, 20X1, Air and Bird decided to liquidate the A&B partnership.
On that date, the partnership condensed balance sheet was as follows:

Cash	15,000	Account payable	10,000
Other assets	90,000	Capital-Air (40%)	50,000
Loan to Bird	5,000	Capital-Bird (60%)	50,000
	$110,000		$110,000

During 20X1, the other assets are sold for $30,000.

⟨A schedule of safe payments⟩

Date	Carrying amount	Sales price
March 15	20,000	10,000
May 3	70,000	20,000

The installment sales approach was used to record the liquidation.

3월 15일 시점의 청산분배금액은 다음과 같다.

[Step-2]

Loss $= 20,000 - 10,000 = 10,000$

⇨ 처분손실 배분후의 각 사원의 자본

Capital-Air $= 50,000 - 10,000 \times 0.4 = 46,000$

Capital-Bird $= 50,000 - 10,000 \times 0.6 = 44,000$

[Step-3]

Possible maximum loss $= 70,000$

⇨ 처분손실 배분후의 각 사원의 자본

Capital-Air $= 46,000 - 70,000 \times 0.4 = 18,000$

Capital-Bird $= 44,000 - 70,000 \times 0.6 - 5,000 = -3,000$

Cash $= 15,000 + 10,000 = 25,000$

⇨ 현금 25,000의 배분 Creditors $= 10,000$

Capital-Air $= 18,000 - 3,000 = 15,000$

Capital-Bird $= 0$

---

02 ▶ Personal financial statements

1 Introduction

(1) Reporting entity

재무제표의 보고실체는 개인이나 가족이며 주로 금융거래나 재무 계획 목적으로 작성한다.

(2) Required financial statements

개인의 재무제표는 다음과 같다.

> (1) Statements of financial condition
> (2) Statement of changes in net worth

기업이나 다른 조직과는 달리 손익계산서와 현금흐름표를 작성하지 않는다.

2 Statements of financial condition

(1) Form

> (1) Estimated current values of assets
> (2) Estimated current amounts of liabilities
> (3) Estimated income taxes on the differences between the estimated current values of assets and the estimated current amounts of liabilities and their tax bases.
> (4) Net worth

James and Jane Person
Statements of Financial Position
December 31, 19X3 amd 19X2

	December 31			
	19X3		19X2	
Assets				
Cash	$	3,700	$	15,600
Bonus receivable		20,000		10,000
Investments				
Marketable securities (Note 2)		160,500		140,700
Stock options (Note 3)		28,000		24,000
Kenbruce Associates (Note 4)		48,000		42,000
DaveKar Company, Inc. (Note 5)		550,000		475,000
Vested interest in deferred profit sharing plan		111,400		98,900
Remainder interest in testamentry trust (Note 6)		171,900		128,800
Cash value of life insurance ($43,600 and $42,900), less loans payable to insurance companies ($38,100 and $37,700) (Note 7)		5,500		5,200
Residence (Note 8)		190,000		180,000
Personal effects (excluding jewelry) (Note 9)		55,000		50,000
Jewelry (Note 9)		40,000		36,500
	$	1,384,000	$	1,206,700

	December 31			
	19X3		19X2	
Liabilities				
Income taxes - current year balance	$	8,800	$	400
Demand 10.5% note payable to bank		25,000		26,000
Mortgage payable (Note 10)		98,200		99,000
Contingent liabilities (Note 11)		-		-
		132,000		125,400
Estimated income taxes on the differences between the estimated current value of assets and the estimated current values of liabilities and their tax bases (Note 12)		239,000		160,000
Net worth		1,013,000		921,300
	$	1,384,000	$	1,206,700

(2) Presentation and recognition

재무상태표의 중요한 표시방법 및 인식기준은 다음과 같다.

1) Assets and liabilities shall be recognized on the accrual basis.

2) Assets and liabilities be presented in the order of liquidity and maturity, without classification as current and non-current.

3) Business interests that constitute a large part of a person's total assets shall be shown separately from other investments.

4) The net investment in a business entity (not its assets and liabilities) shall be presented in the statement of financial condition.

5) Non-cancelable commitments

아래의 조건을 모두 충족하면 부채로 인식한다.

- The commitments are for fixed or determinable amounts.

- The commitments are not contingent on others' life expectancies or the occurrence of a particular event, such as disability or death.

- The commitments do not require future performance of service

(3) Current value or current amount

주요 자산과 부채의 현행가치는 다음과 같다.

Receivables	discounted cash flows
Marketable securities	quoted market price
Life insurance	cash value of the policy less the outstanding loan
Payables and other liabilities	discounted cash flows
Non-cancelable commitments	discounted cash flows

(4) Estimated income taxes on the differences between the estimated current values of assets and the estimated current amounts of liabilities and their tax bases.

재무상태표에 보고된 자산 및 부채의 금액과 세법상의 금액과의 차이에 대한 법인세를 계산한 것으로 기업회계의 이연법인세 부채와 유사한 개념이다.

Example-13

KIM's personal assets :
estimated current value = 800,000, tax bases = 500,000
KIM's personal liabilities :
estimated current amount = 170,000, tax bases = 200,000
Tax rate = 30%
Prepare KIM's statement of financial condition.

> (1) Estimated current values of assets = $800,000
> (2) Estimated current amounts of liabilities = $170,000
> (3) Estimated income taxes = {800,000 − 170,000) − (500,000 − 200,000)} × 30% = $99,000
> (4) Net worth = 800,000 − 170,000 − 99,000 = $531,000

3 Statements of changes in net worth

(1) Major sources of increases in net worth

1) Income

2) Increases in the estimated current values of assets

3) Decreases in the estimated current amounts of liabilities

4) Decreases in estimated income taxes on the differences between the estimated current values of assets and the estimated current amounts of liabilities and their tax bases.

(2) Major sources of decreases in net worth

1) Expenses

2) Decreases in the estimated current values of assets

3) Increases in the estimated current amounts of liabilities

4) Increases in estimated income taxes on the differences between the estimated current values of assets and the estimated current amounts of liabilities and their tax bases.

03 ▶ Task-Based Simulation

[Q 3-1]

A partnership had the following condensed balance sheet:

Cash	$25,000	Liabilities	$95,000
Noncash Assets	185,000	A, Capital (50%)	70,000
		B, Capital (30%)	30,000
		C, Capital (20%)	15,000
Total	$210,000	Total	$210,000

The percentages in parentheses after the partners' capital balances represent their respective interest in profits and losses. Given the above information, respond to each of the following independent fact situations:

1. Assuming new Partner D acquires 30% of Partner B;s interest from B for consideration of $15,000, what is Partner B's capital balance after this transaction?

2. If new Partner D were to acquire a 30% interest in the partnership by making a contribution of assets to the partnership, what would be the suggested value of the consideration?

3. If the above assets were overstated by $24,000, what amount of consideration should new Partner D convey to the partnership in exchange for a 25% interest in capital, keeping in mind that D would also be acquiring a 30% interest in profits?

4. If new Partner D conveyed assets with a fair market value of $70,000 to the partnership in exchange for a one-third interest in capital and a 25% interest in profits, what would be B's capital balance after the transaction, assuming use of the bonus method?

5. Same facts as item 4 above, but assume that the goodwill method is employed.

6. If the tangible assets of the original partnership were understated by $25,000 and new Partner D conveyed assets with a fair market value of $70,000 to the partnership

in exchange for a 30% interest in capital and a 25% interest in profits, what would be A's capital balance after the transaction, assuming use of the bonus method?

7. Same facts as item 6 above, but assume that the goodwill method is employed.

8. If the tangible assets of the original partnership were overstated by $25,000 and new Partner D conveyed tangible assets with a fair market value of $22,000 to the partnership in exchange for a 25% interest in captial and a 20% interest in profits, what would be A's capital balance after the transaction, assuming use of the bonus method?

9. Same facts as item 8 above, but assume that the goodwill method is employed.

[Q 3-2] Partnership Formation

John, Jeff, and Jane decided to engage in a real estate venture as a partnership. John invested $100,000 cash and Jeff provided office equipment that is carried on his books at $82,000. The partners agree that the equipment has a fair value of $110,000. There is a $30,000 note payable remaining on the equipment to be assumed by the partnership. Although Jane has no physical assets to invest in the partnership, both John and Jeff believe that her experience as a real estate appraiser is a valuable skill needed by the partnership and is a basis for granting her a capital interest in the partnership.

• Instructions •

Assuming that each partner is to receive an equal capital interest in the partnership,

(1) Record the partnership formation under the bonus method.

(2) Record the partnership formation under the goodwill method, and assume a total goodwill of $90,000.

[Q 3-3] Allocation of Income or Loss

Jones, Silva, and Thompson form a partnership and agree to allocate income equally after recognition of 10% interest on beginning capital balances and monthly salary allowances of $2,000 to Jones and $1,500 to Thompson. Capital balances on January 1 were as follows:

Jones $40,000

Silva 25,000

Thompson 30,000

• Instructions •

Calculate the net income (loss) allocation to each partner under each of the following independent situations.

(1) Net income for the year is $99,500.

(2) Net income for the year is $38,300.

(3) Net loss for the year is $15,100.

[Q 3-4] Partner Admission

Beth, Steph, and Linda have been operating a small gift shop for several years. After an extensive review of their past operating performance, the partners concluded that the business needed to expand in order to provide an adequate return to the partners. The following balance sheet is for the partnership prior to the admission of a new partner, Mary.

Cash $160,000
Other Assets   640,000
Liabilities $200,000
Beth, Capital (40%)   265,000
Steph, Capital (40%)   215,000
Linda, Capital (20%)   120,000

Figures shown parenthetically reflect agreed profit-and-loss sharing percentages.

• Instructions •

Prepare the necessary journal entries to record the admission of Mary in each of the following independent situations. Some situations may be recorded in more than one way.

(1) Mary is to invest sufficient cash to receive a one–sixth capital interest. The parties agree that the admission is to be recorded without recognizing goodwill or bonus.

(2) Mary is to invest $160,000 for a one–fifth capital interest.

(3) Mary is to invest $160,000 for a one–fourth capital interest.

(4) Mary is to invest $160,000 for a 40% capital interest

Government & Not-For-Profit Accounting For the **US CPA** Exam

Consolidated Financial Statements

Volume
8

Chapter 4

Consolidated Financial Statements

1 Introduction

(1) 의의

사업결합(business combination)은 취득자(acquirer)가 사업(business)에 대한 지배력(control)을 획득하는 거래를 말한다. 사업결합의 유형에는 합병(merger)이나 주식취득(acquisition)이 있다.

Merger (흡수합병)	A+B ⇨ A
Consolidation (신설합병)	A+B ⇨ C
Acquisition (주식인수)	A+B ⇨ A+B : 연결재무제표 작성 대상

합병은 피투자회사(B)의 법률적 실체가 소멸되는 사업결합의 형태로 흡수합병과 신설합병으로 구분되며 주식인수는 피투자회사(B)의 법률적 실체가 유지되어 새무제표의 보고실체가되므로 투자회사(A)의 재무제표와 합산하는 연결재무제표 (consolidated financial statements)를 작성하여야 한다.

(2) 합병과 주식인수의 차이점

	Merger	Acquisition
피투자자(B)의 법률적 실체	소멸	유지
피투자자(B)의 자산 및 부채	투자자(A)의 장부에 기록된다.	피투자자(B)의 장부에 기록된다.
연결재무제표의 작성	No	Yes
취득지분율	100%	50% 초과
회계처리방법	Acquisition method 피투자자의 자산부채를 공정가치로 처리	

(3) 이전대가를 현금인 경우의 회계처리의 비교

투자자(A)는 다음과 같이 회계처리를 한다.

Merger	Acquisition
Asset (B)　　　xxx (FV) Goodwill　　　xxx (plug) 　　　Liability(B)　　　xxx (FV) 　　　Cash　　　xxx	Investment　　　xxx 　　　Cash　　　xxx

2 Acquisition method (ASC 805)

(1) 사업결합은 취득법을 적용하여 다음의 절차를 따른다.

　　1) 취득자의 식별

　　2) 취득일의 결정

　　3) 식별가능한 자산, 부채 및 피취득자에 대한 비지배지분의 인식과 측정

　　4) 영업권 또는 염가매수차익의 인식과 측정

(2) Identifying the acquirer

　　취득자는 피취득자에 대한 지배력(control)을 획득하는 기업이다.

(3) Determining the acquisition date

　　취득자는 취득일을 식별하며, 취득일은 피취득자에 대한 지배력을 획득한 날이 일반적으로 취득자가 법적으로 대가를 이전하여, 피취득자의 자산을 취득하고 부채를 인수한 날인 종료일이다.

(4) Recognizing and measuring assets, liabilities and non-controlling interest (NCI) in the acquiree.

　　취득일 현재, 취득자는 영업권과 분리하여 식별할 수 있는 취득 자산, 인수 부채, 피취득자에 대한 비지배지분을 인식한다. 식별가능한 각 자산과 부채는 취득일의 공정가치로 측정하며, 피취득자에 대한 비지배지분은 취득일의 공정가치로 측정한다.

　　⇨ 피취득자의 기존의 영업권의 공정가치는 "0"이다.

(5) Consideration transferred

사업결합에서 이전대가는 공정가치로 측정하며, 그 공정가치는 취득자가 이전하는 자산, 취득자가 부담하는 부채와 취득자가 발행한 지분의 취득일의 공정가치 합계로 산정한다. 취득일에 공정가치와 장부금액이 다른 취득자의 자산과 부채를 이전대가에 포함하는 경우, 취득자는 이전한 자산이나 부채를 취득일 현재 공정가치로 재측정하고, 그 결과 차손익이 있다면 당기손익으로 인식한다.

> 1) FV of the assets transferred by the acquirer
> 2) FV of the liabilities incurred by the acquirer
> 3) FV of the equity interests issued by the acquirer
> 4) FV of contingent consideration

(6) Non-controlling interest (비지배지분)

비지배지분은 종속기업에 대한 지분 중 지배기업에 직접이나 간접으로 귀속되지 않는 지분으로 취득일 시점의 공정가치로 측정한다. 지배기업은 비지배지분을 연결재무상태표에서 자본에 포함하되 지배기업의 소유주지분과는 구분하여 별도로 표시한다.

지배기업은 당기순손익과 기타포괄손익의 각 구성요소를 지배기업의 소유주와 비지배지분에 귀속시킨다. 또 지배기업은 비지배지분이 부(-)의 잔액이 되더라도 총포괄손익을 지배기업의 소유주와 비지배지분에 귀속시킨다.

(7) Acquisition-related costs

취득관련원가는 취득자가 사업결합을 하기 위해 발생시킨 원가이다. 그러한 원가에는 중개수수료 즉 자문, 법률, 회계, 가치평가 및 그 밖의 전문가 또는 컨설팅 수수료, 내부 취득 부서의 유지 원가를 포함한 일반관리원가, 채무증권과 지분증권의 등록 · 발행 원가를 포함한다.

> 1) Stock issue costs ⇨ decrease APIC
> 2) Bond issue costs ⇨ decrease bond payable
> 3) 나머지 취득관련원가 ⇨ expense

피취득자의 토지나 건물 등의 소유권을 이전하기 위한 취득세 등 특정 자산의 취득에 따른 부대원가는 특정 자산과 직접 관련된 원가이므로 해당 자산의 취득원가로 처리한다.

(8) Business combination achieved in stages

취득자는 때때로 취득일 직전에 지분을 보유하고 있던 피취득자에 대한 지배력을 획득한다. 예를 들어 20X1년 12월 31일에 기업 A는 기업 B에 대한 비지배지분 35%를 보유하고 있고 있다. 동일자에 기업 B의 지분 40%를 추가로 매수하여 기업 B에 대한 지배력을 갖게 된다. 그러한 거래를 단계적 취득이라고도 한다.

단계적으로 이루어지는 사업결합에서, 취득자는 이전에 보유하고 있던 피취득자에 대한 지분을 취득일의 공정가치로 재측정하고 그 결과 차손익이 있다면 당기손익으로 인식한다.

(9) Recognizing and measuring goodwill or a gain from a bargain purchase.

다음 A와 B를 영업권 또는 염가매수차익을 인식한다.

A	① FV of consideration transferred ② FV of non-controlling interest (NCI)
B	FV of net identifiable net assets of acquiree

A > B ⇨ Goodwill = A − B

A < B ⇨ A bargain purchase gain = B − A

영업권의 측정은 영업권에 대한 비지배지분의 몫을 인식해야 하는지 full goodwill method(전부영업권)과 partial goodwill method(부분영업권)으로 구분된다. FASB는 사업결합의 영업권 측정을 full goodwill method를 강제하고 있지만 IASB는 사업결합의 영업권 측정을 full goodwill method과 partial goodwill method 중 선택할 수 있다.

full goodwill method

영업권에 대한 비지배지분의 몫을 인식하며 비지배지분의 측정을 취득시점의 피투자회사의 공정가치로 측정한다.

partial goodwill method

영업권에 대한 비지배지분의 몫을 인식하지 않으며 비지배지분의 측정을 취득시점의 피투자회사의 순자산의 공정가치로 측정한다.

In a business combination to be accounted for as a purchase, Planet Company paid $300,000 for an 75% interest in Sun on January 2, Year 1. At the time, Sun's net assets had a fair value of $280,000.

full goodwill method

NCI (비지배지분) $= 300,000 \times 25\% \div 75\% = \$100,000$

Goodwill $= 300,000 + 100,000 - 280,000 = \$120,000$

partial goodwill method

NCI (비지배지분) $= 280,000 \times 25\% = \$70,000$

Goodwill $= 300,000 + 70,000 - 280,000 = \$90,000$

Comprehensive Example

	Planet (book value)	Star (book value)	Star (fair value)	Difference
		Balance sheets 1/1/20X1 (before combination)		
Cash	231,000	67,000	67,000	0
A/R	34,000	9,000	9,000	0
Inventories	23,000	16,000	20,000	4,000
PPE	179,000	50,000	58,000	8,000
Total Assets	467,000	142,000	154,000	12,000
A/P	4,000	2,000	2,000	
Bond Payable	300,000	34,000	34,000	
Capital stock	100,000	50,000		
APIC	15,000	15,000		
RE	48,000	41,000		
Total	467,000	142,000		

Book value of identifiable net asset of acquiree (Star)= $106,000

Fair value of identifiable net asset of acquiree (Star)= $118,000

On January 2, 20X1, Planet controlled Star by paying cash consideration.

(case−1) 100% merger and consideration = $134,000

(case−2) 100% acquisition and consideration = $134,000

(case−3) 90% acquisition, consideration = $120,600 and FV of NCI = 13,400

• Case 1 Merger (goodwill)

Working sheets (as of 1/2/20X1)				
	Planet	Adjustments		Merger
		Debit	Credit	
Cash	231,000	67,000	134,000	164,000
A/R	34,000	9,000		43,000
Inventory	23,000	20,000		43,000
Equipment	179,000	58,000		237,000
Goodwill	0	16,000		16,000
Total assets	467,000			503,000
A/P	4,000		2,000	6,000
B/P	300,000		34,000	334,000
NCI	0			0
Capital stock	100,000			100,000
APIC	15,000			15,000
R/E	48,000			48,000
Total L & E	467,000			503,000

※ Goodwill = $134,000 - 118,000 = $16,000$

• Case 2 Acquisition (100%)

Journal entry (Planet)	Dr) Investment in Star 134,000 Cr) Cash 134,000

Consolidation entry	Dr) Capital stock (S) 50,000
	    APIC (S) 15,000
	    RE (S) 41,000
	    Inventory 4,000
	    PPE 8,000
	    Goodwill 16,000 (plug)
	      Cr) Investment in Star 134,000

Concepts	Dr) Equity (S) 106,000
	    Differences 12,000
	    Goodwill 16,000 (plug)
	      Cr) Investment in Star 134,000

※ 주식인수는 합병과는 달리 피취득자의 법률적 실체가 소멸되지 않았기 때문에 두 기업의 재무제표를 합산한 후 취득자의 투자주식과 피취득자의 자본을 상계제거하며 자산부채의 시가차이와 영업권을 인식하는 연결재무제표를 작성한다.

※ case-2의 연결재무제표는 case-1의 합병재무제표와 동일하다.

	Planet	Star	Adjustments Debit	Adjustments Credit	Con
Cash	97,000	67,000			164,000
A/R	34,000	9,000			43,000
Inventory	23,000	16,000	4,000		43,000
Equipment	179,000	50,000	8,000		237,000
Investment	134,000			134,000	0
Goodwill	0		16,000		16,000
Total assets	467,000	142,000			503,000
A/P	4,000	2,000			6,000
B/P	300,000	34,000			334,000
NCI	0	0	0		0
Capital stock	100,000	50,000	50,000		100,000
APIC	15,000	15,000	15,000		15,000
R/E	48,000	41,000	41,000		48,000
Total L & E	467,000	142,000			503,000

Working sheets (as of 1/2/20X1)

• Case 3 Acquisition (90%)

FV of Consideration = 134,000 × 90% = 120,600

FV of NCI = 120,600 × 1/9 = 134,000 × 10% = 13,400

Journal entry (Planet)	Dr) Investment in Star 120,600
	Cr) Cash 120,600
Consolidation entry	Dr) Capital stock (S) 50,000
	APIC (S) 15,000
	RE (S) 41,000
	Inventory 4,000
	PPE 8,000
	Goodwill 16,000 (plug)
	Cr) Investment in Star 120,600
	Non-controlling interest 13,400
Concepts	Dr) Equity (S) 106,000
	Differences 12,000
	Goodwill 16,000 (plug)
	Cr) Investment in Star 120,600
	Non-controlling interest 13,400

※ 90%의 주식인수의 연결과정에서는 두 기업의 재무제표를 합산한 후 취득자의 투자주식과 피취득자의 자본을 상계제거하며 자산부채의 시가차이, 영업권 및 비지배지분을 인식하는 연결재무제표를 작성한다.

※ case−2의 연결재무제표는 case−2의 연결재무제표보다 자산과 자본이 각각 13,400 더 크다.

Working sheets (as of 1/2/20X1)					
	Planet	Star	Adjustments		Con
			Debit	Credit	
Cash	110,400	67,000			177,400
A/R	34,000	9,000			43,000
Inventory	23,000	16,000	4,000		43,000
Equipment	179,000	50,000	8,000		237,000
Investment	120,600			120,600	0
Goodwill	0		16,000		16,000
Total assets	467,000	142,000			516,400
A/P	4,000	2,000			6,000
B/P	300,000	34,000			334,000
NCI	0	0	0	13,400	13,400
Capital stock	100,000	50,000	50,000		100,000
APIC	15,000	15,000	15,000		15,000
R/E	48,000	41,000	41,000		48,000
Total L & E	467,000	142,000			516,400

Example-1

On January 1, 20X1, Planet Corp. and Star Corp. had condensed balance sheets as follows:

Accounts	Planet Corp.	Star Corp.
Current assets	100,000	30,000
Non-current assets	120,000	50,000
Current liabilities	60,000	20,000
Non-current liabilities	80,000	10,000
Stockholders' equity	80.000	50,000

On January 2, 20X1, Planet purchased 90% of the outstanding common shares of Star. On that date, the fair value of non-controlling interest was $6,000. The carrying amount of Star's net assets at the purchase date totaled $50,000. Fair values equaled carrying amount for all items except for inventory, for which fair values exceeded carrying amount by $7,000.

Prepare Planet's consolidated balance sheet on January 2,20X1.

On January 2, 20X1, Planet controlled Star
(case-1) By paying cash consideration of $54,000
(case-2) By issuing common stock of $54,000
(case-3) By issuing bond of $54,000

> **Example-2**

Blue Company purchased 80% of the common stock of Red Company for $700,000 plus direct acquisition costs of $30,000. At the time of the purchase, Red Company had the following balance sheet :

Assets		Liabilities and Equity	
Cash	$120,000	Account payable	$200,000
Inventory	200,000	Bond payable	400,000
Land	100,000	Common stock	100,000
Building	450,000	APIC	150,000
Equipment	230,000	Retained earnings	250,000
Total	$1,100,000	Total	$1,100,000

The market values of assets are

Inventory	300,000
Land	200,000
Building	600,000
Equipment	200,000

Prepare the elimination entries that would be made on a consolidated worksheet prepared on the date of purchase.

> **· Answer ·**

(1) Blue's journal entry

Account	Debit	Credit
Investment	700,000	
Expenses	30,000	
Cash		730,000

(2) Blue's consolidation adjustment entry

Account	Debit	Credit
Common Stock	$100,000	
Additional Paid-In Capital	150,000	
Retained Earnings	250,000	
Inventory	100,000	
Land	100,000	
Building	150,000	
Equipment		30,000
Goodwill	55,000	
Investment		700,000
Non-Controlling Interest		175,000

Example-3

On January 1, Year 1, Planet acquired 30% of Star's outstanding common stock for $400,000. During Year 1, Star had net income of $100,000 and paid dividends of $30,000. On January 1, Year 2, Planet acquired an additional 45% interest on Star for $1,012,500. The fair value of Star on January 1, Year 2 was $2,250,000 and the fair value of Star's net assets on January 1, Year 2 was $2,000,000. What amount of gain and goodwill from this transaction will Planet record in Year 2?

• Answer •

Year 1

지분율이 30%이므로 지분법으로 회계 처리하므로 투자주식의 장부금액은 다음과 같다.

$400,000 + (100,000 - 30,000) \times 30\% = \$421,000$

Year 2

취득자는 이전에 보유하고 있던 피취득자에 대한 지분을 취득일의 공정가치로 재측정하고 그 결과는 당기손익으로 인식한다.

이전에 보유하고 있던 피취득자에 대한 지분의 취득일의 공정가치

$= 2,250,000 \times 30\% = \$675,000$

당기손익 $= 675,000 - 421,000 = \$254,000$

75%의 사업결합에 해당되므로 영업권은 다음과 같다.

goodwill $= 2,250,000 - 2,000,000 = \$250,000$

FV of NCI $= 2,250,000 \times 25\% = \$562,500$

02 ▶ Consolidations (ASC 810)

1 Introduction

연결회계는 법적으로 다른 회계 실체들이 하나의 경제적 실체를 형성하는 경우 이들을 하나의 회계실체로 간주하고 단일의 재무제표(consolidated F/S, 연결재무제표)를 작성하는 회계이다. 연결재무제표를 작성하기 위해서는 피투자기업의 형태에 따라 2가지 모형 중 하나를 적용한다.

> Is the legal entity a VIE?
> YES → Variable Interest Model
> NO → Voting Interest Model

2 Voting Interest Model

(1) General

연결재무제표를 작성하기 위해서는 한 기업이 다른 기업의 경영을 좌우할 수 있을 정도의 지배력(control)을 확보하여야 한다.

지배력은 의결권의 과반수 및 실질적 권리를 동시에 고려하여야 한다. 피투자기업의 의결권 과반수를 보유하지 못한 투자자는 지배력(control)이 없으며, 피투자기업의 의결권 과반수를 보유한 투자자는 그 권리가 실질적인가를 평가하여 지배력(control)을 판단한다.

우선주는 의결권이 없으므로 적용되지 않으며, 의결권이 50%인 경우 지배력이 없으므로 투자자는 지분법 회계를 적용한다.

A 기업이 B기업의 지분을 80% 소유하고 B기업이 C기업의 지분을 60% 소유한 경우 A는 C를 간접적으로 지배하고 있기 때문에 B와 C를 모두 연결재무제표에 포함한다.

Voting Interest Model을 적용하는 경우 아래의 순서로 연결재무제표 작성 여부를 판단한다.

(2) Economic entity group

Consolidated statements are presented as if the group of legal entities were one economic entity group because the resources of two or more companies are under the control of the parent company.

(3) Consolidation procedures

The consolidation process eliminates reciprocal items that are shown on both Parent's and Subsidiary's book to avoid double-counting the same items which would misstate the financial statements of the combined entity.

(4) Limitation

Consolidated F/S are prepared from worksheets which begin with the trial balance (T/B) of Parent and Subsidiary.

⇨ 연결조정분개는 정산표에서의 수정이므로 두 기업의 장부를 수정하지 못한다.

3 Presentation

(1) Balance sheet

Non-controlling interest (NCI; 비지배지분)은 대차대조표의 자본에 단일항목으로 표시한다. 따라서 연결대차대조표의 납입자본 및 이익잉여금은 지배기업의 소유주 자본을 표시한다.

(2) Income statement

비지배주주의 귀속 손익을 손익계산서에 구분하여 표시한다.

지배회사가 종속회사를 80%소유하고 지배회사의 당기순이익 = 200, 종속회사의 당기순이익 = 100이라면 연결손익계산서의 당기순이익은 다음과 같이 표시한다.

Net income	300
NI attributable to NCI	20
NI attributable to acquirer	280

(3) Statement of changes in equity

비지배주주의 자본의 증가 또는 감소를 구분하여 표시한다.

지배회사의 배당금 = 40, 종속회사의 배당금 = 20이라면 다음과 같이 표시한다.

	C/S	APIC	R/E	NCI	Total
NI			+280	+20	+300
Dividend			-40	-4	-44

4 Consolidation procedures-subsequent to Acquisition

(Step-1) 지배회사의 투자주식과 종속회사의 자본의 상계제거

(1) 지분법의 제거

    지배회사가 투자주식에 대해여 지분법을 적용하는 경우 지분법을 제거한다.

(2) 지배회사의 투자주식과 종속회사의 자본의 상계제거

    취득시점 기준으로 제거하며 시가차이, 영업권, 비지배지분이 인식된다.

(3) Amortization of differentials

    (2)에서 인식한 시가차이에 대해서 상각을 하여 당기순이익에 반영한다.

(Step-2) 내부거래 및 미실현손익의 제거

(1) 다음의 내부거래를 제거하며 관련 미실현손익을 제거한다.

    1) Inventory
    2) PPE
    3) Bond

(2) 내부거래를 상향판매와 하향판매로 구별한다.

    1) Upstream (상향판매) : 종속회사가 지배회사에게 판매
    2) Downstream (하향판매) : 지배회사가 종속회사에게 판매

(Step-3) 비지배주주 귀속 손익의 측정

비지배주주 귀속 손익은 다음과 같이 측정한다.

NI attributable to NCI

= (종속회사의 NI − 시가차이 상각 − 상향판매 미실현이익) × 지분율

03 ▶ Intercompany Transactions

1 Elimination of intercompany transactions

내부거래(intercompany transactions)는 지배기업과 종속기업 간의 거래를 말한다. 연결실체의 관점에서는 지배기업과 종속기업 간의 거래는 동일한 기업실체 내의 거래이므로 연결재무제표에 반영되어서는 안된다. 따라서 연결조정분개를 할 때 내부거래는 제거되어야 한다.

내부거래는 연결순이익에 영향을 미치는 거래도 있고 영향을 미치지 않는 거래도 있다. 연결순이익에 영향을 미치는 내부거래의 제거로 발생하는 미실현손익 및 실현손익은 지배회사의 순이익과 종속회사의 순이익에 미치는 영향을 고려하여야 한다.

내부거래로 인식한 자산 또는 부채가 연결실체에 남아 있는 경우 내부거래로 발생한 손익은 미실현손익이다. 내부거래로 인식한 자산 또는 부채가 연결실체 외부로 판매되거나 사용하여 소멸하는 경우 발생한 손익은 실현손익이다.

내부거래는 하향내부거래(downstream)과 상향내부거래(upstream)고 구분한다.
seller = parent company → Downstream
seller = subsidiary company → Upstream

내부거래 손익 조정

하향내부거래(downstream)
미실현손익과 실현손익 모두 지배회사의 순이익이 원천이므로
NI attributable to acquirer에서 조정한다.

상향내부거래(upstream)
미실현손익과 실현손익 모두 종속회사의 순이익이 원천이므로
NI attributable to acquirer 및 NI attributable to NCI에서 조정한다.

2 Inventory-Downstream

(1) 미실현이익이 없는 경우

On January 2, 20X1, Planet purchased 80% of the outstanding common shares of Star. During 20X1, Planet sold merchandise that cost $2,700 to Star for $3,600 and Star sold all of this merchandise to its customers for $4,200 on account. And Star paid $2,000 to Planet.

합산재무제표와 연결 실체 입장에서의 금액을 비교하면, 매출과 매출원가가 동시에 $3,600이 과대되어 있으며, 매출채권과 매입채무가 $1,600이 과대되어 있으므로 연결분개는 다음과 같다.

Accounts	DR	CR
① 매출 및 매출원가제거		
Sales revenue	3,600	
COGS		3,600
② 채권 및 채무제거		
Accounts payable	1,600	
Accounts receivable		1.600

지배기업이 종속기업에 20X1에 판매한 재고자산을 종속기업은 20X1에 판매하여 미실현이익은 없다. 따라서 연결순이익에는 영향이 없으며 NI attributable to acquirer 및 NI attributable to NCI도 달라지지 않으므로 조정하지 않는다.

내부거래 미실현손익이 없으므로 연결순이익은 달라지지 않지만 연결손익계산서 매출과 매출원가는 각각 $3,600씩 감소하며, 연결재무상태표 매출채권과 매입채무는 각각 $1,600씩 감소한다.

	Planet	Star	Adjusting	Con
Income Statement				
Sales revenue	3,600	4,200	−3,600	4,200
COGS	2,700	3,600	−3,600	2,700
Net income	900	600		1,500
NI attributable to NCI				120
NI attributable to acquirer				1,380
Balance sheet				
Accounts receivable	1,600	4,200	−1,600	4,200
Accounts payable	0	1,600	−1,600	0

NI attributable to NCI $= 600 \times 20\% = 120$

NI attributable to acquirer $= 1,500 - 120 = 1,380$

(2) 미실현이익이 있는 경우

On January 2, 20X1, Planet purchased 80% of the outstanding common shares of Star. During 20X1, Planet sold merchandise that cost \$2,700 to Star for \$3,600 and Star sold all but \$600 of this merchandise to its customers for \$3,500 on account. And Star paid \$2,000 to Planet.

지배기업이 종속기업에 20X1에 판매한 재고자산을 종속기업은 20X1에 판매하지 않았기 때문에 미실현이익이 있다. 종속회사는 취득원가 \$600의 재고자산을 20X2년에 판매할 것이며 이때 미실현이익은 \$150이다.

미실현이익의 계산 방법은 다음 두 가지 방법이 있다.

1) 미실현이익 = 판매자의 매출총이익률 × 구매자의 기말재고금액

$\qquad = 25\% \times 600 = 150$

2) 미실현이익 = 판매자의 매출총이익 × 구매자의 기말재고비율

$\qquad = 900 \times 600/3600 = 150$

합산재무제표와 연결 실체 입장에서의 금액을 비교하면, 매출은 $3,600이 과대되어 있고, 매출원가는 $3,450이 과대되어 있고, 재고자산은 $150과소되어 있다. 매출채권과 매입채무가 $1,600이 과대되어 있으므로 연결분개는 다음과 같다. 재고자산 내부거래 분개는 먼저 내부거래한 재고자산 판매금액만큼 매출과 매출원가를 취소하고(①), 미실현이익만큼 재고자산을 감소시키면서 매출원가를 인식한다(③).

Accounts	DR	CR
① 매출 및 매출원가제거		
Sales revenue	3,600	
COGS		3,600
② 채권 및 채무제거		
Accounts payable	1,600	
Accounts receivable		1.600
③ 미실현이익 제거		
COGS	150	
Inventory		150

하향내부거래(downstream)이므로 미실현이익 $150은 NI attributable to acquirer에서만 조정하며 NI attributable to NCI에서는 조정하지 않는다.

	Planet	Star	Adjust-ing	Con
Income Statement				
Sales revenue	3,600	3,500	-3,600	3,500
COGS	2,700	3,000	-3,450	2,250
Net income	900	500		1,250
NI attributable to NCI				100
NI attributable to acquirer				1,150
Balance sheet				
Inventory	0	600	-150	450
Accounts receivable	1,600	3,500	-1,600	3,500
Accounts payable	0	1,600	-1,600	0

NI attributable to NCI $= 500 \times 20\% = 100$

NI attributable to acquirer $= 1,250 - 100 = 1,150 (= 900 + 500 \times 80\% -150)$

(3) 미실현이익의 실현

　20X1년 내부거래로 발생한 미실현이익 \$150은 지배기업 이익잉여금에 반영하고 있다. 또한 종속기업은 20X2년에 판매하면서 인식한 매출원가 \$600에 미실현이익 \$150이 포함되어 있다. 따라서 20X2년 연결조정분개는 다음과 같다. 즉, 지배기업의 이익잉여금 \$150을 감소시키고, 종속기업이 인식한 매출원가 \$150을 감소시키는 분개를 한다.

Accounts	DR	CR
④ 미실현이익의 실현		
Retained earnings(P)	150	
COGS(S)		150

　20X2년 미실현이익의 실현 분개를 통해서 매출원가 \$150이 감소하여 연결순이익이 \$150이 증가한다. 미실현이익의 실현이익 \$150은 하향내부거래로 발생하였으므로 NI attributable to acquirer에서 조정하며 \$150 증가한다.

Example-4

P Company owns 80% of the outstanding stock of S Company. During 20X1, S Company reported net income of $525,000 and declared no dividends. At the end of the year, S Company's inventory included $487,500 in unrealized profit on purchases from P Company. Intercompany sales for 20X1 totaled $2,700,000.

(1) Prepare in general journal form all consolidated financial statement workpaper entries necessary at the end of the year to eliminate the effects of the 20X1 intercompany sales.

(2) Calculate the amount of the noncontrolling interest to be deducted from consolidated income in arriving at 20X1 controlling interest in consolidated net income.

• Answer •

(1) 재고자산 내부거래 분개는 먼저 내부거래한 재고자산 판매금액만큼 매출과 매출원가를 취소하고(①), 미실현이익만큼 재고자산을 감소시키면서 매출원가를 인식한다(③).

Accounts	DR	CR
① 매출 및 매출원가제거		
Sales revenue	2,700,000	
COGS		2,700,000
③ 미실현이익 제거		
COGS	487,500	
Inventory		487,500

(2) 하향내부거래(downstream) 미실현이익 NI attributable to NCI에서 조정하지 않는다.
 NI attributable to NCI = 525,000 x 20% = 105,000

3 Inventory-Upstream

(1) 미실현이익이 없는 경우

On January 2, 20X1, Planet purchased 80% of the outstanding common shares of Star. During 20X1, Star sold merchandise that cost $2,700 to Planet for $3,600 and Planet sold all of this merchandise to its customers for $4,200 on account. And Planet paid $2,000 to Star.

합산재무제표와 연결 실체 입장에서의 금액을 비교하면, 매출과 매출원가가 동시에 $3,600이 과대되어 있으며, 매출채권과 매입채무가 $1,600이 과대되어 있으므로 연결분개는 다음과 같다.

Accounts	DR	CR
① 매출 및 매출원가제거		
Sales revenue	3,600	
COGS		3,600
② 채권 및 채무제거		
Accounts payable	1,600	
Accounts receivable		1.600

종속기업이 지배기업에 20X1에 판매한 재고자산을 지배기업은 20X1에 판매하여 미실현이익은 없다. 따라서 연결순이익에는 영향이 없으며 NI attributable to acquirer 및 NI attributable to NCI도 달라지지 않으므로 조정하지 않는다.

내부거래 미실현손익이 없으므로 연결순이익은 달라지지 않지만 연결손익계산서 매출과 매출원가는 각각 $3,600씩 감소하며, 연결재무상태표 매출채권과 매입채무는 각각 $1,600씩 감소한다.

	Planet	Star	Adjusting	Con
Income Statement				
Sales revenue	4,200	3,600	-3,600	4,200
COGS	3,600	2,700	-3,600	2,700
Net income	600	900		1,500
NI attributable to NCI				180
NI attributable to acquirer				1,320
Balance sheet				
Accounts receivable	4,200	1,600	-1,600	4,200
Accounts payable	1,600	0	-1,600	0

NI attributable to NCI = 900 × 20% = 180

NI attributable to acquirer= 1,500 − 180 = 1,320

(2) 미실현이익이 있는 경우

On January 2, 20X1, Planet purchased 80% of the outstanding common shares of Star. During 20X1, Star sold merchandise that cost $2,700 to Planet for $3,600 and Planet sold all but $600 this merchandise to its customers for $3,500 on account. And Planet paid $2,000 to Star.

종속기업이 지배기업에 20X1에 판매한 재고자산을 지배기업은 20X1에 판매하지 않았기 때문에 미실현이익이 있다. 지배회사는 취득원가 $600의 재고자산을 20X2년에 판매할 것이며 이때 미실현이익은 $150이다.

합산재무제표와 연결 실체 입장에서의 금액을 비교하면, 매출은 $3,600이 과대되어 있고, 매출원가는 $3,450이 과대되어 있고, 재고자산은 $150과소되어 있다. 매출채권과 매입채무가 $1,600이 과대되어 있으므로 연결분개는 다음과 같다. 재고자산 내부거래 분개는 먼저 내부거래한 재고자산 판매금액만큼 매출과 매출원가를 취소하고(①), 미실현이익만큼 재고자산을 감소시키면서 매출원가를 인식한다(③).

Accounts	DR	CR
① 매출 및 매출원가제거		
Sales revenue	3,600	
COGS		3,600
② 채권 및 채무제거		
Accounts payable	1,600	
Accounts receivable		1.600
③ 미실현이익 제거		
COGS	150	
Inventory		150

상향내부거래(upstream)이므로 미실현이익 $150은 NI attributable to acquirer 및 NI at-tributable to NCI에서 조정한다.

	Planet	Star	Adjusting	Con
Income Statement				
Sales revenue	3,500	3,600	−3,600	3,500
COGS	3,000	2,700	−3,450	2,250
Net income	500	900		1,250
NI attributable to NCI				150
NI attributable to acquirer				1,100
Balance sheet				
Inventory	600	0	−150	450
Accounts receivable	3,500	1,600	−1,600	3,500
Accounts payable	1,600	0	−1,600	0

NI attributable to NCI $= (900 - 150) \times 20\% = 150$

NI attributable to acquirer$= 1,350 - 150 = 1,100 \ (= 500 + (900-150) \times 80\%)$

(3) 미실현이익의 실현

20X1년 내부거래로 발생한 미실현이익 $150은 종속기업 이익잉여금에 반영하고 있다. 또한 지배기업은 20X2년에 판매하면서 인식한 매출원가 $600에 미실현이익 $150이 포함되어 있다. 따라서 20X2년 연결조정분개는 다음과 같다. 즉, 종속업의 이익잉여금 $120을 감소시키고, 비지배지분 $30을 감소하고, 지배기업이 인식한 매출원가 $150을 감소시키는 분개를 한다.

Accounts	DR	CR
④ 미실현이익의 실현		
Retained earnings(S)	120	
NCI	30	
COGS(P)		150

20X2년 미실현이익의 실현 분개를 통해서 매출원가 $150이 감소하여 연결순이익이 $150이 증가한다. 미실현이익의 실현이익 $150은 상향내부거래로 발생하였으므로 NI attributable to acquirer 및 NI attributable to NCI에서 각각 $120 및 $30의 증가로 조정한다.

Example-5

P Company owns 80% of the outstanding stock of S Company. During 20X1, S Company reported net income of $525,000 and declared no dividends. At the end of the year, P Company's inventory included $487,500 in unrealized profit on purchases from S Company. Intercompany sales for 20X1 totaled $2,700,000.

(1) Prepare in general journal form all consolidated financial statement workpaper entries necessary at the end of the year to eliminate the effects of the 20X1 intercompany sales.

(2) Calculate the amount of the noncontrolling interest to be deducted from consolidated income in arriving at 20X1 controlling interest in consolidated net income.

• Answer •

(1) 재고자산 내부거래 분개는 먼저 내부거래한 재고자산 판매금액만큼 매출과 매출원가를 취소하고(①), 미실현이익만큼 재고자산을 감소시키면서 매출원가를 인식한다(③).

Accounts	DR	CR
① 매출 및 매출원가제거		
Sales revenue	2,700,000	
COGS		2,700,000
③ 미실현이익 제거		
COGS	487,500	
Inventory		487,500

(2) 상향내부거래(upstream) 미실현이익은 NI attributable to NCI에서 미실현이익의 20% 조정한다.

NI attributable to NCI = $(525,000 - 487,500) \times 20\% = 7,500$

Example-6

On January 1, 20X1, Mountain Company purchased 90% of the common stock of Garden Corporation. During 20X1, Garden sold all of its production to Mountain Company for $400,000, a price that includes a 20% gross profit. 20X1 is the first year that such intercompany sales were made. By year-end, Mountain sold 70% of the goods it had purchased at a markup on cost of 25%.

1. Determine the gross profit on sales recorded by both Garden and Mountain companies and to be shown on the consolidated income statement.

2. Prepare the eliminations and adjustments that would be made on the December 31, 20X1 and 20X2 consolidated worksheet as a result of this transaction.

• Answer •

1. Garden's gross profit = $400,000 \times 0.2 = \$80,000$
   Mountain' gross profit = $400,000 \times 0.25 \times 0.7 = \$70,000$

2. Consolidation adjustment entry for 20X1

Account	Debit	Credit
Sales	$400,000	
COGS		376,000
Inventory		24,000

Unrealized profit = $400,000 \times 0.3 \times 0.2 = \$24,000$

※ 종속기업이 처분한 상향내부거래이므로 미실현이익과 미실현이익의 실현은 지분율에 비례하여 지배기업소유주 귀속 순이익과 비지배지분 귀속 순이익에서 조정한다.

NI attributable to NCI : $24,000 \times 0.1 = 2,400$ decrease

NI attributable to acquirer : $24,000 \times 0.9 = 21,600$ decrease

Consolidation adjustment entry for 20X2

Account	Debit	Credit
Retained Earnings	$24,000	
Inventory		24,000

내부거래로 구입한 재고자산을 20X2에 판매하였다면 다음과 같이 연결조정분개를 한다.

4 Property, Plant and Equipment

(1) Downstream sales

하향판매의 손익인식기업은 지배기업이므로 미실현이익 전액을 지배기업의 소유주가 부담하며 이익잉여금에서 차감된다.

On January 1, 20X1, Planet purchased 80% of the outstanding common shares of Star. On January 2, 20X1, Planet sold machinery with an original cost of $2,000 and a carrying amount of $1,200 to Star for $1,500. Planet had owned the machinery for two years and used a five-year straight line depreciation with no residual value. Star is using straight-line depreciation over three years with no residual value. Star reported net income of $3,000 and Planet reported net income of $5,000 during 20X1.

1) 하향판매의 연결조정분개

```
Dr) Gain on disposal of PPE        300
    PPE—machinery                  500
    Cr) Accumulated depreciation         700
        Depreciation expense             100
```

유형자산 내부거래 분개는 먼저 유형자산처분이익 $300이 미실현이익이므로 제거되고, 매년 감가상각비가 $100씩 제거되어 실현된다.

2) 미실현이익 = 300 − 100 = $200

3) Net income = 5,000 + 3,000 − 200 = $7,800

4) NI attributable to NCI = 3,000 × 20% = $600

5) NI attributable to acquirer = 7,800 − 600 = $7,200

미실현이익은 처분이익과 감가상각비의 차이금액이며 하향판매의 미실현이익 $200은 지배회사의 이익에서 조정한다.

(2) Upstream sales

상향판매의 손익인식기업은 종속회사이므로 미실현이익 전액을 지배기업의 소유주와 비지배주주가 지분율에 비례하여 배분하여 각각 이익잉여금과 비지배지분에서 차감된다.

On January 1, 20X1, Planet purchased 80% of the outstanding common shares of Star. On January 2, 20X1, Star sold machinery with an original cost of $2,000 and a carrying amount of $1,200 to Planet for $1,500. Star had owned the machinery for two years and used a five-year straight line depreciation with no residual value. Planet is using straight-line depreciation over three years with no residual value. Star reported net income of $3,000 and Planet reported net income of $5,000 during 20X1.

1) 상향판매의 연결조정분개

Dr) Gain on disposal of PPE   300
    PPE−machinery   500
      Cr) Accumulated depreciation   700
        Depreciation expense   100

유형자산 내부거래 분개는 먼저 유형자산처분이익 $300이 미실현이익이므로 제거되고, 매년 감가상각비가 $100씩 제거되어 실현된다.

2) 미실현이익 = 300 − 100 = $200

3) Net income = 5,000 + 3,000 − 200 = $7,800

4) NI attributable to NCI = (3,000-200) × 20% = $560

5) NI attributable to acquirer = 7,800 − 560 = $7,240

미실현이익은 처분이익과 감가상각비의 차이금액이며 상향판매의 미실현이익 $200은 종속회사의 이익에서 조정한다.

Example-7

Planet owns 80% of the outstanding common stock of Star. On January 2, 20X1, Planet sold equipment to Star for $500,000. The equipment cost Planet $780,000 and had accumulated depreciation of $400,000 on the date of the sale.

The management of Star estimated that the equipment had a remaining useful life of four years from January 2, 20X1. In 20X1, Planet reported $300,000 and Star reported $200,000 in net income from their independent operations (including sales to affiliates).

(1) Prepare in general journal form the workpaper entries necessary because of the intercompany sale of equipment in the consolidated financial statements workpaper for the year ended December 31, 20X1.

(2) Calculate the balances to be reported in the consolidated income statement for the year ended December 31, 20X1, for the following items:

    1) Consolidated income.

    2) Noncontrolling interest in consolidated income.

    3) Controlling interest in consolidated income

• Answer •

(1) 유형자산 내부거래 분개는 먼저 유형자산처분이익 $120,000이 미실현이익이므로 제거되고, 매년 감가상각비가 $30,000씩 제거되어 실현된다.

Accounts	DR	CR
Gain on disposal of equipment ①	120,000	
Equipment ③	280,000	
Depreciation expense ②		30,000
Accumulated depreciation		370,000(plug)

    ① $= 500,000 - (780,000 - 400,000) = 120,000$

    ② $= 120,000/4 \text{ years} = 30,000$

    ③ $= 780,000 - 500,000 = 280,000$

(2) downstream unrealized profit $= 120,000 - 30,000 = 90,000$

    1) Consolidated income $= 300,000 + 200,000 - 90,000 = 410,000$

    2) NCI in consolidated income $= 200,000 \times 20\% = 40,000$

    3) Controlling interest in consolidated income $= 410,000 - 40,000 = 370,000$

Example-8

Planet owns 80% of the outstanding common stock of Star. On June 30, 20X1, Planet sold equipment to Star for $500,000. The equipment cost Planet $780,000 and had accumulated depreciation of $400,000 on the date of the sale.

The management of Star estimated that the equipment had a remaining useful life of four years from On June 30, 20X1. In 20X1, Planet reported $300,000 and Star reported $200,000 in net income from their independent operations (including sales to affiliates).

(1) Prepare in general journal form the workpaper entries necessary because of the intercompany sale of equipment in the consolidated financial statements workpaper for the year ended December 31, 20X1.

(2) Calculate the balances to be reported in the consolidated income statement for the year ended December 31, 20X1, for the following items:

    1) Consolidated income.

    2) Noncontrolling interest in consolidated income.

    3) Controlling interest in consolidated income

• Answer •

(1) 유형자산 내부거래 분개는 먼저 유형자산처분이익 $120,000이 미실현이익이므로 제거되고, 매년 감가상각비가 $15,000씩 제거되어 실현된다.

Accounts	DR	CR
Gain on disposal of equipment ①	120,000	
Equipment ③	280,000	
Depreciation expense ②		15,000
Accumulated depreciation		385,000(plug)

    ① $= 500,000 - (780,000 - 400,000) = 120,000$

    ② $= 120,000/4 \text{ years} \times 6/12 = 15,000$

    ③ $= 780,000 - 500,000 = 280,000$

(2) downstream unrealized profit $= 120,000 - 15,000 = 105,000$

    1) Consolidated income $= 300,000 + 200,000 - 105,000 = 395,000$

    2) NCI in consolidated income $= 200,000 \times 20\% = 40,000$

    3) Controlling interest in consolidated income $= 395,000 - 40,000 = 355,000$

Example-9

Planet owns 80% of the outstanding common stock of Star. On January 2, 20X1, Star sold equipment to Planet for $500,000. The equipment cost Star $780,000 and had accumulated depreciation of $400,000 on the date of the sale.

The management of Planet estimated that the equipment had a remaining useful life of four years from January 2, 20X1. In 20X1, Planet reported $300,000 and Star reported $200,000 in net income from their independent operations (including sales to affiliates).

(1) Prepare in general journal form the workpaper entries necessary because of the intercompany sale of equipment in the consolidated financial statements workpaper for the year ended December 31, 20X1.

(2) Calculate the balances to be reported in the consolidated income statement for the year ended December 31, 20X1, for the following items:

  1) Consolidated income.
  2) Noncontrolling interest in consolidated income.
  3) Controlling interest in consolidated income

• Answer •

(1) 유형자산 내부거래 분개는 먼저 유형자산처분이익 $120,000이 미실현이익이므로 제거되고, 매년 감가상각비가 $30,000씩 제거되어 실현된다.

Accounts	DR	CR
Gain on disposal of equipment	120,000	
Equipment	280,000	
Depreciation expense		30,000
Accumulated depreciation		370,000(plug)

(2) upstream unrealized profit = 120,000 − 30,000 = 90,000

  1) Consolidated income = 300,000 + 200,000 − 90,000 = 410,000
  2) NCI in consolidated income = (200,000 − 90,000) × 20% = 22,000
  3) Controlling interest in consolidated income = 410,000 − 22,000 = 388,000

Example-10

On January 1, 20X1, Bark Company sold a machine to Fan Company for $25,000. The machine had an original cost of $24,000, and depreciation on the asset had accumulated to $9,000 at the time of the sale. The machine has a 5-year remaining life and will be depreciated on a straight-line basis with no salvage value. Bark Company is an 90%-owned subsidiary of Fan Company.

Prepare the eliminations and adjustments that would be made on the December 31, 20X1 and 20X2 consolidated worksheet as a result of this sale.

• Answer •

미실현이익 : 유형자산처분이익 = 25,000 − (24,000 − 9,000) = 10,000
미실현이익의 실현 : 감가상각비 = 10,000/5년 = 2,000

Consolidation adjustment entry for 20X1

Account	Debit	Credit
Gain on sale of machine	$10,000	
Depreciation		2,000
Machine (PPE)		1,000
Accumulated Depreciation		7,000

※ 종속기업이 처분한 상향내부거래이므로 미실현이익과 미실현이익의 실현은 지분율에 비례하여 지배기업소유주 귀속 순이익과 비지배지분 귀속 순이익에서 조정한다.

NI attributable to NCI : 8,000 × 0.1 = 800 decrease
NI attributable to acquirer : 8,000 × 0.9 = 7,200 decrease

Account	Debit	Credit
Retained Earnings	$8,000	
Depreciation		2,000
Machine (PPE)		1,000
Accumulated Depreciation		5,000

5 Bond

(1) 의의

연결실체내의 한 기업이 회사채를 발행하고 다른 기업이 그 회사채를 취득하면 이는 내부 거래에 해당한다. 따라서 지배기업과 종속기업이 개별 재무제표에 인식한 자산(debt investment)과 부채(bond payable) 및 수익(interest revenue)과 비용(interest expense)는 연결분개를 통해서 제거되어야 한다.

연결실체내의 한 기업이 회사채를 발행하고 다른 기업이 그 회사채를 취득하면 연결실체 입장에서는 회사채를 상환하는 것에 해당하므로 연결분개를 통해서 상환손익을 인식하여야 한다.

지배기업이 회사채를 발행하고 종속기업이 그 회사채를 취득한 경우는 하향내부거래이며, 종속기업이 회사채를 발행하고 지배기업이 그 회사채를 취득한 경우는 상향내부거래이다.

(2) Downstream sales

하향판매의 손익인식기업은 지배기업이므로 미실현이익 전액을 지배기업의 소유주가 부담 하며 이익잉여금에서 차감된다.

On January 1, 20X1, Planet purchased 80% of the outstanding common shares of Star. On January 2, 20X1, Star purchased the $10,000 face amount, 8% bond of Planet for $8,500 to yield 10%. These bonds represented 10 percent of the outstanding class of bonds issued at par by Planet. Star intends to hold the bonds until maturity. Star reported net income of $3,000 and Planet reported net income of $5,000 during 20X1.

1) 하향판매의 연결조정분개

Dr) Interest revenue   850
  Bond payable   10,000
   Cr) Interest expense   800
    Investment-HTM   8,550
    Gain on retirement of S bond   1,500 (plug)

2) 미실현이익 = 1,500 − 850 + 800 = 1,450

3) Net income = 5,000 + 3,000 + 1,450 = $9,450

4) NI attributable to NCI = 3,000 × 20% = $600

5) NI attributable to acquirer = $9,450 − 600 = $8,850

미실현이익은 상환이익과 이자수익 및 이자비용의 차이금액이며 하향판매의 미실현이익은 지배회사의 이익에서 조정한다.

(3) Upstream sales

상향판매의 손익인식기업은 종속회사이므로 미실현이익 전액을 지배기업의 소유주와 비지배주주가 지분율에 비례하여 배분하여 각각 이익잉여금과 비지배지분에서 차감된다.

On January 1, 20X1, Planet purchased 80% of the outstanding common shares of Star. On January 2, 20X1, Planet purchased the $10,000 face amount, 8% bond of Star for $8,500 to yield 10%. These bonds represented 10 percent of the outstanding class of bonds issued at par by Star. Planet intends to hold the bonds until maturity. Star reported net income of $3,000 and Planet reported net income of $5,000 during 20X1.

1) 상향판매의 연결조정분개

Dr) Interest revenue   850
　　Bond payable   10,000
　　Cr) Interest expense   800
　　　　Investment−HTM   8,550
　　　　Gain on retirement of S bond   1,500 (plug)

2) 미실현이익 = 1,500 − 850 + 800 = 1,450

3) Net income = 5,000 + 3,000 + 1,450 = $9,450

4) NI attributable to NCI = (3,000 + 1,450) × 20% = $890

5) NI attributable to acquirer = $9,450 − 890 = $8,560

미실현이익은 상환이익과 이자수익 및 이자비용의 차이금액이며 상향판매의 미실현이익은 종속회사의 이익에서 조정한다.

Example-11

Green Company is an 90%-owned subsidiary of Black Corporation. Green Company issued $100,000 of 10%, 8-year bonds for $102,000 on January 1, 20X1. Annual interest is paid on January 1. Black Corporation purchased the bonds on January 2, 20X5, for $99,400. Black intends to hold the bonds until maturity. Both companies are using the straight-line method to amortize the premium/discount on the bonds.

Prepare the eliminations and adjustments that would be made on the December 31, 20X5 consolidated worksheet as a result of this purchase.

• Answer •

채권 발행자의 기말 장부금액 = $100,000 + 2,000 \times 3/8 = 100,750$
채권 발행자의 이자비용 = $100,000 \times 10\% - 2,000 \times 1/8 = 9,750$
채권 투자자의 기말 장부금액 = $99,400 + 600 \times 1/4 = 99,550$
채권 투자자의 이자수익 = $100,000 \times 10\% + 600 \times 1/4 = 10,150$

Consolidation adjustment entry for 20X5

Account	Debit	Credit
Bond Payable (net)	$100,750	
Interest Revenue	10,150	
Investment (net)		99,550
Interest Expense		9,750
Gain on retirement of bond		1,600

※ 종속기업이 처분한 상향내부거래이므로 미실현이익과 미실현이익의 실현은 지분율에 비례하여 지배기업소유주 귀속 순이익과 비지배지분 귀속 순이익에서 조정한다.
미실현이익 및 실현이익 = $1,600 + 9,750 - 10,150 = 1,200$
NI attributable to NCI : $1,200 \times 0.1 = 120$ increase
NI attributable to acquirer : $1,200 \times 0.9 = 1,080$ increase

6 지분법의 제거

지배회사의 개별재무제표는 외부에 공표되지 않기 때문에 연결재무제표 정산표의 지배회사의 투자주식은 지분법 또는 원가법 모두 가능하다. 따라서 지분법의 경우 종속회사의 당기순이익이 연결당기순이익에서 중복이 되어 있기 때문에 연결정산표에서 지분법을 제거하며 원가법의 경우 배당수익의 중복을 제거한다.

(1) Equity method

On January 1, 20X1, Planet paid $80,000 for 80% of the common stock of Star. On this date, the carrying amount of Star's net assets was $90,000 ($60,000 C/S and $30,000 R/E) and approximated their fair value except for patent, for which fair exceeded book value by $10,000. The patent has a 10 year life.

Star's net income and dividends are as follows during 20X1

NI = $ 25,000, Dividends = $15,000

- 지분법 회계처리 (Planet)

```
Dr) Investment           7,200(plug)
    Cash                12,000*
    Cr) Investment income            19,200**
```

* 배당 = 15,000 × 80% = 12,000

** 지분법 이익 = (25,000 − 10,000/10년) × 80% = 19,200

(Step-1) 지배회사의 투자주식과 종속회사의 자본의 상계제거

(1) 지분법의 제거

Dr) Investment income	19,200	
NCI	3,000	
Cr) Retained earnings		15,000
Investments in S		7,200

(2) 지배회사의 투자주식과 종속회사의 자본의 상계제거

Dr) Common stock(S)	60,000	
Retained earnings (S)	30,000	
Patent	10,000	
Cr) Investments in S		80,000
NCI		20,000

(3) Amortization of differentials

Dr) Amortization expenses	1,000	
Cr) Patent		1,000

(Step-2) 내부거래 및 미실현손익의 제거

없음

(Step-3) 비지배주주 귀속 손익의 측정

NI attributable to NCI
$= (25,000 - 1,000) \times 20\% = \$4,800$

⟨Income statement⟩

	P	S	Adjustment	Consolidated
Revenue	250,000	65,000		315,000
Investment income	19,200		-19,200	0
Expenses	200,000	40,000	+1,000	241,000
NI	69,200	25,000		74,000
NI-NCI				4,800
NI-P				69,200

⟨Statement of R/E⟩

	P	S	Adjustment	Consolidated
Beginning R/E	5,000	30,000	-30,000	5,000
NI	69,200	25,000		69,200
Dividends	30,000	15,000	-15,000	30,000
Ending R/E	44,200	40,000		44,200

⟨Balance sheet⟩

	P	S	Adjustment	Consolidated
Current asset	130,000	60,000		190,000
Investment in S	87,200		-87,200	0
PPE	250,000	70,000		320,000
Patents			+9,000	9,000
Liabilities	73,000	30,000		103,000
Common stock	350,000	60,000	-60,000	350,000
R/E	44,200	40,000		44,200
NCI			+21,800	21,800

※ NCI (12/31)

= 취득시점의 공정가치 + 비지배주주 귀속 순이익 − 비지배주주 배당

= 20,000 + 4,800 − 3,000 = $21,800

(2) Cost method

- 원가법 회계처리 (Planet)

> Dr) Cash   12,000*
>   Cr) Dividend revenue   12,0000

(Step-1) 지배회사의 투자주식과 종속회사의 자본의 상계제거

> (1) 배당수익의 제거
>
> Dr) Dividend revenue   12,000
>   NCI   3,000
>   Cr) Retained earnings   15,000
>
> ---
>
> (2) 지배회사의 투자주식과 종속회사의 자본의 상계제거
>
> Dr) Common stock(S)   60,000
>   Retained earnings (S)   30,000
>   Patent   10,000
>   Cr) Investments in S   80,000
>   NCI   20,000
>
> ---
>
> (3) Amortization of differentials
>
>   Dr) Amortization expenses   1,000
>   Cr) Patent   1,000

(Step-2) 내부거래 및 미실현손익의 제거

> 없음

(Step-3) 비지배주주 귀속 손익의 측정

> NI attributable to NCI
> $= (25,000 - 1,000) \times 20\% = \$4,800$

⟨Income statement⟩

	P	S	Adjustment	Consolidated
Revenue	250,000	65,000		315,000
Investment income	12,000		-12,000	0
Expenses	200,000	40,000	+1,000	241,000
NI	62,000	25,000		74,000
NI-NCI				4,800
NI-P				69,200

⟨Statement of R/E⟩

Beginning R/E	5,000	30,000	-30,000	5,000
NI	62,000	25,000		69,200
Dividends	30,000	15,000	-15,000	30,000
Ending R/E	37,000	40,000		44,200

⟨Balance sheet⟩

Current asset	130,000	60,000		190,000
Investment in S	80,000		-80,000	0
PPE	250,000	70,000		320,000
Patents			+9,000	9,000
Liabilities	73,000	30,000		103,000
Common stock	350,000	60,000	-60,000	350,000
R/E	37,000	40,000		44,200
NCI			+21,800	21,800

※ NCI (12/31)

= 취득시점의 공정가치 + 비지배주주 귀속 순이익 − 비지배주주 배당

= 20,000 + 4,800 − 3,000 = \$21,800

7 Combined Financial Statements

(1) Scope

1) Companies are under common control

개인이 다수의 기업을 지배하는 상황에서 연결재무제표를 작성할 수 없는 경우 공동 지배 하의 기업의 재무제표를 합산

2) A group of unconsolidated subsidiaries

(2) Procedure

적용절차는 연결재무제표와 동일하며 적용대상이 다를 뿐이다.

- Intercompany transaction, balances, unrealized G/L
- NCI, foreign operation, different fiscal periods, income tax etc.

Example-12

Case-1

Alpha Corp. owns 100% of the capital stock of both Beta Corp. and Charlie .Corp. Beta purchases merchandise from Charlie at 40% markup on Charlie's cost. During 20X1, merchandise that cost Charlie $30,000 was sold to Beta. Beta sold all of this merchandise to unrelated customers for $75,000 during 20X1.

Case-2

Alpha Corp. owns 100% of the capital stock of both Beta Corp. and Charlie .Corp. Beta purchases merchandise from Charlie at 40% markup on Charlie's price. During 20X1, merchandise that cost Charlie $30,000 was sold to Beta. Beta sold all of this merchandise to unrelated customers for $75,000 during 20X1.

Determine the gross profit on sales recorded by both Beta and Charlie companies and to be shown on the 20X1 combined income statement for Beta and Charlie.

• Answer •

Case-1

Charlie's gross profit = $30,000 \times 0.4 = \$12,000$

Beta's gross profit = $75,000 - 30,000 \times 1.4 = \$33,000$

Combined gross profit = $75,000 - 30,000 = \$45,000$

Case-2

Charlie's gross profit = $30,000 \times 0.4/0.6 = \$20,000$

Beta's gross profit = $75,000 - 30,000 / 0.6 = \$25,000$

Combined gross profit = $75,000 - 30,000 = \$45,000$

8 Comprehensive Example(100% Acquisition)

Planet acquired all of the outstanding $10 par value voting common stock of Star on January 1, 20X1 by issuing 25,000 shares of its $10 par value voting common stock. On January 1, 20X1, Planet's common stock had a closing market price of $30 per share on a national stock exchange.

There were no changes in the common stock and additional paid-in capital accounts during 20X1 except the one necessitated by Planet's acquisition of Star.

At the acquisition date, the fair value of Star's machinery exceeded its book value by $54,000. The excess cost will be amortized over the estimated average remaining life of six years. The fair values of all of Star's other assets and liabilities were equal to their book values.

During 20X1, Planet purchased merchandise from Star at an aggregate invoice price of $180,000, which included a 25% markup on Star's cost. At December 31, 20X1, Planet owed Star $86,000 on these purchases, and $36,000 of this merchandise remained in Planet's inventory.

On July 1, 20X1, Planet sold equipment with an original cost of $60,000 a carrying value of $42,000 to Star for $72,000. The equipment had a remaining life of three years and was depreciated using the straight-line method by both companies.

On December 31, 20X1, the companies had condensed financial statements as follows:

⟨Income statement⟩

	Planet Dr. (Cr.)	Star Dr. (Cr.)
Net sales	$(3,800,000)	$(1,500,000)
Dividends from Star	(40,000)	0
Gain on sale of PPE	(30,000)	0
Cost of goods sold	2,360,000	870,000
Operating expenses	1,100,000	440,000
Net income	$(410,000)	$(190,000)

⟨Statement of R/E⟩

	Planet Dr. (Cr.)	Star Dr. (Cr.)
Beginning R/E	$(440,000)	$(156,000)
NI	(410,000)	(190,000)
Dividends	100,000	40,000
Ending R/E	(750,000)	(306,000)

⟨Balance sheet⟩

	Planet Dr. (Cr.)	Star Dr. (Cr.)
Cash	$470,000	$150,000
Accounts receivable	860,000	350,000
Inventory-merchandise	1,060,000	410,000
Land, plant and equipment	1,320,000	680,000
Accumulated depreciation	(370,000)	(210,000)
Investment in Star (at cost)	750,000	0
Total Assets	$4,090,000	$1,380,000
Accounts payable	$(1,340,000)	$(594,000)
Common stock ($10 par)	(1,700,000)	(400,000)
Additional paid-in capital	(300,000)	(80,000)
Retained earnings	(750,000)	(306,000)
Total liabilities & equity	$(4,090,000)	$(1,380,000)

(Step-1) 지배회사의 투자주식과 종속회사의 자본의 상계제거

Account	Debit	Credit
(1) 배당수익의 제거		
Dividend revenue(P)	40,000	
NCI	0	
Retained earnings(S)		40,000
(2) 지배회사의 투자주식과 종속회사의 자본의 상계제거		
Common stock(S)	400,000	
APIC(S)	80,000	
Retained earnings(S)	156,000	
Machinery(S)	54,000	
Goodwill(S)	60,000	
Investments in S(P)		750,000
NCI		0
(3) Amortization of differentials		
Depreciation expense(S)	9,000	
Accumulated depreciation(S)		9,000

(Step-2) 내부거래 및 미실현손익의 제거

Account	Debit	Credit
(1)재고자산 내부거래		
Sales	180,000	
Cost of goods sold		180,000
Accounts payable	86,000	
Accounts receivable		86,000
Cost of goods sold	7,200	
Inventory		7,200
(2) 유형자산 내부거래		
Gain on sale of PPE	30,000	
PPE		12,000
Depreciation expense		5,000
Accumulated depreciation		13,000

(Step-3) 비지배주주 귀속 손익의 측정

Account	Debit	Credit
Retained earnings(S)	0	
NCI		0

⟨Income statement⟩

	P	S	Adjustment	Consolidated
Net Sales	3,800,000	1,500,000	(180,000)	5,120,000
Dividends from Star	40,000	-	(40,000)	-
Gain on sale of PPE	30,000	-	(30,000)	-
COGS	2,360,000	870,000	(172,800)	3,057,200
S&A expense	1,100,000	440,000	4,000	1,544,000
Net income	410,000	190,000		518,800

⟨Statemen of RE⟩

	P	S	Adjustment	Consolidated
1/1 RE	440,000	156,000	(156,000)	440,000
Net income	410,000	190,000		518,800
Dividend paid	100,000	40,000	(40,000)	100,000
12/31 RE	750,000	306,000		858,800

⟨Balance Sheet⟩

	P	S	Adjustment	Consolidated
Cash	470,000	150,000	0	620,000
A/R	860,000	350,000	(86,000)	1,124,000
Inventory	1,060,000	410,000	(7,200)	1,462,800
PPE	1,320,000	680,000	42,000	2,042,000
AD	370,000	210,000	(22,000)	602,000
Investment	750,000	-	(750,000)	-
Goodwill	-	-	60,000	60,000
Total	4,090,000	1,380,000		4,706,800
A/P	1,340,000	594,000	(86,000)	1,848,000
CS	1,700,000	400,000	(400,000)	1,700,000
APIC	300,000	80,000	(80,000)	300,000
RE	750,000	306,000		858,800
NCI	-	-		-
Total	4,090,000	1,380,000		4,706,800

9 Consolidated Financial Statements

(1) Incomes Statement

Consolidated revenue and expense

= 지배회사 금액 + 종속회사 금액 ± 순자산 과소평가 당기 상각액 ± 내부거래 제거금액

---

1) Consolidated income

  = 지배회사 순이익 + 종속회사 순이익 − 지분법이익(배당수익)
   − 순자산 과소평가 당기 상각액 ± 내부거래 미실현손익

2) 지배회사 연결 순이익

  = 지배회사 순이익 − 지분법이익(배당수익) ± 내부거래 미실현손익(downstream)

3) 종속회사 연결 순이익

  = 종속회사 순이익 − 순자산 과소평가 당기 상각액 ± 내부거래 미실현손익
   (upstream)

4) NCI in consolidated income = 3) x NCI 지분율

5) CI in consolidated income = 1) − 4) = 2) + 3) x CI 지분율

※ 지배회사가 지분법을 사용하는 경우 CI in consolidated income = 지배회사 순이익

(2) Statement of retained earnings

---

1) Beginning RE = 지배회사 금액

2) Net income = CI in consolidated income

3) Dividend = 지배회사 금액

4) Ending RE = 1) + 2) − 3)

※ 지배회사가 지분법을 사용하는 경우 Ending RE = 지배회사 금액

---

(3) Balance sheet

1) Consolidated assets and liabilities excluding investment in subsidiary & goodwill
   = 지배회사 금액+종속회사 금액 ± 순자산 과소평가 상각후 금액 ± 내부거래 제거금액

2) Investment in subsidiary = 0

3) Goodwill = 연결조정분개에서 인식한 금액

4) Paid-in capital = 지배회사 금액

5) Retained earnings = 자본변동표 기말금액

6) Non-controlling interest (NCI) = ① + ② − ③

   ① Beginning NCI = 취득시점의 공정가치

   ② NCI in consolidated income

   ③ 종속회사 배당금 × NCI 지분율

04 ❯❯ Tasked-Based Simulation(TBS)

[Q 4-1] Non-controlling interest

In a business combination to be accounted for as a purchase, Planet Company paid $1,300,000 for an 80% interest in Sun on January 2, Year 1. At the time, Sun's net assets had a book value of $1,000,000, while the market value of Sun's patents was $200,000 more than book value. All other assets and liabilities had book values equal to market value. Sun depreciates its assets on a straight-line basis. Both tangible and intangible assets are amortized over 10 years. For the current year, Sun had net income of $400,000 and declared and paid dividends of $100,000.

• Instructions •

(1) In its Year 1 consolidated balance sheet, what amount should Planet report as goodwill under full goodwill method ?

(2) What is the non-controlling interest that will be reported on Planet's Year 1 consolidated balance sheet?

[Q 4-2] Acquisition and goodwill

On January 1, Year 1, Planet and Star had the following balance sheet.

	Planet	Star
Cash	231,000	47,000
A/R	34,000	9,000
Inventories	23,000	16,000
PPE	179,000	50,000
Intangible assets	0	0
Total Assets	467,000	122,000
A/P	4,000	2,000
Bond Payable	300,000	14,000
Capital stock ($10par)	100,000	50,000
APIC	15,000	15,000
RE	48,000	41,000
Total liabilities and equity	467,000	112,600

Fair values of Star's assets were follows:
Inventory : $15,000, PPE : 63,000

(Case I)

Planet issued 3,000 shares of $10 par value common stock for 100% of the common stock of Star and Star ceased to operate as separate business. The market value of Planet's stock is $50.

Cost incurred in relationship to the purchase are as follows:

Finder's fees =$4,000, Appraisal fees=1,000, Stock registration fees = 3,000

Prepare Planet's consolidated B/S.

(Case 2)

Planet issued 2,400 shares of $10 par value common stock for 80% of the common stock of Star and the market value of Planet's stock is $50.

Prepare Planet's consolidated B/S.

[Q 4-3] Consolidation subsequent to acquisition

On January 2, Year 1, the carrying amount of Star's net assets was $650,000. The fair values of Star's net assets were the same as their carrying amounts. At the acquisition date, the fair value of Star's machinery exceeded its book value by $60,000. The excess cost will be amortized over the estimated average remaining life of six years. The fair values of all of Sun's other assets and liabilities were equal to their book values.

During Year 1, Planet purchased merchandise from Star at an aggregate invoice price of $180,000, which included a 20% markup on Star's cost. At December 31, Year 1, Planet owed Star $86,000 on these purchases, and $36,000 of this merchandise remained in Planet's inventory.

⟨Situation I⟩

On January 2, Year 1, Planet Corp. acquired 100% of Star Corp.'s common stock for $750,000. Planet used cost method for the investment.

⟨Situation II⟩

On January 2, Year 1, Planet Corp. acquired 100% of Star Corp.'s common stock for $750,000. Planet used equity method for the investment.

• Situation I •

⟨Income statement⟩

	Planet	Star	Adjustments	Consolidated
Net sales	$3,800,000	$1,500,000		
Dividends from Star	54,000	0		
Gain on sale of PPE	42,000	0		
Cost of goods sold	2,300,000	870,000		
S&A expense	900,000	440,000		
Net income	$696,000	$190,000		

⟨Statement of retained earnings⟩

	Planet	Star	Adjustments	Consolidated
Balance, 1/1/Year 1	$500,000	$170,000		
Net income	696,000	190,000		
Dividends paid	346,000	54,000		
Balance, 12/31/Year 1	$850,000	$306,000		

⟨Balance sheet⟩

	Planet	Star	Adjustments	Consolidated
Cash	$570,000	$150,000		
Accounts receivable	860,000	350,000		
Inventories	1,060,000	410,000		
PPE	1,320,000	680,000		
Accumulated Dep.	370,000	210,000		
Investment in Star	750,000			
Goodwill	0	0		
Total Assets	$4,190,000	$1,380,000		
Accounts payable	$340,000	$394,000		
Bond payable	1,000,000	200,000		
Common stock ($10)	1,700,000	400,000		
APIC	300,000	80,000		
Retained earnings	850,000	306,000		
NCI	0	0		
Total	$4,190,000	$1,380,000		

⟨Income statement⟩

	Planet	Star	Adjustments	Consolidated
Net sales	$3,800,000	$1,500,000		
Investment income	174,000	0		
Gain on sale of PPE	42,000	0		
Cost of goods sold	2,300,000	870,000		
S&A expense	900,000	440,000		
Net income	$816,000	$190,000		

⟨Statement of retained earnings⟩

	Planet	Star	Adjustments	Consolidated
Balance, 1/1/Year 1	$500,000	$170,000		
Net income	816,000	190,000		
Dividends paid	346,000	54,000		
Balance, 12/31/Year 1	$970,000	$306,000		

⟨Balance sheet⟩

	Planet	Star	Adjustments	Consolidated
Cash	$570,000	$150,000		
Accounts receivable	860,000	350,000		
Inventories	1,060,000	410,000		
PPE	1,320,000	680,000		
Accumulated Dep.	370,000	210,000		
Investment in Star	870,000			
Goodwill	0	0		
Total Assets	$4,310,000	$1,380,000		
Accounts payable	$340,000	$394,000		
Bond payable	1,000,000	200,000		
Common stock ($10)	1,700,000	400,000		
APIC	300,000	80,000		
Retained earnings	970,000	306,000		
NCI	0	0		
Total	$4,310,000	$1,380,000		

[Q 4-4] Consolidation subsequent to acquisition

On January 2, Year 1, Planet purchased 10% of the outstanding common shares of Star for $20,000 cash and classified them as FVTNI Investment . The carrying amount of Star's net assets on January 2, Year 1 totaled $180,000. Fair values equaled carrying amounts for all items. During Year 1, Star reported net income of $50,000. On January 1, Year 2, Planet purchase additional 50% of the outstanding common shares of Star for $140,000 cash. During Year 2, Star reported net income of $60,000.

• Instructions •

(1) Prepare the journal entry for Planet on January 1, Year 2.

(2) In its Year 2 consolidated balance sheet, what amount should Planet report as goodwill under US GAAP?

(3) What is the non-controlling interest that will be reported on Planet's Year 2 consolidated balance sheet?

[Q 4-5] Consolidation subsequent to acquisition

On January 2, Year 1, Planet purchased 20% of the outstanding common shares of Star for $40,000 cash and classified them as equity method. The carrying amount of Star's net assets on January 2, Year 1 totaled $180,000. Fair values equaled carrying amounts for all items. During Year 1, Star reported net income of $50,000. On January 1, Year 2, Planet purchase additional 50% of the outstanding common shares of Star for $140,000 cash. During Year 2, Star reported net income of $60,000.

• Instructions •

(1) Prepare the journal entry for Planet on January 1, Year 2.

(2) In its Year 2 consolidated balance sheet, what amount should Planet report as goodwill under US GAAP?

(3) What is the non-controlling interest that will be reported on Planet's Year 2 consolidated balance sheet?

[Q 4-6] Intercompany transactions

Planet sold a press to its 80%-owned subsidiary, Star for $5,000 on January 1, Year 2. The press originally was purchased by Planet on January 1, Year 1, for $20,000, and $6,000 of depreciation for 20X1 had been recorded. The fair market value of the press on January 1, Year 2, was $10,000. Star proceeded to depreciate the press on a straight-line basis, using a 5-year life and no salvage value.

• Instructions •

Prepare all worksheet eliminations that would be made on the Year 2 consolidated worksheet.

[Q 4-7] Intercompany transactions

Gander Corporation is a wholly owned subsidiary of Mountain Company. During Year 1, Gander sold all of its production to Mountain Company for $400,000, a price that includes a 25% gross profit. Year 1 is the first year that such intercompany sales were made. By year-end, Mountain sold 80% of the goods it had purchased at a markup on cost of 20%.

• Instructions •

1. Determine the gross profit on sales recorded by both Gander and Mountain companies.
2. Determine the gross profit to be shown on the consolidated income statement.

[Q 4-8] Consolidated statements : date of acquisition

Kippers Steel has approached the management of Gage Company and has made an offer to acquire 90% of Gage's outstanding stock on July 1, Year 1. Kippers Steel will give 20,000 shares of its previously unissued, $1 par, $35 market value, common stock in exchange for a 90% ownership interest. Out-of-pocket costs of the acquisition incurred by Kippers Steel would be as follows:

Legal fees and finder's fees : $27,000   Stock issuance costs : 18,000

Comparative balance sheets just prior to the combination are as follows:

	Kippers Steel	Gage
Cash	$200,000	$80,000
Other current assets	650,000	180,000
Marketable securities	180,000	50,000
Property, plant, and equipment (net)	2,500,000	800,000
Patents	240,000	60,000
Total assets	$3,770,000	$1,170,000
Current liabilities	$410,000	$320,000
Bonds payable	1,000,000	300,000
Common stock($1par)	300,000	
Common stock($25par)		25,000
Paid-in capital in excess of par	1,200,000	275,000
Retained earnings	860,000	250,000
Total liabilities and equity	$3,770,000	$1,170,000

On July 1, Gage's book values approximate market values, except for the following:

Marketable securities $60,000   Bonds payable   296,000
Property, plant, and equipment   950,000   Patents   80,000

• Instructions •

Prepare a consolidated balance sheet for July1, Year 1, immediately subsequent to the acquisition.

[Q 4-9] Equity method & Cost method

On January 1, Planet Corporation purchased 90% of the common stock of Star Company for $1,500,000. The following information relates to Star at the date of acquisition.

Cash	$50,000
Inventory	250,000
Land	100,000
Building	700,000
Liabilities	100,000

Additional information relating to the purchase is shown below.

1. Both the book value and the fair value are the same for the inventory and liabilities.
2. The fair market value of the building is $800,000 and the fair market value of the land is $200,000.
3. Star Company depreciates its assets on a straight-line basis. Both tangible and intangible assets are amortized over 10 years.
4. For the current year, Star Company had net income of $400,000 and declared and paid dividends of $100,000.

• Instructions •

1. Prepare the eliminations and adjustments that would be made on the On January 2, 20X1 consolidated worksheet.

2. Prepare the eliminations and adjustments that would be made on the December 31, 20X1 consolidated worksheet if Planet accounted for the investment using equity method.

3. Prepare the eliminations and adjustments that would be made on the December 31, 20X1 consolidated worksheet if Planet accounted for the investment using cost method.

4. What amount of non−controlling interest would Planet report in its December 31, 20X1 consolidated balance sheet?

[Q 4-10] Intercompany transactions

Planet Company owns 90% of the outstanding capital stock of Star Company. During 20X1 and 20X2 Star sold merchandise to Planet at a markup of 25% of selling price. The selling price of the merchandise sold during the two years was $20,800 and $25,000, respectively.

At the end of each year, Planet had in its inventory one-fourth of the goods purchased that year from Star. Star reported net income of $30,000 in 20X1 and $35,000 in 20X2.

• Instructions •

Determine the amount of the noncontrolling interest in consolidated income to be reported for 20X1 and 20X2.

[Q 4-11] Comprehensive example

On January 2, 20X1, Planet purchased a 90% interest in Star for $1,400,000. At that time Star had capital stock outstanding of $800,000 and retained earnings of $425,000. The difference between book value of equity acquired and the value implied by the purchase price was allocated to the following assets:

Inventory : $ 41,667

Plant and Equipment (net) : 200,000

Goodwill : 88,889

The inventory was sold in 20X1. The plant and equipment had a remaining useful life of 10 years on January 2, 20X1.

During 20X1 Star sold merchandise with a cost of $950,000 to Planet at a 20% markup above cost. At December 31, 20X1, Planet still had merchandise in its inventory that it purchased from Star for $576,000.

In 20X1, Star Company reported net income of $410,000 and declared no dividends.

• Instructions •

(1) Prepare in general journal form all entries necessary on the consolidated financial statements workpaper to eliminate the effects of the intercompany sales, to eliminate the investment account, and allocate the difference between book value of equity acquired and the value implied by the purchase price

(2) Assume that Planet reports net income of $2,000,000 from its independent operations. Calculate controlling interest in consolidated net income

[Q 4-12] Intercompany transactions

On January 1, 20X1, Planet purchased an 80% interest in the capital stock of Star for $2,460,000. At that time, Star had capital stock of $1,500,000 and retained earnings of $300,000. The difference between book of value Star equity and the value implied by the purchase price was attributed to specific assets of Star as follows:
* $1,275,000 to equipment of Star with a five-year remaining life.

At year-end 20X1 and 20X2, Star had in its inventory merchandise that it had purchased from Planet at a 25% markup on cost during each year in the following amounts:
20X1 : $ 90,000. 20X2 : $105,000
During 20X1, Planet reported net income from independent operations (including sales to affiliates) of $1,500,000, while Star reported net income of $600,000. In 20X2, Planet's net income from independent operations (including sales to affiliates) was $1,800,000 and Star's was $750,000.

• Instructions •

Calculate the controlling interest in consolidated net income for 20X1 and 20X2.

[Q 4-13] Intercompany transactions

Payne Company owns all the outstanding common stock of Sierra Company and 80% of the outstanding common stock of Santa Fe Company. The amount of intercompany profit included in the inventories of Payne Company on December 31, 20X1, and December 31, 20X2, is indicated here:

	Intercompany Profit on Goods Purchased From	
	Sierra Company	Santa Fe Company
Inventory, 12/31/20X1	$3,800	$4,600
Inventory, 12/31/20X2	4,800	2,300

The three companies reported net income from their independent operations (including sales to affiliates) for the year ended December 31, 20X2, as follows:

Payne Company : $280,000

Sierra Company : 172,000

Santa Fe Company : 120,000

• Instructions •

Calculate the controlling interest in consolidated net income for the year ended December 31, 20X2

Government & Not-For-Profit Accounting For the **US CPA** Exam

SEC Reporting

Volume
8

Chapter 5 SEC Reporting

01 SEC Reporting

1 Form 10-K (Annual report)

A Form 10-K is an annual report required by the SEC that gives a comprehensive summary of a company's financial performance. Form 10-K must be filed annually by registered companies. Pursuant to the Securities Exchange Act of 1934, the 10-K is an SEC filing that must be filed annually with the SEC.

Part	Items
1	(1) Business including risk factors (2) Properties (3) Legal Proceedings (4) Mine Safety Disclosures
2	(5) Market information for the registrant's common stock and related security matters and issuer purchases of equity securities (6) Selected financial information (7) MD&A (8) Audited F/S and supplementary information (9) Changes in and Disagreements With Accountants on Accounting and Financial Disclosure
3	(10) Directors, Executive Officers and Corporate Governance (11) Executive Compensation (12) Security Ownership of Certain Beneficial Owners and Management and Related Stockholder Matters (13) Certain Relationships and Related Transactions, and Director Independence (14) Principal Accounting Fees and Services
4	(15) Exhibits, Financial Statement Schedules Signatures

CASE STUDY

Amazon's 10–k report

UNITED STATES
SECURITIES AND EXCHANGE COMMISSION
Washington, D.C. 20549

FORM 10-K

(Mark One)

☒   **ANNUAL REPORT PURSUANT TO SECTION 13 OR 15(d) OF THE SECURITIES EXCHANGE ACT OF 1934**

For the fiscal year ended December 31, 2017

or

☐   **TRANSITION REPORT PURSUANT TO SECTION 13 OR 15(d) OF THE SECURITIES EXCHANGE ACT OF 1934**

For the transition period from   to   .

Commission File No. 000-22513

AMAZON.COM, INC.

(Exact name of registrant as specified in its charter)

Delaware	91-1646860
(State or other jurisdiction of incorporation or organization)	(I.R.S. Employer Identification No.)

410 Terry Avenue North
Seattle, Washington 98109-5210
(206) 266-1000
(Address and telephone number, including area code, of registrant's principal executive offices)

Securities registered pursuant to Section 12(b) of the Act:

Title of Each Class	Name of Each Exchange on Which Registered
Common Stock, par value $.01 per share	Nasdaq Global Select Market

Securities registered pursuant to Section 12(g) of the Act:
None

Indicate by check mark if the registrant is a well-known seasoned issuer, as defined in Rule 405 of the Securities Act.   Yes ☒   No ☐

Indicate by check mark if the registrant is not required to file reports pursuant to Section 13 or Section 15(d) of the Exchange Act.   Yes ☐   No ☒

Indicate by check mark whether the registrant (1) has filed all reports required to be filed by Section 13 or 15(d) of the Securities Exchange Act of 1934 during the preceding 12 months (or for such shorter period that the registrant was required to file such reports), and (2) has been subject to such filing requirements for the past 90 days.   Yes ☒   No ☐

Indicate by check mark whether the registrant has submitted electronically and posted on its corporate Web site, if any, every Interactive Data File required to be submitted and posted pursuant to Rule 405 of Regulation S-T during the preceding 12 months (or for such shorter period that the registrant was required to submit and post such files).   Yes ☒   No ☐

Indicate by check mark if disclosure of delinquent filers pursuant to Item 405 of Regulation S-K is not contained herein, and will not be contained, to the best of registrant's knowledge, in definitive proxy or information statements incorporated by reference in Part III of this Form 10-K or any amendment to this Form 10-K. ☒

Indicate by check mark whether the registrant is a large accelerated filer, an accelerated filer, a non-accelerated filer, smaller reporting company, or an emerging growth company. See definitions of "large accelerated filer," "accelerated filer," "smaller reporting company," and "emerging growth company" in Rule 12b-2 of the Exchange Act.

Large accelerated filer	☒	Accelerated filer	☐
Non-accelerated filer	☐ (Do not check if a smaller reporting company)	Smaller reporting company	☐
		Emerging growth company	☐

If an emerging growth company, indicate by check mark if the registrant has elected not to use the extended transition period for complying with any new or revised financial accounting standards provided pursuant to Section 13(a) of the Exchange Act. ☐

Indicate by check mark whether the registrant is a shell company (as defined in Rule 12b-2 of the Exchange Act).   Yes ☐   No ☒

Aggregate market value of voting stock held by non-affiliates of the registrant as of June 30, 2017	$	387,327,844,190
Number of shares of common stock outstanding as of January 24, 2018		484,107,183

DOCUMENTS INCORPORATED BY REFERENCE

The information required by Part III of this Report, to the extent not set forth herein, is incorporated herein by reference from the registrant's definitive proxy statement relating to the Annual Meeting of Shareholders to be held in 2018, which definitive proxy statement shall be filed with the Securities and Exchange Commission within 120 days after the end of the fiscal year to which this Report relates.

AMAZON.COM, INC.
FORM 10-K
For the Fiscal Year Ended December 31, 2017
INDEX

2 Form 10-Q

Form 10-Q is a quarterly report mandated by the SEC to be filed by publicly traded corporations. Pursuant to the Securities Exchange Act of 1934, the 10-Q is an SEC filing that must be filed quarterly with the SEC.

It contains similar information to the annual form 10-K, however the information is generally less detailed, and the financial statements are generally unaudited. Information for the final quarter of a firm's fiscal year is included in the 10-K, so only three 10-Q filings are made each year.

Part	Items
1	Financial information (1) Unaudited Financial Statements (2) MD&A (3) Quantitative and Qualitative Disclosures About Market Risk. (4) Controls and Procedures.
2	Other information (1) Risk factors (2) Unregistered Sales of Equity Securities and Use of Proceeds. (3) Defaults Upon Senior Securities. (4) Mine Safety Disclosures (5) Other information (6) Exhibits

3 Filing Deadline

(1) Large accelerated filer

1) float : $700 million or more

2) 10-K : within **60 days** after the end of the fiscal year

3) 10-Q : within **40 days** after the end of the fiscal quarter

(2) Accelerated filer

1) float : $75million~$700 million

2) 10-K : within **75 days** after the end of the fiscal year

3) 10-Q : within **40 days** after the end of the fiscal quarter

(3) Non-accelerated filer

1) float : less than $75 million or more

2) 10-K : within **90 days** after the end of the fiscal year

3) 10-Q : within **45 days** after the end of the fiscal quarter

4 Registered statements

When a company issues new securities, it is required to submit a registration statement to the SEC under the Securities Act of 1933.

(1) A description of the company's properties and business

(2) A description of the security to be offered for sale

(3) Information about the management of the company

(4) Financial statements certified by independent accountants

5 Form 8-K

Form 8-K must be filed to report major events.

(1) Completion of Acquisition or Disposition of Assets

(2) Unregistered Sales of Equity Securities

(3) Changes in Registrant's Certifying Accountant

(4) Changes in Corporate Governance and Management

6 Filing Size

Companies that are required to file documents with the SEC

(1) Companies whose stocks are traded on a national stock exchange

(2) Companies with assets of over $10 million and have at least 500 shareholders

(3) Companies that have sold securities to the public pursuant to a registration, such as an initial public offering.

02 ▶ Form 10-K Sample

Item 1. Business

(1) General

We seek to be Earth's most customer–centric company. We are guided by four principles: customer obsession rather than competitor focus, passion for invention, commitment to operational excellence, and long–term thinking. In each of our segments, we serve our primary customer sets, consisting of consumers, sellers, developers, enterprises, content creators, advertisers, and employees.

We have organized our operations into three segments: North America, International, and Amazon Web Services ("AWS"). These segments reflect the way the Company evaluates its business performance and manages its operations. Information on our net sales is contained in Item 8 of Part II, "Financial Statements and Supplementary Data — Note 10 — Segment Information."

(2) Consumers
(3) Sellers
(3) Developers and Enterprises
(4) Content Creators
(5) Advertisers

Item 1A. Risk Factors

Business and Industry Risks

1) We Face Intense Competition

2) Our Expansion into New Products, Services, Technologies, and Geographic Regions Subjects Us to Additional Risks

3) Our International Operations Expose Us to a Number of Risks

4) The Variability in Our Retail Business Places Increased Strain on Our Operations

Operating Risks

1) Our Expansion Places a Significant Strain on our Management, Operational, Financial, and Other Resources

2) We Experience Significant Fluctuations in Our Operating Results and Growth Rate

3) We Face Risks Related to Successfully Optimizing and Operating Our Fulfillment Network and Data Centers

Legal and Regulatory Risks

Government Regulation Is Evolving and Unfavorable Changes Could Harm Our Business

Claims, Litigation, Government Investigations, and Other Proceedings May Adversely Affect Our Business and Results of Operations

Item 1B. Unresolved Staff Comments

None.

Item 2. Properties

Description of Use	Leased Square Footage	Owned Square Footage	Location
Office space	xxx	xxx	North America
Office space	xxx	xxx	International
Physical stores	xxx	xxx	North America
Physical stores	xxx	xxx	International
Fulfillment, data centers	xxx	xxx	North America
Fulfillment, data centers	xxx	xxx	International

Item 3. Legal Proceedings

See Item 8 of Part II, "Financial Statements and Supplementary Data – Note 7 – Commitments and Contingencies – Legal Proceedings."

Item 4. Mine Safety Disclosures

Not applicable.

Item 5. Market for the Registrant's Common Stock, Related Shareholder Matters, and Issuer Purchases of Equity Securities

1) Market Information

Our common stock is traded on the Nasdaq Global Select Market under the symbol "AMZN."

2) Holders

As of January 25, 2023, there were 10,845 shareholders of record of our common stock, although there is a much larger number of beneficial owners.

3) Recent Sales of Unregistered Securities

None.

4) Issuer Purchases of Equity Securities

None.

Item 6. Reserved

Item 7. Management's Discussion and Analysis of Financial Condition and Results of Operations

(1) Overview

(2) Critical Accounting Estimates

(3) Liquidity and Capital Resources

(4) Results of Operations

(5) Non-GAAP Financial Measures

(6) Guidance

Item 7A. Quantitative and Qualitative Disclosures About Market Risk

(1) Interest Rate Risk

(2) Foreign Exchange Risk

(3) Equity Investment Risk

Item 8. Financial Statements and Supplementary Data

(1) Report of Ernst & Young LLP, Independent Registered Public Accounting Firm

(2) Consolidated Statements of Cash Flows

(3) Consolidated Statements of Operations

(4) Consolidated Statements of Comprehensive Income (Loss)

(5) Consolidated Balance Sheets

(6) Consolidated Statements of Stockholders' Equity

(7) Notes to Consolidated Financial Statements

Item 9. Changes in and Disagreements with Accountants On Accounting and Financial Disclosure

None.

Item 9A. Controls and Procedures

Item 9B. Other Information

Item 9C. Disclosure Regarding Foreign Jurisdictions that Prevent Inspections

Item 10. Directors, Executive Officers, and Corporate Governance

Information regarding our Executive Officers required by Item 10 of Part III is set forth in Item 1 of Part I "Business — Information About Our Executive Officers."

Information required by Item 10 of Part III regarding our Directors and any material changes to the process by which security holders may recommend nominees to the Board of Directors is included in our Proxy Statement relating to our 2023 Annual Meeting of Shareholders, and is incorporated herein by reference.

Information relating to our Code of Business Conduct and Ethics and, to the extent applicable, compliance with Section 16(a) of the 1934 Act is set forth in our Proxy Statement relating to our 2023 Annual Meeting of Shareholders and is incorporated herein by reference. To the extent permissible under Nasdaq rules, we intend to disclose amendments to our Code of Business Conduct and Ethics, as well as waivers of the provisions thereof, on our investor relations website under the heading "Corporate Governance" at amazon.com/ir.

Item 11. Executive Compensation

Information required by Item 11 of Part III is included in our Proxy Statement relating to our 2023 Annual Meeting of Shareholders and is incorporated herein by reference.

Item 12. Security Ownership of Certain Beneficial Owners and Management and Related Shareholder Matters

Information required by Item 12 of Part III is included in our Proxy Statement relating to our 2023 Annual Meeting of Shareholders and is incorporated herein by reference.

Item 13. Certain Relationships and Related Transactions, and Director Independence

Information required by Item 13 of Part III is included in our Proxy Statement relating to our 2023 Annual Meeting of Shareholders and is incorporated herein by reference.

Item 14. Principal Accountant Fees and Services

Information required by Item 14 of Part III is included in our Proxy Statement relating to our 2023 Annual Meeting of Shareholders and is incorporated herein by reference.

01. Which of the following is the SEC form used by issuer companies to file as an annual report with the SEC?

    a. Form 10-Q   b. Form 8-K

    c. Form 10-K   d. From S-1

02. Which of the following is the SEC form used by issuer companies to file as a quarterly report with the SEC?

    a. Form 10-Q   b. Form 8-K

    c. Form 10-K   d. From S-1

03. Which of the following is the SEC form used by issuer companies to file information about mergers and acquisitions?

    a. Form 10-Q   b. Form 8-K

    c. Form 10-K   d. From S-1

04. Which of the following is the SEC form used by issuer companies to file information about changes in directors?

    a. Form 10-Q   b. Form 8-K

    c. Form 10-K   d. From S-1

05. A company is an accelerated filer that is required to file Form 10-k.
What is the maximum number of days after the company's fiscal year-end?

    a. 60 days   b. 75 days

    c. 90 days   d. 120 days

06. A company is a large accelerated filer that is required to file Form 10-k.

What is the maximum number of days after the company's fiscal year-end?

a. 60 days   b. 75 days

c. 90 days   d. 120 days

07. A company is an accelerated filer that is required to file Form 10-Q.

What is the maximum number of days after the company's fiscal quarter?

a. 60 days   b. 75 days

c. 90 days   d. 40 days

Government & Not-For-Profit Accounting For the US CPA Exam

Chapter 06

Fair value measurements

Volume
8

Fair Value Measurements

01 Fair Value

1 Definition of Fair Value

> the price that would be received to sell an asset or paid to transfer a liability in an orderly transaction between market participants at the measurement date.

2 The Asset or Liability

A fair value measurement is for a particular asset or liability. Therefore, when measuring fair value a reporting entity should take into account the characteristics of the asset or liability if market participants would take those characteristics into account when pricing the asset or liability at the measurement date.

(공정가치 측정은 특정 자산이나 부채에 대한 것이다. 따라서 공정가치를 측정할 때에는 시장참여자가 측정일에 자산이나 부채의 가격을 결정할 때 고려하는 그 자산이나 부채의 특성을 고려한다.)

Fair value is a market-based measure, not an entity-based measure.
(공정가치는 시장에 근거한 측정치이며 기업 특유의 측정치가 아니다.)

The asset or liability measured at fair value might be either of the following:
a) A standalone asset or liability

(for example, a financial instrument or a nonfinancial asset)

A company may apply fair value to financial instruments on an instrument-by-instrument basis, but once elected, fair value measurement will be used until the asset/liability is disposed

3 The Transaction

(1) Orderly Transaction (정상거래)

A fair value measurement assumes that the asset or liability is exchanged in an orderly transaction between market participants to sell the asset or transfer the liability at the measurement date under current market conditions.
(공정가치는 측정일 현재의 시장 상황에서 자산을 매도하거나 부채를 이전하는 시장참여자 사이의 정상거래에서 자산이나 부채가 교환되는 것으로 가정하여 측정한다.)

Orderly Transaction is a transaction that assumes exposure to the market for a period before the measurement date to allow for marketing activities that are usual and customary for transactions involving such assets or liabilities; it is not a forced transaction (for example, a forced liquidation or distress sale).
(정상거래는 측정일 전의 일정 기간에 해당 자산이나 부채와 관련되는 거래를 위하여 통상적이고 관습적인 마케팅 활동을 할 수 있도록 시장에 노출되는 것을 가정한 거래를 말한다. 따라서 강제 청산이나 재무적 어려움에 따른 매각 등과 같은 강제된 거래는 정상거래가 아니다.)

Buyers and sellers in the principal (or most advantageous) market for the asset or liability that have all of the following characteristics:

a) They are independent of each other, that is, they are not related parties, although the price in a related-party transaction may be used as an input to a fair value measurement if the reporting entity has evidence that the transaction was entered into at market terms

b) They are knowledgeable, having a reasonable understanding about the asset or liability and the transaction using all available information, including information that might be obtained through due diligence efforts that are usual and customary

c) They are able to enter into a transaction for the asset or liability

d) They are willing to enter into a transaction for the asset or liability, that is, they are motivated but not forced or otherwise compelled to do so.

A fair value measurement assumes that the transaction to sell the asset or transfer the liability takes place either:

① In the principal market for the asset or liability

② In the absence of a principal market, in the most advantageous market for the asset or liability.

(공정가치 측정은 자산을 매도하거나 부채를 이전하는 거래가 다음 중 어느 하나의 시장에서 이루어지는 것으로 가정한다.)

① 주된 시장(principal market)

② 주된 시장이 없는 경우 가장 유리한 시장(most advantageous market)

(2) Principal Market (주된 시장)

1) 거래하는 규모가 가장 크고 빈도가 가장 잦은 시장

The market with the greatest volume and level of activity for the asset or liability.

2) 반증이 없는 한 통상적으로 거래하는 시장

In the absence of evidence to the contrary, the market in which the reporting entity normally would enter into a transaction to sell the asset or to transfer the liability is presumed to be the principal market.

3) 다른 시장의 가격이 더 유리하더라도 주된 시장의 가격이 공정가치

If there is a principal market for the asset or liability, the fair value measurement should represent the price in that market, even if the price in a different market is potentially more advantageous at the measurement date.

4) 기업 간의 관점에서 고려/기업 간의 차이 허용

The principal market should be considered from the perspective of the reporting entity, thereby allowing for differences between and among entities with different activities.

(3) Most Advantageous Market (가장 유리한 시장)

The market that maximizes the amount that would be received to sell the asset or minimizes the amount that would be paid to transfer the liability, after taking into account transaction costs and transportation costs.

(거래원가나 운송원가를 고려했을 때자산을 매도할 때 받는 금액을 최대화하거나 부채를 이전할 때 지급하는 금액을 최소화하는 시장)

4 Market Participants (시장참여자)

A reporting entity should measure the fair value of an asset or a liability using the assumptions that market participants would use in pricing the asset or liability, assuming that market participants act in their economic best interest. In developing those assumptions, a reporting entity need not identify specific market participants.

(기업은 시장참여자(market participants)가 경제적으로 최선의 행동을 한다는 가정 하에, 시장참여자가 자산이나 부채의 가격을 결정할 때 사용할 가정에 근거하여 자산이나 부채의 공정가치를 측정하여야 한다. 그러나 그러한 가정을 위하여 특정 시장참여자를 식별할 필요는 없다.)

5 The Price (가격)

Fair value is the price that would be received to sell an asset or paid to transfer a liability in an orderly transaction in the principal (or most advantageous) market at the measurement date under current market conditions (an exit price) regardless of whether that price is directly observable or estimated using another valuation technique.

(공정가치는 측정일 현재의 시장 상황에서 주된 시장에서의 정상거래에서 자산을 매도하면서 받거나 부채를 이전하면서 지급하게 될 유출가격(exit price)이다. 이때, 그 가격은 직접 관측가능할 수도 있으며 다른 가치평가기법을 이용하여 추정할 수도 있다.)

Entry Price

the price that would be paid to acquire the asset or received to assume the liability

Exit Price

the price that would be received to sell the asset or paid to transfer the liability

The price in the principal (or most advantageous) market used to measure the fair value of the asset or liability should not be adjusted for transaction costs.

(자산이나 부채의 공정가치를 측정하기 위하여 사용하는 주된 시장의 가격에는 거래원가를 조정하지 않는다.)

Transaction costs are not a characteristic of an asset or a liability; rather, they are specific to a transaction and will differ depending on how a reporting entity enters into a transaction for the asset or liability.

(거래원가는 자산이나 부채를 거래하는 주된 시장에서 자산을 매도하거나 부채를 이전할 때 발생하는 원가로서 자산이나 부채의 특성이 아니라 거래에 특정된 것이어서 자산이나 부채를 어떻게 거래하는지에 따라 달라진다.)

Transaction costs do not include transportation costs. If location is a characteristic of the asset (for example, for a commodity), the price in the principal (or most advantageous) market should be adjusted for the costs, if any, that would be incurred to transport the asset from its current location to that market.

(거래원가는 운송원가를 포함하지 않는다. 운송원가(transport costs)는 현재의 위치에서 주된 시장으로 자산을 운송하는데 발생하는 원가를 말한다. 예를 들어 상품의 경우처럼 위치가 자산의 특성에 해당한다면 현재의 위치에서 시장까지 자산을 운송하는 데에 드는 원가가 있을 경우 주된 시장에서의 가격을 그 원가만큼 조정한다.)

Fair Value = Exit Price − Transportation costs

NRV = Fair value − Transaction costs

Transaction costs	Transportation costs
should not be adjusted for FV	should be adjusted for FV
specific to a transaction	specific to assets or liabilities

[Example-1] Financial assets

ABC Company owns stock in XYZ Company. The stock is traded on the New York Stock Exchange and the London Stock Exchange. Stock price information from the two stock exchanges on December 31 is as follows:

Exchange	Quoted Stock Price	Transaction Costs
New York	$26	$3
London	$25	$1

Q1) What is the fair value of the XYZ stock on December 31 if New York is principal market for the stock?

Q2) What is the fair value of the XYZ stock on December 31 if London is principal market for the stock?

Q3) What is the fair value of the XYZ stock on December 31 if there is no principal market for the stock?

· Answer ·

Q1) New York Exchange가 주된 시장이라면
→ 자산의 공정가치 = $26

Q2) London Exchange가 주된 시장이라면
→ 자산의 공정가치 = $25

Q3) 가장 유리한 시장은 거래원가와 운송원가를 고려했을 때, 자산의 매도로 받게 될 금액을 최대화하는 시장이므로 London Exchange가 가장 유리한 시장이다
→ 자산의 공정가치 = $25

[Example-2] Financial liabilities

XYZ Company issued bond. The bond is traded on the New York Bond Exchange and the London Stock Exchange. Bond price information from the two exchanges on December 31 is as follows:

Exchange	Quoted Price	Transaction Costs
New York	$26	$3
London	$25	$1

Q1) What is the fair value of the XYZ stock on December 31 if New York is principal market for the bond?

Q2) What is the fair value of the XYZ stock on December 31 if London is principal market for the bond?

Q3) What is the fair value of the XYZ stock on December 31 if there is no principal market for the bond?

• Answer •

Q1) New York Exchange가 주된 시장이라면
　　› 부채의 공정가치 = $26

Q2) London Exchange가 주된 시장이라면
　　→ 부채의 공정가치 = $25

Q3) 가장 유리한 시장은 거래원가와 운송원가를 고려했을 때, 부채를 이전할 때 지급하는 금액을 최소화하는 시장이므로 London Exchange가 가장 유리한 시장이다
　　→ 부채의 공정가치 = $25

[Example-3] Non-Financial assets

Commodity is traded on the market A and the market B. The price information from the two markets on December 31 is as follows:

Market	Quoted Price	Transaction Costs	Transportation costs
A	$26	$3	$2
B	$25	$1	$2

Q1) What is the fair value of the Commodity on December 31 if Market A is principal market for the commodity?

Q2) What is the fair value of the Commodity on December 31 if Market B is principal market for the commodity?

Q3) What is the fair value of the Commodity on December 31 if there is no principal market for the commodity?

· Answer ·

Q1) 시장 A가 그 자산에 대한 주된 시장이라면
→ 자산의 공정가치 = $24

Q2) 시장 B가 그 자산에 대한 주된 시장이라면
→ 자산의 공정가치 = $23

Q3) 가장 유리한 시장은 거래원가와 운송원가를 고려했을 때, 자산의 매도로 받게 될 금액을 최대화하는 시장이므로 시장 B가 가장 유리한 시장이다.
→ 자산의 공정가치 = $23

02 Valuation Techniques

1 Valuation Techniques

(1) Valuation Techniques

The objective of using a valuation technique is to estimate the price at which an orderly transaction to sell the asset or to transfer the liability would take place between market participants at the measurement date under current market conditions. Three widely used valuation approaches are the market approach, cost approach, and income approach.

(가치평가기법을 사용하는 목적은 측정일에 현행 시장 상황에서 시장참여자 사이에 이루어지는 자산을 매도하거나 부채를 이전하는 정상거래에서의 가격을 추정하는 것이다.)

Valuation techniques used to measure fair value should be applied consistently. However, a change in a valuation technique or its application is appropriate if the change results in a measurement that is equally or more representative of fair value in the circumstance.

(공정가치 측정을 위해 사용하는 가치평가기법은 일관되게 적용한다. 그러나 가치평가기법이나 그 적용방법을 변경하는 것이 그 상황에서 공정가치를 똑같이 또는 더 잘 나타내는 측정치를 산출해낸다면 이러한 변경은 적절하다.)

Revisions resulting from a change in the valuation technique or its application should be accounted for as a change in accounting estimate.

(가치평가기법이나 그 적용방법이 바뀜에 따른 수정은 회계추정의 변경으로 회계처리한다.)

(2) Market Approach (시장접근법)

The market approach uses prices and other relevant information generated by market transactions involving identical or comparable assets, liabilities, or a group of assets and liabilities, such as a business.

1) market multiples derived from a set of comparables.

2) matrix pricing

(3) Cost Approach (원가접근법)

> The cost approach reflects the amount that would be required currently to replace the service capacity of an asset (often referred to as current replacement cost).

(4) Income Approach (이익접근법 또는 소득접근법)

> The income approach converts future amounts (for example, cash flows or income and expenses) to a single current (that is, discounted) amount. When the income approach is used, the fair value measurement reflects current market expectations about those future amounts.

1) Present value techniques

2) Option-pricing models, such as the Black-Scholes-Merton formula or a binomial model

3) The multiperiod excess earnings method, which is used to measure the fair value of some intangible assets.

2 Inputs to Valuation Techniques

Inputs are the assumptions that market participants would use when pricing the asset or liability, including assumptions about risk. Inputs may be observable or unobservable.
(투입변수(inputs)는 자산이나 부채의 가격을 결정할 때 시장참여자가 사용할 가정을 말하며, 관측가능하거나 관측가능하지 않을 수 있다.)

A reporting entity should use valuation techniques that are appropriate in the circumstances and for which sufficient data are available to measure fair value, maximizing the use of relevant observable inputs and minimizing the use of unobservable inputs.

(공정가치를 측정하기 위해 사용하는 가치평가기법은 관련된 관측할 수 있는 관련된 투입변수를 최대한으로 사용하고 관측할 수 없는 투입변수를 최소한으로 사용한다.)

Observable Inputs

Inputs that are developed using market data, such as publicly available information about actual events or transactions, and that reflect the assumptions that market participants would use when pricing the asset or liability.

(실제 사건이나 거래에 관해 공개적으로 구할 수 있는 정보와 같은 시장 자료를 사용하여 개발하였으며 자산이나 부채의 가격을 결정할 때 시장참여자가 사용할 가정을 반영한 투입변수)

Unobservable Inputs

Inputs for which market data are not available and that are developed using the best information available about the assumptions that market participants would use when pricing the asset or liability.

(시장 자료를 구할 수 없는 경우에 자산이나 부채의 가격을 결정할 때 시장참여자가 사용할 가정에 대해 구할 수 있는 최선의 정보를 사용하여 개발된 투입변수)

3 Fair Value Hierarchy

공정가치 측정 및 관련 공시에서 일관성과 비교가능성을 높이기 위하여, 공정가치를 측정하기 위하여 사용하는 가치평가기법에의 투입변수를 3수준으로 분류하는 공정가치 서열체계(fair value hierarchy)를 정한다.

The fair value hierarchy prioritizes the inputs to valuation techniques, not the valuation techniques used to measure fair value.

(공정가치 서열체계는 가치평가기법에의 투입변수에 우선순위를 부여하는 것이지, 공정가치를 측정하기 위해 사용하는 가치평가기법에 우선순위를 부여하는 것은 아니다.)

(1) Level 1 Inputs

Level 1 inputs are quoted prices (unadjusted) in active markets for identical assets or liabilities that the reporting entity can access at the measurement date.

수준 1 투입변수는 측정일에 동일한 자산이나 부채에 대한 접근 가능한 활성시장의 (조정되지 않은) 공시가격이다.
예) 거래소시장, 딜러시장, 중개시장, 직거래 시장

(2) Level 2 Inputs

Level 2 inputs are inputs other than quoted prices included within Level 1 that are observable for the asset or liability, either directly or indirectly

1) Quoted prices for similar assets or liabilities in active markets
2) Quoted prices for identical or similar assets or liabilities in markets that are not active
3) Inputs other than quoted prices that are observable
   : interest rates and yield curves, volatilities, credit spreads

수준 2의 투입변수는 수준 1의 공시가격 이외에 자산이나 부채에 대해 직접적으로 또는 간접적으로 관측가능한 투입변수이다.
예) 보유하여 사용하고 있는 건물의 경우 비슷한 위치의 비교할 수 있는 건물과 관련된 관측할 수 있는 거래의 가격에서 도출한 배수에서 도출한 건물의 제곱미터당 가격

(3) Level 3 Inputs

Level 3 inputs are unobservable inputs for the asset or liability.

수준 3의 투입변수는 자산이나 부채에 대한 관측가능하지 않은 투입변수이다.
예) 현금창출단위의 경우 기업 자신의 자료를 사용하여 개발한 재무예측

If an observable input requires an adjustment using an unobservable input and that adjustment results in a significantly higher or lower fair value measurement, the resulting measurement would be categorized within Level 3 of the fair value hierarchy.

(관측할 수 있는 투입변수를 관측할 수 없는 투입변수를 사용해 조정해야 하고 그러한 조정으로 공정가치 측정치가 유의적으로 더 높아지거나 더 낮아진다면, 그러한 측정치는 공정가치 서열체계 중 수준 3으로 분류할 것이다.)

03 ▷ Disclosures

Apple의 2023년 재무제표에 공시된 사례는 다음과 같다.

Note 4 – Financial Instruments

Cash, Cash Equivalents and Marketable Securities

The following tables show the Company's cash, cash equivalents and marketable securities by significant investment category as of September 30, 2023 and September 24, 2022 (in millions):

	2023						
	Adjusted Cost	Unrealized Gains	Unrealized Losses	Fair Value	Cash and Cash Equivalents	Current Marketable Securities	Non-Current Marketable Securities
Cash	$ 28,359	$ —	$ —	$ 28,359	$ 28,359	$ —	$ —
Level 1:							
Money market funds	481	—	—	481	481	—	—
Mutual funds and equity securities	442	12	(26)	428	—	428	—
Subtotal	923	12	(26)	909	481	428	—
Level 2 [(1)]:							
U.S. Treasury securities	19,406	—	(1,292)	18,114	35	5,468	12,611
U.S. agency securities	5,736	—	(600)	5,136	36	271	4,829
Non-U.S. government securities	17,533	6	(1,048)	16,491	—	11,332	5,159
Certificates of deposit and time deposits	1,354	—	—	1,354	1,034	320	—
Commercial paper	608	—	—	608	—	608	—
Corporate debt securities	76,840	6	(5,956)	70,890	20	12,627	58,243
Municipal securities	628	—	(26)	602	—	192	410
Mortgage- and asset-backed securities	22,365	6	(2,735)	19,636	—	344	19,292
Subtotal	144,470	18	(11,657)	132,831	1,125	31,162	100,544
Total [(2)]	$ 173,752	$ 30	$ (11,683)	$ 162,099	$ 29,965	$ 31,590	$ 100,544

Government & Not-For-Profit Accounting For the **US CPA** Exam

Miscellaneous

Volume
8

Chapter 7

Miscellaneous

01 > Foreign Currency Transactions

1 Foreign currency accounting

(1) ASC 830

ASC 830의 외환회계는 외환거래와 외화표시재무제표의 환산으로 구분하여 환율변동으로 인한 손익을 다르게 보고한다.

1) Foreign currency transaction

Transactions whose terms are denominated in a currency other than the entity's functional currency.

※ 외화로 결제되지 않는 해외거래에서는 환율변동손익이 발생하지 않는다.

2) Foreign currency translation

The process of expressing in the reporting currency of the reporting entity those amounts that are denominated or measured in a different currency.

(2) Objectives of foreign currency translation

1) Provide information that is generally compatible with the expected economic effects of a rate change on a reporting entity's cash flows and equity

2) Reflect in consolidated statements the financial results and relationships of the individual consolidated entities as measured in their functional currencies in conformity with U.S. GAAP.

(3) 환율의 기초

1) 환율표시방법

Direct method	1 foreign currency = 0.50 USD
Indirect method	1 USD = 2 foreign currency

2) 거래시점에 의한 환율의 분류

Spot rate (현물환율)	현재시점에서 거래되는 환율
Forward rate (선도환율)	미래시점에서 거래되는 약정환율

3) 환율의 변동

Appreciation (평가절상)	외화의 가치가 상승 ⇒ 외화 자산 환차익, 외화 부채 환차손
Depreciation (평가절하)	외화의 가치가 하락 ⇒ 외화 자산 환차손, 외화 부채 환차익

2 Foreign Currency Transactions

(1) Foreign currency transactions

외화거래는 외화로 결제되어야 하는 거래로서 다음을 포함한다.

– 외화로 가격이 표시되어 있는 재화나 용역의 매매

– 지급하거나 수취할 금액이 외화로 표시된 자금의 차입이나 대여

– 외화로 표시된 자산의 취득이나 처분, 외화로 표시된 부채의 발생이나 상환

(2) Initial measurement

기능통화로 외화거래를 최초로 인식하는 경우에 거래일의 외화와 기능통화 사이의 현물환율을 외화금액에 적용하여 기록한다.

(3) Subsequent measurement

매 보고기간 말 화폐성 외화항목은 마감환율로 환산한다.

(4) Changes in exchange rate

화폐성항목의 결제시점에 생기는 외환차이 또는 화폐성항목의 환산에 사용한 환율이 회계 기간 중 최초로 인식한 시점이나 전기의 재무제표 환산시점의 환율과 다르기 때문에 생기는 외환차이는 그 외환차이가 생기는 회계기간의 손익으로 인식한다.

⇒ income from continuing operation

※ 외화로 결제되지 않는 거래는 환율변동손익을 인식하지 않는다.

Example-1

On 12/1/20X1, KIMCPA purchased goods from foreign company. The purchase in the amount of 1,000 EUR is to paid for on 2/1/20X2 in EUR. The exchange spot rates for EUR are as follows:

October 1, 20X1	1 euro = 1.15 USD
December 1, 20X1	1 euro = 1.20 USD
December 31, 20X1	1 euro = 1.30 USD
February 1, 20X2	1 euro = 1.35 USD

10/1/20X1	No entry		
12/1/20X1	Inventory	1,200	
	Account payable		1,200
12/31/20X1	Exchange loss	100*	
	Account payable		100
2/1/20X2	Exchange loss	50**	
	Account payable		50
Settlement	Account payable	1,350	
	Cash		1,350

* 1,000 EUR × (1.30-1.20) = $100
** 1,000 EUR × (1.35-1.30) = $50

※ Tax reconciliation

20X1	* 세무조정 : +100 ⇨ 이연법인세 자산의 증가
20X2	* 세무조정 : −100 ⇨ 이연법인세 자산의 감소

> **Example-2**

On 12/1/20X1, KIMCPA sold goods to foreign company. The sale in the amount of 1,000 EUR is to paid for on 2/1/20X2 in EUR. The exchange rates for EUR are as follows:

December 1, 20X1	1 euro = 1.20 USD
December 31, 20X1	1 euro = 1.30 USD
February 1, 20X2	1 euro = 1.35 USD

12/1/20X1	Account receivable	1,200	
	Sales revenue		1,200
12/31/20X1	Account receivable	100*	
	Exchange gain		100
2/1/20X2	Account receivable	50**	
	Exchange gain		50
Settlement	Cash	1,350	
	Account receivable		1,350

* 1,000 EUR × (1.30-1.20) = $100
** 1,000 EUR × (1.35-1.30) = $50

※ Tax reconciliation

20X1	* 세무조정 : -100 ⇨ 이연법인세 부채의 증가
20X2	* 세무조정 : +100 ⇨ 이연법인세 부채의 감소

Example-3

On 12/1/20X1, KIMCPA purchased goods from foreign company. The purchase in the amount of 1,000 EUR is to paid for on 2/1/20X2 in EUR. The exchange rates for EUR are as follows:

December 1, 20X1	1 USD = 1.20 euro
December 31, 20X1	1 USD = 1.30 euro
February 1, 20X2	1 USD = 1.35 euro

12/1/20X1	Inventory	833*	
	Account payable		833
12/31/20X1	Account payable	64**	
	Exchange gain		64
2/1/20X2	Account payable	28***	
	Exchange gain		28
Settlement	Account payable	741	
	Cash		741

* 1,000 EUR ÷ 1.2 = 833

** (1,000 EUR ÷ 1.30) − (1,000 EUR ÷ 1.20) = − 64

*** (1,000 EUR ÷ 1.35) − (1,000 EUR ÷ 1.30) = − 28

3 Foreign currency transactions-exceptions

다음 외환거래의 환율변동손익은 당기손익이 아닌 기타포괄손익(OCI)에 보고한다.

⇨ be reported in other comprehensive income

(1) Economic hedges

Foreign currency transactions that are designated as, and are effective as, economic hedges of a net investment in a foreign entity, commencing as of the designation date

(2) Available-for-sale debt securities

The entire change in the fair value of foreign-currency-denominated available-for-sale debt securities be reported in other comprehensive income.

매도가능 금융자산의 공정가치 평가에서 생긴 손익을 기타포괄손익으로 인식하는 경우에 그 손익에 포함된 환율변동효과는 당기손익이 아닌 기타포괄손익(OCI)에 보고한다.

금융자산의 환율변동손익의 표시방법을 요약하면 다음과 같다.

HTM, Trading, FVTNI, FVO ⇨ 당기손익(NI)

AFS ⇨ 기타포괄손익(OCI)

02 ▶ Discontinued Operations

1 Component

중단영업의 성과는 손익계산서에 별도로 표시하여야 하며 중단영업의 대상을 기업의 구분단위 (component of an entity)라고 한다.

(1) Definition of component of an entity

A component of an entity comprises operations and cash flows that can be clearly distinguished, operationally and for financial reporting purposes, from the rest of the entity. (재무보고 목적뿐만 아니라 영업상으로도 기업의 나머지와 명확히 구별되는 영업 및 현금흐름을 기업의 구분단위하고 한다.)

A component of an entity may be a reportable segment or an operating segment, a reporting unit, a subsidiary, or an asset group.

(2) Operating segment

A component of a public entity

(3) Reporting unit

The level of reporting at which goodwill is tested for impairment. A reporting unit is an operating segment or one level below an operating segment.

(4) Asset group

An asset group is the unit of accounting for a long-lived asset or assets to be held and used, which represents the lowest level for which identifiable cash flows are largely independent of the cash flows of other groups of assets and liabilities.

2 Reporting discontinued operation

(1) Criteria of discontinued operation

중단영업은 이미 처분되었거나 매각예정으로 분류되는 기업의 구분단위이다.

The results of operations of a component of an entity that either has been disposed of or is classified as held for sale shall be reported in discontinued operations if both of the following conditions are met:

> a. The operations and cash flows of the component have been (or will be) **eliminated** from the ongoing operations of the entity as a result of the disposal transaction.
>
> b. The entity will **not** have any significant **continuing involvement** in the operations of the component after the disposal transaction.

(2) Components of discontinued operation

1) Gain or loss from operations of discontinued component for the period

2) Gain or loss on disposal of discontinued component

3) Income tax expense or tax benefit

Income from continuing operations before income taxes	$ XXXX	
Income taxes	XXX	
Income from continuing operations		$ XXXX
Discontinued operations (Note X)		
Loss from operations of discontinued Component X (including loss on disposal of $XXX)		XXXX
Income tax benefit		XXXX
Loss on discontinued operations		XXXX
Net income		$ XXXX

(3) Comparative F/S

The income statement presented for each previous year must be adjusted retroactively to enhance consistency.

3 Long-lived asset classified as "held-for-sale"

(1) 매각예정의 분류기준

비유동자산의 장부금액이 계속사용이 아닌 매각거래를 통하여 주로 회수될 것이라면 이를 매각예정으로 분류하며 다음 조건을 모두 충족하여야 한다.

a) Management commits to a plan of disposal
   적절한 지위의 경영진이 자산의 매각계획을 확약하여야 한다.
b) The assets are available for sale
   현재의 상태에서 즉시 매각 가능하여야 한다.
c) An active program to locate a buyer have been initiated
   매수자를 물색하고 매각계획을 이행하기 위한 적극적인 업무진행을 이미 시작하였어야 한다.
d) The sale is probable
   매각될 가능성이 매우 높아야 한다.
e) The asset is being actively marketed for sale a fair price
   합리적인 가격 수준으로 적극적으로 매각을 추진하여야 한다.
f) It is unlikely that the disposal plan will significantly change
   매각 계획이 유의적으로 변경되거나 철회될 가능성이 낮아야 한다.

(2) Measurement

매각예정으로 분류된 비유동자산은 순공정가치(NRV)와 장부금액 중 작은 금액으로 측정하며 감가상각(또는 상각)하지 아니한다.

CASE STUDY

GE 2017 annual report

Held—for—sale

On September 25, 2017, we signed an agreement to sell our Industrial Solutions business within our Power segment with assets of $2,201 million and liabilities of $548 million, to ABB for approximately $2,600 million. The transaction is targeted to close in mid-2018.

FINANCIAL INFORMATION FOR ASSETS AND LIABILITIES OF BUSINESSES HELD FOR SALE	
December 31 (In millions)	2017
Assets	
Current receivables(a)	$ 703
Inventories	1,039
Property, plant, and equipment – net	931
Goodwill	1,619
Other intangible assets – net	403
Contract assets	858
Valuation allowance on disposal group classified as held for sale(b)	(1,378)
Other	67
Assets of businesses held for sale	$ 4,243
Liabilities	
Accounts payable	$ 602
Progress collections and price adjustments accrued	38
Other current liabilities	450
Non-current compensation and benefits	162
Other	87
Liabilities of businesses held for sale	$ 1,339

Discontinued operations

Discontinued operations primarily relate to our financial services businesses as a result of the GE Capital Exit Plan (our plan announced in 2015 to reduce the size of our financial services businesses) and were previously reported in the Capital segment.

FINANCIAL INFORMATION FOR DISCONTINUED OPERATIONS						
(In millions)		2017		2016		2015
Operations						
Total revenues and other income (loss)	$	182	$	2968	$	23,003
Earnings (loss) from discontinued operations before income taxes	$	(731)	$	(162)	$	887
Benefit (provision) for income taxes(a)		295		460		(791)
Earnings (loss) from discontinued operations, net of taxes	$	(437)	$	298	$	96
Disposals						
Gain (loss) on disposals before income taxes	$	306	$	(750)	$	(6,612)
Benefit (provision) for income taxes(a)		(178)		(502)		(979)
Gain (loss) on disposals, net of taxes	$	128	$	(1,252)	$	(7,591)
Earnings (loss) from discontinued operations, net of taxes(b)(c)	$	(309)	$	(954)	$	(7,495)

Example-4

On October 5, 20X1, Planet sold its electronics division at a loss of $24,000.

The disposal meets the requirements to be classifies as discontinued operations.

For the period January 1 through October 4 20X1, the component had revenues of $600,000 and expense of $700,000.

> 20X1년도에 매각으로 중단영업요건을 만족하였기 때문에 영업손실과 매각손실을 중단영업손익으로 보고한다.
>
> 1) Gain or loss from operations of discontinued component for 20X1
>
>   = 600,000 − 700,000 = −100,000
>
> 2) Gain or loss on disposal of discontinued component for 20X1
>
>   = −24,000

Example-5

On May 5, 20X1, Planet committed to plan to dispose its electronics division.

The disposal meets the requirements to be classifies as discontinued operations.

For the period January 1 through December 31 20X1, the component had revenues of $600,000 and expense of $700,000. On December 31 20X1, the carrying amount of the division was $40,000 and Planet estimated the fair value to be $30,000 and the cost to sell the division to be $5,000.

> 20X1년도에 매각예정으로 중단영업요건을 만족하였기 때문에 영업손실과 손상차손을 중단영업손익으로 보고한다.
>
> 1) Gain or loss from operations of discontinued component for 20X1
>
>   = 600,000 − 700,000 = −100,000
>
> 2) Gain or loss on its disposal of discontinued component for 20X1
>
>   = 40,000 − 25,000 = −15,000

Example-6

On May 5, 20X1, Planet committed to plan to dispose its electronics division. The disposal meets the requirements to be classifies as discontinued operations. For the period January 1 through December 31 20X1, the component had revenues of $600,000 and expense of $700,000. On December 31 20X1, the   carrying amount of the division was $40,000 and Planet estimated the fair value to be $50,000 and the cost to sell the division to be $5,000.

> 20X1년도에 매각예정으로 중단영업요건을 만족하였기 때문에 영업손실을 중단영업손익으로 보고하고 손상차손은 발생하지 않았다.
>
> 1) Gain or loss from operations of discontinued component for 20X1
>   = 600,000 - 700,000 = -100,000
> 2) Gain or loss on its disposal of discontinued component for 20X1
>   = 0

Example-7

On May 5, 20X1, Planet committed to plan to dispose its electronics division. The disposal meets the requirements to be classifies as discontinued operations. For the period January 1 through December 31 20X1, the component had revenues of $700,000 and expense of $600,000. On December 31 20X1, the   carrying amount of the division was $40,000 and Planet estimated the fair value to be $30,000 and the cost to sell the division to be $5,000.

> 20X1년도에 매각예정으로 중단영업요건을 만족하였기 때문에 영업이익과 손상차손을 중단영업손익으로 보고한다.
>
> 1) Gain or loss from operations of discontinued component for 20X1
>   = 700,000 - 600,000 = +100,000
> 2) Gain or loss on its disposal of discontinued component for 20X1
>   = 40,000 - 25,000 = -15,000

03 ▷ Notes to Financial Statements

1 Summary of significant accounting policies

The summary of significant accounting policies includes disclosures of:

1) Measurement bases used in preparing the financial statements.
2) Specific accounting principles and methods used during the period, including:
  - Basis of consolidation
  - Depreciation methods
  - Amortization of intangibles
  - Inventory pricing
  - Use of estimates
  - Fiscal year definition
  - Special revenue recognition issues (e.g., long-term construction contracts, franchising, leasing operations, etc.)

2 Items Not Included

The summary of significant accounting policies would not include the following items:

1) Composition and detailed dollar amounts of account balances
2) Details relating to changes in accounting principles
3) Dates of maturity and amounts of long-term debt
4) Yearly computation of depreciation, depletion, and amortization

3 Other Disclosures

The remaining notes contain all other information relevant to decision makers.

These notes are used to disclose facts not presented in either the body of the financial statements or in the Summary of Significant Accounting Policies. Examples of relevant note information include the following:

1) Material information regarding inventory, property, plant, and equipment, and other significant asset/liability balances that require specific disclosures;

2) Changes in stockholders' equity, including capital stock, paid-in capital, retained earnings, treasury stock, stock dividends, and other capital changes;

3) Required marketable securities disclosure, including carrying value and gross unrealized gains and losses;

4) Fair value estimates;

5) Contingency losses;

6) Contingency gains (if highly probable, but care should be exercised to avoid misleading implications as to the likelihood of realization);

7) Contractual obligations (including bonds payable and notes payable), including restrictions on specific assets or liabilities;

8) Pension plan description;

9) Segment reporting;

10) Subsequent events;

11) Changes in accounting principles or implementation of new accounting standards update.

4 Disclosure of Risks and Uncertainties

(1) Nature of Operations

The footnotes should include a description of the entity's major products or services and its principal markets, including the locations of those markets. If the entity operates multiple businesses, the disclosure should describe the relative importance of each business.

(2) Use of Estimates in the Preparation of Financial Statements

The preparation of financial statements in conformity with generally accepted accounting principles (GAAP) requires management to make estimates and assumptions that affect the reported amounts of assets and liabilities, the disclosure of contingent assets and liabilities at the date of the financial statements, and the reported amounts of revenues and expenses during the reporting period. Actual results could differ from those estimates.

(3) Certain Significant Estimates

When it is reasonably possible that an estimate will change in the near term and that the effect of the change will be material, an estimate of the effect of the change should be disclosed.

The following are examples of assets and liabilities and related revenues and expenses, including gain and loss contingencies that may be based on estimates that are particularly sensitive to change:

1) Inventory or equipment subject to rapid technological obsolescence.
2) Deferred tax asset valuation allowances.
3) Capitalized computer software costs.
4) Loan valuation allowances.
5) Litigation−related obligations.
6) Amounts reported for long−term obligations, such as pension and postretirement benefits.
7) Amounts reported in long−term contracts.

(4) Current Vulnerability Due to Certain Concentrations

1) Definition

Vulnerability due to concentrations arise when an entity is exposed to risk of loss that could be mitigated through diversification.

2) Disclosure Requirements

Concentrations should be disclosed if all of the following criteria are met:

- The concentration exists at the financial statement date.
- The concentration makes the entity vulnerable to the risk of a near-term severe impact (a significant financially disruptive effect on the normal functioning of an entity).
- It is at least reasonably possible that the events that could cause the severe impact will occur in the near term.

3) Examples of Concentrations

The following are common examples of concentrations:

- Concentrations in the volume of business transacted with a particular customer, supplier, lender, grantor, or contributor.

- Concentrations in revenue from particular products, services, or fund-raising events.

- Concentrations in the available supply of resources, such as materials, labor, or services.

- Concentrations in market or geographic area.

04 ▷▷ Tasked-Based Simulation(TBS)

[Q 7-1] Importing and Exporting

AIFA, a U.S. Company, imports and exports tools, shop equipment, and industrial construction supplies. The company uses a periodic inventory system. During April the company entered into the following transactions. All rate quotations are direct exchange rates.

⟨April 3⟩

Purchased power tools from a wholesaler in Japan, on account, at an invoice cost of 1,600,000 yen. On this date the exchange rate for the yen was $.0072.

⟨April 5⟩

Sold hand tools on credit that were manufactured in the U.S. to a retail outlet located in West Germany. The invoice price was $2,800. The exchange rate for euros was $1.25.

⟨April 9⟩

Sold electric drills on account to a retailer in New Zealand. The invoice price was 16,800 U.S. dollars and the exchange rate for the New Zealand dollar was $.76.

⟨April 11⟩

Purchased drill bits on account from a manufacturer located in Belgium. The billing was for 801,282 euros. The exchange rate for euro was $1.26.

⟨April 16⟩

Paid 1,000,000 yen on account to the wholesaler for purchases made on April 3. The exchange rate on this date was $.0067.

⟨April 18⟩

Settled the accounts payable with the Belgium manufacturer. The exchange rate was $1.28.

〈April 22〉

Received full payment from the New Zealand retailer. The exchange rate was $.74.

〈April 30〉

Completed payment on the April 3 purchase. The exchange rate for yen was $.0078.

• Instructions •

Prepare journal entries on the books of AIFA to record the transactions listed above.

[Q 7-2] Importing and Exporting

During December of the current year, AIFA, Inc., a company based in Seattle, Washington, entered into the following transactions:

⟨Dec 10⟩

Sold seven office computers to a company located in Colombia for 8,541,000 pesos. On this date, the spot rate was 365 pesos per U.S. dollar.

⟨Dec 12⟩

Purchased computer chips from a company domiciled in Taiwan. The contract was denominated in 500,000 Taiwan dollars. The direct exchange spot rate on this date was $.0391.

• Instructions •

(1) Prepare journal entries to record the transactions above on the books of AIFA, Inc. The company uses a periodic inventory system.

(2) Prepare journal entries necessary to adjust the accounts as of December 31. Assume that on December 31 the direct exchange rates were as follows:
Colombia peso : $.00268
Taiwan dollar : $.0351

(3) Prepare journal entries to record settlement of both open accounts on January 10. Assume that the direct exchange rates on the settlement dates were as follows:
Colombia peso : $.00320
Taiwan dollar : $.0398

(4) Prepare journal entries to record the December 10 transaction, adjust the accounts on December 31, and record settlement of the account on January 10, assuming that the transaction was denominated in dollars rather than pesos. Assume the same exchange rates as those given.

Government & Not-For-Profit Accounting For the **US CPA** Exam

Chapter 08

Ratio Analysis

Volume
8

01 Financial Statements

1 Income Statement

KIM Corporation

Income Statement for Year Ended December 31, Year 2

($ in millions)

Sales	$2,311
Cost of goods sold	1,144
Gross profit	1,167
Operating expenses excluding depreciation	200
Depreciation expenses	276
Earnings before interest and taxes (EBIT)	691
Interest expense	141
Earnings before taxes (EBT)	550
Federal and state income taxes (34%)	187
Net income	**$ 363**

Additional information

Total dividends : $121 millions

Shares outstanding : 33 millions

Stock price per share at the end of the year : $88

2 **Balance Sheet** (Financial Position)

KIM Corporation
Balance Sheet as of December 31, Year 1and Year 2
($ in millions)

Accounts	Year 1	Year 2
Cash	84	98
Accounts receivable	165	188
Inventory	393	422
Total current assets	$642	$708
Net plant & equipment	$2,731	$2,880
Total assets	**$3,373**	**$3,588**

Accounts	Year 1	Year 2
Accounts payable	312	344
Notes payable	231	196
Total current liabilities	$543	$540
Long-term debt	531	457
Total liabilities	$1,074	$997
Common stock	500	550
Retained earnings	1,799	2,041
Total equity	$2,299	$2,591
Total liabilities and equity	**$3,373**	**$3,588**

3 | Statement of Cash Flows

KIM Corporation
Statement of Cash Flows for Year Ended December 31, Year 2
($ in millions)

Operating activity	
Net income	$363
Depreciation	276
Increase in accounts receivable	−23
Increase in inventory	−29
Increase in accounts payable	32
Net cash from operating activity	**$619**
Investing activity	
Plant & equipment acquisition	−$425
Net cash from investing activity	**−$425**
Financing activity	
Decrease in notes payable	−$35
Decrease in long-term debt	−74
Dividend paid	−121
Increase in common stock	50
Net cash from financing activity	**−$180**
Net increase in cash	$14
Cash, beginning of year	$84
Cash, end of year	$98

02 ❯ Ratio Analysis

Ratio analysis is a quantitative method of gaining insight into a company's liquidity, operational efficiency, and profitability by comparing information contained in its financial statements.

(1) Liquidity ratio

(2) Long-term solvency (Leverage) ratio

(3) Activity ratio

(4) Profitability ratio

(5) Growth ratio

(6) Market value ratio

1 Liquidity Measures

유동성 비율(Liquidity ratios)은 기업의 단기 채무를 상환할 수 있는 능력을 측정하는 재무비율로 단기 안정성(short−term solvency)이라고도 한다. 유동성 비율이 높을수록 단기적인 채무지급능력은 뛰어나지만 수익성은 낮아지기 때문에 적정수준은 기업의 상황에 따라 달라진다.

(1) Working Capital

순운전자본은 유동자산에서 유동부채를 차감한 잔액으로 일상적인 영업활동에 필요한 자금을 말하며, 단기부채를 지급하기 위해 단기자산의 여력이 얼마나 되는가를 판단하는 지표로 활용된다.

working capital	current assets - current liabilities

For KIM, the Year 2 working capital = $708 - $540 = $168

the Year 1 working capital = $642 - $543 = $99

(2) Current Ratio

유동비율은 유동자산을 유동부채로 나눈 비율이다. 회사의 지불능력을 판단하기 위해서 사용하는 분석지표로 유동부채의 몇 배의 유동자산을 가지고 있는가를 나타내며 이 비율이 높을수록 지불능력이 커진다.

current ratio (working capital ratio)	$\dfrac{\text{current assets}}{\text{current liabilities}}$

For KIM, the Year 2 current ratio = $708 ÷ $540 = 1.31 times

- If a current ratio is less than one, a company has negative working capital with potential liquidity problems.
- A high current ratio isn't always a good thing. It might indicate that the business has too much inventory or is not investing its excess cash.

(3) Quick Ratio

당좌비율은 당좌자산을 유동부채로 나눈 비율이다. 당좌자산은 유동자산에서 재고자산과 선급비용을 제외한 자산으로 단기간에 환금할 수 있는 자산만을 포함한다. 당좌비율을 계산하는 데 있어서 재고자산을 제외하는 이유는 재고자산은 판매과정을 거쳐야 현금화할 수 있으므로 현금, 예금 또는 외상매출금 등과 같은 당좌자산과 비교할 때 유동성이 낮으며, 재고자산은 평가방법에 따라 그 가치가 다르게 나타나는 경우가 있기 때문이다.

※ Quick assets = current assets − inventory − prepaid expenses

= cash & equivalents + marketable securities + accounts receivable

Quick ratio (Acid-test ratio)	$\dfrac{\text{quick assets}}{\text{current liabilities}}$

For KIM, the Year 2 quick ratio = ($708 − 422) ÷ $540 = 0.53 times

- The quick ratio indicates a company's capacity to pay its current liabilities without needing to sell its inventory or get additional financing.
- The quick ratio is considered a more conservative measure than the current ratio.

(4) Cash Ratio

현금비율은 현금자산을 유동부채로 나눈 비율로 기업의 초단기 채무지급능력을 가늠할 수 있는 지표이다. 현금자산은 현금, 현금성자산 및 단기금융상품을 말하며, 당좌자산에서 매출채권을 제외한 자산이다.

cash ratio	$\dfrac{\text{cash \& cash equivalents + marketable securities}}{\text{current liabilities}}$

For KIM, the Year 2 cash ratio = $98 ÷ $540 = 0.18 times

- The cash ratio is more conservative than other liquidity ratios because it only considers a company's most liquid resources.

(5) Other Liquidity Ratio

operating cash flow ratio	$\dfrac{\text{cash flow from operations}}{\text{current liabilities}}$
working capital to total assets	$\dfrac{\text{working capital}}{\text{total assets}}$
defensive interval	$\dfrac{\text{quick assets}}{\text{average daily expenditures}}$

JOHNSON & JOHNSON has current assets equal to $3 million. The company's current ratio is 1.5 and its quick ratio is 1.0. What is the firm's level of inventories.

Solution

Current liabilities = $3 million ÷ 1.5 = $2 million.

Quick assets = 1.0 × $2 million = $2 million.

Inventory = Current assets − Quick assets

$\qquad$ = $3 million − $2 million = $1 million

Example-2

American Express Co. has $1,400,000 in current assets and $500,000 in current liabilities. Its initial inventory level is $500,000 and it will raise funds as additional notes payable and use them to increase inventory. How much can the firm's short-term debt increase without pushing its current ratio below 2.0? What will be the firm's quick ratio after the firm has raised the maximum amount of short-term funds?

Solution

Current assets = $1,400,000 + X

Current liabilities = $500,000 + X

$1,400,000 + X = 2 × ($500,000 + X) → X = $400,000

After refinancing

Quick assets = $1,400,000 − $500,000 = $900,000

Current liabilities = $500,000 + $400,000 = $900,000

Quick ratio = $900,000 ÷ $900,000 = 1.00 (100%)

2 Long-term Solvency Measures

장기안정성 비율은 기업의 장기채무지급능력의 측정치로 재무레버리지 비율(financial leverage ratios) 또는 레버리지 비율(leverage ratios, gearing ratio)이라고도 한다.

(1) Debt ratio

부채비율은 타인자본과 자산 또는 자기자본 간의 관계를 나타내는 대표적인 안정성 지표로서 이 비율이 낮을수록 재무구조가 건전하다고 판단할 수 있다.

total debt ratio	$\dfrac{\text{total liabilities}}{\text{total assets}}$
debt-to-equity ratio	$\dfrac{\text{total liabilities}}{\text{total equity}}$
equity multiplier	$\dfrac{\text{total assets}}{\text{total equity}}$

For KIM, the Year 2

total debt ratio = \$997 ÷ \$3,588 = 0.28 times

debt-to-equity ratio = \$997 ÷ \$2,591= 0.39 times

equity multiplier = \$3,588 ÷ \$,591= 1.39 times

- Investors can use the debt ratio to evaluate how much leverage a company is using.

- Higher leverage ratios tend to indicate a company with higher risk to shareholders.

- Ambiguity between the terms "debt" and "liabilities"

  Total debt = long–term and shirt–term debt

  Total liabilities = total debt + operating liabilities such as accounts payable

  For KIM, the Year 2

  total debt ratio = (\$997 − 344) ÷ \$3,588 = 0.18 times

(2) Times-Interest-Earned (Interest Coverage) Ratio

이자보상비율은 이자지급에 필요한 수익의 창출능력을 측정하기 위한 지표로 이자부담능력을 판단하는데 유용하게 쓰인다.

TIE ratio (times-interest-earned)	$\dfrac{EBIT}{\text{interest expense}}$

For KIM, the Year 2 TIE ratio = $691 ÷ $141 = 4.9 times

(3) EBITDA Coverage Ratio (=Cash Coverage)

현금보상비율은 기업의 영업현금흐름을 측정치인 EBITDA를 이용한 현금주의 이자보상비율이다.

EBITDA coverage ratio	$\dfrac{EBITDA}{\text{interest expense}}$

For KIM, the Year 2 cash coverage = ($691 + 276) ÷ $141 = 6.9 times

(4) Other Leverage Ratio

debt-to-capital ratio	$\dfrac{\text{total debt}}{\text{total capital}}$
비유동장기적합률	$\dfrac{\text{non-current assets}}{\text{equity + non-current liabilities}}$
fixed charge coverage	$\dfrac{\text{EBIT + lease payments}}{\text{interest payments + lease payments}}$

Example-3

WELLS FARGO has a total debt ratio of 0.62.
What is its debt-equity ratio? What is its equity multiplier??

Solution

$D/A = D/E \times E/A = D/E \times (1 - D/A)$
$0.62 = D/E \times (1-0.62) \rightarrow D/E = 1.63$
$A/E = 1 + D/E = 1 + 1.63 = 2.63$

Example-4

Caterpillar Inc. has $500,000 of debt outstanding and it pays an interest rate of 10% annually. The company's sales are $2 million, its average tax rate is 30% and its net profit margin on sales is 7%. If the company does not maintain a TIE ratio of at least 4 times, its bank will refuse to renew loan, and bankruptcy will result. What is the company's ratio?

Solution

Net income $= \$2,000,000 \times 7\% = \$140,000$
EBT $= \$140,000 \div 0.7 = \$200,000$
Interest $= \$500,000 \times 10\% = \$50,000$
EBIT $= \$200,000 + \$50,000 = \$250,000$
TIE $= \$250,000 \div \$50,000 = 5$ times
$\rightarrow$ The bank will not refuse to renew loan.

Example-5

When compared to a debt-to-assets ratio, a debt-to-equity ratio is
a. the same as the debt-to-assets ratio.
b. higher than the debt-to-assets ratio.
c. lower than the debt-to-assets ratio.
d. unrelated to the debt-to-assets ratio.

Solution

Assets $\rangle$ Equity $\rightarrow$ D/A $\langle$ D/E

정답 : b

Example-6

Calvin Klein's net income for the most recent year was $8,175. The tax rate was 34 percent. The firm paid $2,380 in total interest expense and deducted $1,560 in depreciation expense. What was Calvin Klein's interest coverage ratio and cash coverage ratio for the year?

Solution

EBIT = $8,175 ÷ 0.66 + 2,380 = $14,766
interest coverage ratio = $14,766 ÷ $2,380 = 6.2 times
EBITDA = 14,766 + 1,560 = $16,326
cash coverage ratio = $16,326 ÷ $2,380 = 6.9 times

3 Activity Measures

활동성 비율은 기업에 투하된 자본이 기간 중 얼마나 활발하게 운용되었는가를 나타내는 비율로서 회전율(turnover ratio) 또는 자산 이용률(asset utilization ratios)이라고도 한다. 활동성 분석의 재무상태표 항목은 일반적으로 평균금액을 기준으로 구한다. 하지만 AICPA 시험에서는 기말금액을 기준으로 회전율을 계산하도록 요구하기도 한다.

(1) Asset Turnover Ratios

총자산회전율(total asset turnover)은 총자산이 1년 동안 몇 번 회전하였는가를 나타내는 비율로서 기업에 투하한 총자산의 운용효율을 총괄적으로 표시하는 지표이다.

total asset turnover	$\dfrac{\text{sales}}{\text{average total assets}}$

For KIM, the Year 2

average total assets = (3,373 + 3,588) ÷ 2 = $3,480

total asset turnover = $2,311 ÷ $3,480 = 0.66 times

유형자산 회전율(fixed asset turnover) 유형자산의 이용도를 나타내는 지표로서 기업이 보유하고 있는 설비자산의 적정성 여부를 판단하는데 유용하다.

fixed asset turnover	$\dfrac{\text{sales}}{\text{average net fixed assets}}$

For KIM, the Year 2

average net fixed assets = (2,731 + 2,880) ÷ 2 = $2,806

fixed asset turnover = $2,311 ÷ $2,806 = 0.82 times

운전자본 회전율(working capital turnover) 운전자본의 이용도를 나타내는 지표로서 기업이 보유하고 있는 운전자본의 적정성 여부를 판단하는데 유용하다.

working capital turnover	$\dfrac{\text{sales}}{\text{average working capital}}$

For KIM, the Year 2

average working capital = (99 + 168) ÷ 2 = $134

working capital turnover = $2,311 ÷ $134 = 17.3 times

(2) Receivables Turnover and Days Sales Outstanding (DSO)

매출채권 회전율은 매출채권의 현금화 속도를 측정하는 비율로서 높을수록 매출채권의 현금화 속도가 빠르다는 것을 의미한다. 매출채권회전율의 역수를 취하여 365일을 곱하면 평균회수기간을 계산할 수 있는데 이 기간이 짧을수록 매출채권이 효율적으로 관리되어 판매자금이 매출채권에 오래 묶여 있지 않음을 뜻하며, 반대의 경우에는 가공매출 또는 고객의 지급불능의 신호가 된다.

그러나 기업이 시장점유율 확대를 위해 판매 전략을 강화하는 경우에도 매출채권회전율이 낮게 나타날 수 있으므로 기업의 목표회수기간이나 판매조건과 비교하여 적정성을 평가하여야 할 것이다.

receivable turnover	$\dfrac{\text{sales}}{\text{average A/R}}$
days sales outstanding (DSO)	$\dfrac{365}{\text{receivable turnover}}$
	$\dfrac{\text{average A/R}}{\text{sales per day}}$
	$\dfrac{\text{ending A/R(net)}}{\text{sales per day}}$

For KIM, the Year 2

average receivable = (165 + 188) ÷ 2 = $177

receivable turnover = $2,311 ÷ $177 = 13.1 times

days sales outstanding = 365 ÷ 13.1 times = 28 days (평균 매출채권기준)

days sales outstanding = 188 ÷ (2,311 ÷ 365) = 30 days (기말 매출채권기준)

(3) Inventory Turnover and Days Inventory Outstanding (DIO)

재고자산회전율은 매출액을 재고자산으로 나눈 비율로서 재고자산의 회전속도, 즉 재고자산이 현금 등 당좌자산으로 변화하는 속도를 나타낸다. 일반적으로 이 비율이 높을수록 상품의 재고손실 방지 및 보험료, 보관료의 절약 등 재고자산의 관리가 효율적으로 이루어지고 있음을 의미한다. 이 비율이 낮다는 것은 재고자산이 과다하다는 것을 의미하며, 이 비율이 높다는 것은 생산 및 판매활동이 효율적으로 수행되고 있다는 의미이다. Just-in-time (JIT) system을 도입한 기업은 재고자산 회전율은 높아지고, 재고자산 회전기간은 짧아진다.

그러나 재고를 정상적인 영업활동에 필요한 적정수준 이하로 유지하여 수요변동에 적절히 대처하지 못하는 경우에도 이 비율은 높게 나타날 수가 있으므로 해석에

유의할 필요가 있다.

또한 원재료의 가격이 상승추세에 있는 기업이나 재고자산의 보유수준이 크게 높아지는 기업들의 경우에는 주로 후입선출법(LIFO)에 의해 재고자산을 평가함으로써 재고자산회전율이 높게 나타나는 경향이 있다.

따라서 재고자산회전율에 대한 상대적인 차이에 대해서는 실제로 재고자산이 효율적으로 관리되었는지, 생산기간이 단축되어 재공품이 감소하였는지, 기업의 재고보유 방침이 바뀌었는지, 또한 재고자산 평가방법을 다르게 채택하고 있는지를 비교 분석하여 판단하여야 할 것이다.

inventory turnover	$\dfrac{\text{cost of goods sold}}{\text{average inventory}}$
days inventory outstanding (DIO)	$\dfrac{365}{\text{inventory turnover}}$
	$\dfrac{\text{average inventory}}{\text{COGS per day}}$
	$\dfrac{\text{ending inventory}}{\text{COGS per day}}$

For KIM, the Year 2

average inventory = (393 + 422) ÷ 2 = $408

inventory turnover = \$1,144 ÷ \$408 = 2.8 times

days inventory outstanding = 365 ÷ 2.8 times = 130 days (평균 재고자산 기준)

days inventory outstanding = 422 ÷ (1,144 ÷ 365) = 134 days (기말 재고자산 기준)

(4) Payable Turnover and Days Payable Outstanding (DPO)

매입채무회전율은 매입채무의 지급속도를 측정하는 지표로서 기업의 부채 중에서도 특히 매입채무가 원활히 결제되고 있는가의 여부를 나타낸다. 매입채무회전율을 측정하는 기본항목은 매출원가 또는 매입금액이다.

매입채무회전율이 높을수록 결제속도가 빠름을 의미하나 회사의 신용도가 저하되어 신용 매입기간을 짧게 제공받는 경우에도 이 비율이 높게 나타날 수 있기 때문에 운전자본의 압박가능성 등을 보다 정확하게 분석하기 위해서는 매출채권회전율도 함께 비교 · 검토하는 것이 요구된다.

payable turnover	$\dfrac{\text{cost of goods sold}}{\text{average A/P}}$
days payable outstanding (DPO)	$\dfrac{365}{\text{payable turnover}}$
	$\dfrac{\text{average A/P}}{\text{COGS per day}}$
	$\dfrac{\text{ending A/P}}{\text{COGS per day}}$

For KIM, the Year 2

average A/P = (312 + 344) ÷ 2 = \$328

payable turnover = \$1,144 ÷ \$328 = 3.5 times

days payable outstanding = 365 ÷ 3.5 times = 104 days (평균 매입채무 기준)

days payable outstanding = 344 ÷ (1,144 ÷ 365) = 110 days (기말 매입채무 기준)

(5) Cash Conversion Cycle (CCC)

The Cash Conversion Cycle (CCC) is a metric that shows the amount of time it takes a company to convert its investments in inventory to cash. The cash conversion cycle formula measures the amount of time, in days, it takes for a company to turn its resource inputs into cash.

The cash conversion cycle formula is aimed at assessing how efficiently a company is managing its working capital. The shorter the cash conversion cycle, the better the company is at selling inventories and recovering cash from these sales while paying suppliers.

DIO

the average number of days that a company holds its inventory before selling it.

DSO

the average number of days for a company to collect payment after a sale.

DPO

the average number of days for a company to pay its invoices from suppliers.

cash conversion cycle	DIO + DSO - DPO

For KIM, the Year 2

Cash Conversion Cycle = 130 + 28 - 104 = 54 days

→ it takes approximately 54 days to turn its initial cash investment in inventory back into cash.

Example-7

The following financial ratios and calculations were based on information from Boeing Co.'s financial statements for the current year :

Accounts receivable turnover : Ten times during the year

Total assets turnover : Two times during the year

Average receivables during the year : $200,000

What was firm's average total assets for the year?

Solution

Sales = $200,000 × 10 times = $2,000,000

Total average assets = $2,000,000 ÷ 2.0 times = $1,000,000

Example-8

Accounts receivable turnover will normally decrease as a result of

a. The write-off of an uncollectible account.

b. A significant sales volume decrease near the end of the accounting period.

c. An increase in cash sales in proportion to credit sales.

d. A change in credit policy to lengthen the period for cash discounts.

Solution

a. 이미 대손충당금을 설정하였기 때문에 매출채권의 순액에 영향을 주지 않는다.

b. 기말의 매출감소는 기말매출채권을 급격히 감소시키므로 매출채권 회전율이 증가.

c. 현금매출의 증가는 매출채권의 감소이므로 회전율의 증가.

d. 현금할인 기간이 증가하면 회수기간이 길어지므로 회전율은 감소.

정답 : d

Example-9

CHANEL's receivable turnover is ten times, the inventory turnover is five times and the payable turnover is nine times. What is firm's cash conversion cycle?

Solution

DIO = 365 ÷ 5 times = 73 days

DSO = 365 ÷ 10 times = 37 days

DPO = 365 ÷ 9 times = 41 days

CCC = 73 + 37 − 41 = 69 days

4 Profitability Measures

수익성 비율은 일정기간 동안의 기업의 경영성과를 측정하는 비율로서 투자된 자본 또는 자산, 매출수준에 상응하여 창출한 이익의 정도를 나타내므로 자산이용의 효율성, 이익창출능력 등에 대한 평가는 물론 영업성과를 요인별로 분석·검토

하기 위한 지표로 이용된다. 수익성 분석의 재무상태표 항목은 일반적으로 평균금액을 기준으로 구한다. 하지만 AICPA 시험에서는 기말금액을 기준으로 수익성 비율을 계산하도록 요구하기도 한다.

(1) Profit Margin Ratios

매출액 이익률은 일정기간 동안의 기업의 경영성과를 측정하는 비율로서 매출수준에 상응하여 창출한 이익의 정도를 나타낸다.

gross profit margin	$\dfrac{\text{gross profit}}{\text{sales}}$
operating profit margin	$\dfrac{\text{operating profit}}{\text{sales}}$
net profit margin	$\dfrac{\text{net income}}{\text{sales}}$

For KIM, the Year 2

gross profit margin = 1,167 ÷ 2,311 = 50.5%

operating profit margin = 691 ÷ 2,311 = 29.9%

net profit margin = 363 ÷ 2,311 = 15.7%

(2) Return on Assets (ROA)

총자산순이익률은 당기순이익의 총자산에 대한 비율로, 기업 관점에서의 투자수익률을 의미한다. 기업의 계획과 실적 간 차이 분석을 통한 경영활동의 평가나 경영전략 수립 등에 많이 활용된다.

return on assets (ROA)	$$\dfrac{\text{net income}}{\text{average total assets}}$$

For KIM, the Year 2

average assets = (3,373 + 3,588) ÷ 2 = $3,481

return on assets = $363 ÷ $3,481 = 10.43%

(3) Return on Equity (ROE)

자기자본순이익률은 자기자본에 대한 당기순이익의 비율로서, 주주 관점에서의 투자수익률을 의미한다. 자본조달 특성에 따라 동일한 자산구성 하에서도 서로 다른 결과를 나타낼 수 있으므로 자본구성과의 관계도 동시에 고려해야 한다.

return on equity (ROE)	$$\dfrac{\text{net income}}{\text{average equity}}$$

For KIM, the Year 2

average equity = (2,299 + 2,591) ÷ 2 = $2,445

return on equity = $363 ÷ $2,445 = 14.85%

Du Pont identity (듀퐁항등식)

화학업체 듀퐁에서 근무하던 Donaldson Brown이 1920년대 고안한 재무 분석 기법

ROE = NI / Equity = (NI / Sales) × (Sales / Assets) × (Assets / Equity)

return on equity (ROE)	profit margin × asset turnover × equity multipliers
	ROA × equity multipliers

For KIM, the Year 2

profit margin = 15.7%, asset turnover = 0.664 times,

average equity multipliers = $3,481 ÷ $2,445 = 1.42 times

ROE = 15.7% × 0.664 × 1.42 = 14.8%

Popular expression breaking ROE into three parts:

1. Operating efficiency (as measured by profit margin)

2. Asset use efficiency (as measured by total asset turnover)

3. Financial leverage (as measured by the equity multiplier)

Example–10

Dimler-Benz Corp. has a profit margin of 7 percent, total asset turnover of 1.09, and ROE of 23.70 percent. What is this firm's debt-equity ratio?

Solution

23.70% = 7% × 1.09 × equity multipliers → equity multipliers = 3.1

A/E = 1 + D/E → 3.1 = 1 + D/E → D/E = 2.1

Example–11

PRADA has a debt-equity ratio of 1.10. Return on assets is 8.4 percent, and total equity is $440,000. What is the equity multiplier? Return on equity? Net income?

Solution

equity multipliers = 1 + D/E = 1+ 1.10 = 2.10

ROE = 8.4% × 2.10 = 17.64%

NI = $440,000 × 0.1764 = $77,616

Example-12

Coca-Cola Co.'s ROE last year was only 3%, but its management has developed a new operating plan designed to improve things. The new plan calls for a total debt ratio of 60%, which will result in interest charge of $300,000 per year. Management projects an EBIT of $1,000,000 on sales of $10,000,000 and it expects to have a total assets turnover of 2.0. Under these condition, the tax rate will be 40%. If the changes are made, what ROE will the company earn?

Solution

net income = ($1,000,000 − $300,000) × (1 − 0.4) = $420,000

profit margin = $420,000 ÷ $10,000,000 = 4.2%

equity multiplier = Assets ÷ Equity = 100% ÷ 40% = 2.5times

ROE = 4.2% × 2.0 × 2.5 = 21%

5 Growth Measures

(1) Sales Growth

매출액 증가율은 전기 매출액에 대한 당기 매출액의 증가율로서 기업의 외형 신장세를 판단하는 대표적인 지표이다.

sales growth	$\dfrac{\text{current sales - prior sales}}{\text{prior sales}}$

(2) Profit Growth

순이익증가율은 전기 순이익에 대한 당기 순이익의 증가율로서 기업의 수익성 신장세를 판단하는 대표적인 지표이다.

profit growth	$\dfrac{\text{current net income - prior net income}}{\text{prior net income}}$

(3) Assets Growth

자산증가율은 기업에 투하된 총자산이 얼마나 증가하였는가를 나타내는 비율로서 기업의 전체적인 성장성을 측정하는 지표이다.

assets growth	$\dfrac{\text{current assets - prior assets}}{\text{prior assets}}$

(4) Payout Ratio

배당성향은 기업이 당기순이익 중 어느 정도를 배당금으로 지급하였는가를 나타내는 지표로 배당금을 당기순이익으로 나누어 측정하거나 주당배당금을 주당이익으로 나누어 측정한다.

payout ratio	$\dfrac{\text{total dividends}}{\text{net income}}$
	$\dfrac{\text{dividend per share (DPS)}}{\text{earning per share (EPS)}}$

For KIM, the Year 2 payout ratio = 121 ÷ 363 = 33.3%

(5) Retention Ratio (RR)

유보율은 당기순이익 중에서 배당으로 처분되지 않고 기업내부에 유보된 금액의 비율을 나타내며, 1001에서 배당성향을 차감하여 산출된다.

retention ratio	1 - payout ratio

For KIM, the Year 2 retention ratio = 100% − 33.3% = 66.7%

(6) Sustainable Growth Rate (SGR)

배당 성장률은 당기 배당대비 향후 배당이 얼마나 증가할 것인지를 나타내는 비율로서, 기업의 유보율에 자기자본이익률(ROE)을 곱하여 측정한다.

sustainable growth rate	ROE × retention ratio

For KIM, the Year 2 SGR = 66.7% × 14.85% = 9.9%

Example-13

Volvo has a dividend payout ratio of 40%, a net profit margin of 10%, an asset turnover of 0.9 times and an equity multiplier of 1.2times. What is the firm's sustainable growth rate?

Solution

ROE $= 10\% \times 0.9 \times 1.2 = 10.8\%$
Retention rate $= 1 - 0.4 = 0.6$
SGR $= 10.8\% \times 0.6 = 6.48\%$

Example-14

Two companies are identical except for different dividend payout ratio. The company with the lower dividend payout ratio is most likely to have?

a. lower stock price   b. higher debt-to-equity ratio
c. less rapid growth of EPS   d. more rapid growth of EPS

Solution

배당성향이 낮은 기업은 자기자본이 더 크기 때문에 부채비율은 작고, 유보율이 높기 때문에 이익성장률이 높으며, 주가는 더 높을수도 있고 낮을 수도 있다.

정답 : d

6 Market Value Measures

(1) Price-to-Earnings Ratio (P/E Ratio)

주가수익률은 주가를 주당이익(EPS)으로 나눈 값을 말하며, 이는 기업의 주당순이익이 증권시장에서 몇 배의 주가로 평가되고 있는가를 나타낸다. 예를 들어, 주당이익이 1,000원이고 주가가 12,000원이라면 PER는 12이다.

P/E ratio	$\dfrac{\text{price per share}}{\text{earning per share}}$
	$\dfrac{\text{market value}}{\text{net income}}$

For KIM, the Year 2
EPS = $363 ÷ 33 = $11
P/E = $88 ÷ $11 = 8 times

- High P/E : 주식의 시장가격이 과대평가 또는 성장주(growth stock)
- Low P/E : 주식의 시장가격이 과소평가 또는 가치주(value stock)
- Forward P/E : uses forecasted earnings for the P/E calculation
- Trailing P/E : uses last 12 months of actual earnings for the P/E calculation
- TTM : Trailing 12 Months
- MRQ : Most Recent Quarter

목표기업의 주가를 추정하는 경우 목표기업의 주당이익에 목표기업이 속한 산업평균 P/E ratio를 곱하여 산출할 수 있다.

$$Price^{target} = EPS^{target} \times P/E^{industry}$$

The earnings yield (which is the inverse of the P/E ratio) shows the percentage of each dollar invested in the stock that was earned by the company.

earnings yield (EY)	$\dfrac{\text{earning per share}}{\text{price per share}}$

For KIM, the Year 2 earnings yield = \$11 ÷ \$88 = 12.5%

The price/earnings to growth ratio (PEG ratio) is a stock's price-to-earnings (P/E) ratio divided by the growth rate of its earnings for a specified time period. The PEG ratio is considered to be an indicator of a stock's true value, and a lower PEG may indicate that a stock is undervalued.

PEG ratio	$\dfrac{\text{price-to-earnings ratio}}{\text{EPS growth}}$

For KIM, the Year 2 PEG ratio = 8 ÷ 9.9 = 0.81

(2) Price-to-Book Ratio (P/B ratio, Market-to-Book Ratio)

주가순자산배율은 주가를 주당순자산으로 나눈 값을 말하며, 이는 기업의 주당순자산이 증권시장에서 몇 배의 주가로 평가되고 있는가를 나타낸다.

P/B ratio	$\dfrac{\text{price per share}}{\text{book value per share}}$
	$\dfrac{\text{market value}}{\text{equity}}$

For KIM, the Year 2
book value per share = \$2,591 ÷ 33 = \$78.5
P/B = \$88 ÷ \$78.5 = 1.12 times

- High P/B : 주식의 시장가격이 과대평가 또는 성장주(growth stock)
- Low P/B : 주식의 시장가격이 과소평가 또는 가치주(value stock)

목표기업의 주가를 추정하는 경우 목표기업의 주당순자산에 목표기업이 속한 산업평균 P/B ratio 를 곱하여 산출할 수 있다.

$$\text{Price}^{\text{target}} = \text{BPS}^{\text{target}} \times \text{P/B}^{\text{industry}}$$

The P/B ratio can also be used for firms with positive book values and negative earnings since negative earnings render price-to-earnings ratios useless, and there are fewer companies with negative book values than companies with negative earnings. However, when accounting standards applied by firms vary, P/B ratios may not be comparable, especially for companies from different countries. Additionally, P/B ratios can be less useful for service and information technology companies with little tangible assets on their balance sheets. Finally, the book value can become negative because of a long series of negative earnings, making the P/B ratio useless for relative valuation.

(3) Price-to-Sales Ratio (P/S Ratio)

주가매출배율은 주가를 주당매출액으로 나눈 값을 말하며, 이는 기업의 주당매출액이 증권시장 에서 몇 배의 주가로 평가되고 있는가를 나타낸다.

P/S ratio	$\dfrac{\text{price per share}}{\text{sales per share}}$
	$\dfrac{\text{market value}}{\text{sales}}$

For KIM, the Year 2
sales per share = $2,311 ÷ 33 = $70.0
P/S = $88 ÷ $70 = 1.26 times

The P/S ratio provides a way to value a company with little or no profits. A higher (lower) P/S ratio relative to peers or the industry may suggest a company is overvalued (undervalued).

(4) Price-to-Cash Flow Ratio (P/CF Ratio)

주가현금흐름배율은 주가를 주당영업현금흐름으로 나눈 값을 말하며, 이는 기업의 주당영업현금흐름이 증권시장에서 몇 배의 주가로 평가되고 있는가를 나타낸다.

P/CF ratio	$\dfrac{\text{price per share}}{\text{operating cash flow per share}}$
	$\dfrac{\text{market value}}{\text{operating cash flow}}$

The price-to-cash flow multiple works well for companies that have large non-cash expenses such as depreciation. A low multiple implies that a stock may be undervalued.

Example-15

LVMH group had additions to retained earnings for the year just ended of $275,000. The firm paid out $150,000 in cash dividends, and it has ending total equity of $6 million. If LVMH currently has 125,000 shares of common stock outstanding, what are earnings per share? Book value per share? If the stock currently sells for $95 per share, what is the market-to-book ratio? The price-earnings ratio?

Solution

net income = 275,000 + 150,000 = $425,000

EPS = $425,000 ÷ 125,000 = $3.4

BPS = $6,000,000 ÷ 125,000 = $48

market−to−book ratio = $95 ÷ $48 = 1.98 times

price−earnings ratio = $95 ÷ $3.4 = 27.9 times

Example-16

A company has an EPS of \$2.00, a cash flow per share of \$3.00, and a price/cash flow ratio of 8.0. What is its P/E ratio?

Solution

price per share = \$3 × 8 = \$24
price—earnings ratio = \$24 ÷ \$2 = 12 times

Example-17

Volkswagen recently reported net income of \$2 million. It has 500,000 shares of common stock, which currently trades at \$40 a share. Volkswagen continues to expand and anticipates that 1 year from now its net income will be \$3.25 million. Over the next year it also anticipates issuing an additional 150,000 shares of stock, so that 1 year from now it will have 650,000 shares of common stock. Assuming its price/earnings ratio remains at its current level, what will be its stock price 1 year from now?

Solution

EPS = \$2,000,000 ÷ 500,000 = \$4
price—earnings ratio = \$40 ÷ \$4 = 10 times
EPS 1 year from now = \$3,250,000 ÷ 650,000 = \$5
price per share = \$5 × 10 = \$50
market value = \$50 × 650,000 = \$32,500,000

7 Limitations of Financial Statement Analysis

(1) Different accounting practices

기업마다 회계처리 방법이 다르기 때문에 비율분석을 통한 비교만으로는 충분하지 않다. 비교대상 기업의 재고자산 평가방법이나 감가상각 방법이 상이하다면 정확한 비교정보를 얻을 수 없을 것이다. 예를 들면 물가 상승시에 FIFO방법은 LIFO방법보다 기말재고와 이익을 더 높게 보고한다.

(2) Large firms operating different divisions in different industries.

다양한 산업을 영위하는 대기업의 경우 적절한 벤치마킹을 결정하기가 어렵다. 예를 들면 삼성전자의 비교대상이 되는 산업평균은 반도체인지 가전제품인지의 판단이 어려울 것이다.

(3) It is difficult to generalize about whether a particular ratio is good or bad.

종합적인 재무비율이 양호한지 불량한지의 여부를 일반화하기가 어렵다. 예를 들면 현금을 많이 보유하고 있으면 유동성은 좋지만, 수익성은 감소한다.

(4) Window dressing technique.

회계연도 말에 경영자가 재무제표의 수치를 고의로 왜곡시키는 분식회계를 말한다.

예를 들면 연말에 기업이 은행으로부터 장기차입을 하여 현금을 보유하고 있다면, 유동성은 양호해 보인다. 그리고 다음연도 초에 차입금을 상환한다면, 또한 이러한 행위를 매년 반복한다면, 이 기업의 유동성 비율은 매년 분식을 하는 셈이다.

(5) Only financial measures.

재무비율 분석은 기업의 재무적인 성과만을 보는 것이다. 하지만 경영자의 자질, 시장점유율, 브랜드 가치 등의 비재무적인 질적 요인들은 재무제표에 수치화 할 수 없다.

Example-18

Which of the following is not a limitation of ratio analysis?

a. Different accounting practices
b. Different fiscal years.
c. Window dressing
d. Liquidity cannot be analyzed.

Solution

유동비율이나 당좌비율 등으로 기업의 유동성을 평가할 수 있다.

정답 : d

03 ▷ **Multiple Choice**

01. For a given level of sales, and holding all other financial statement items constant, a company's return on equity (ROE) will (CMA)

    a. increase as their debt ratio decreases.

    b. decrease as their cost of goods sold as a percent of sales decrease.

    c. decrease as their total assets increase.

    d. increase as their equity increases.

02. The following financial information applies to Sycamore Company.

Cash	$10,000
Marketable securities	18,000
Accounts receivable	120,000
Inventories	375,000
Prepaid expenses	12,000
Accounts payable	75,000
Long-term debt – current portion	20,000
Long-term debt	400,000
Sales	1,650,000

What is the acid-test (or quick) ratio for Sycamore? (CMA)

    a. 1.56   b. 1.97

    c. 2.13   d. 5.63

03. A bondholder would be most concerned with which one of the following ratios? (CMA)

    a. Inventory turnover   b. Times interest earned

    c. Quick ratio   d. Earnings per share

04. Anderson Cable wishes to calculate their return on assets. You know that the return on equity is 12% and that the debt ratio is 40%. What is the ROA? (CMA)

    a. 4.8%   b. 7.2%

    c. 12.0%   d. 20.0%.

05. Peggy Monahan, controller, has gathered the following information regarding Lampasso Company.

	Beginning of the year	End of the year
Inventory	$6,400	$7,600
Accounts receivable	2,140	3,060
Accounts payable	3,320	3,680

Total sales for the year were $85,900, of which $62,400 were credit sales. The cost of goods sold was $24,500. Lampasso's accounts receivable turnover ratio for the year was (CMA)

    a. 9.4 times   b. 20.4 times

    c. 24.0 times   d. 33.0 times

06. Davis Retail Inc. has total assets of $7,500,000 and a current ratio of 2.3 times before purchasing $750,000 of merchandise on credit for resale. After this purchase, the current ratio will (CMA)

a. remain at 2.3 times.

b. be higher than 2.3 times.

c. be lower than 2.3 times.

d. be exactly 2.53 times.

07. Markowitz Company increased its allowance for uncollectable accounts. This adjustment will (CMA)

a. increase the acid test ratio.

b. increase working capital.

c. reduce debt-to-asset ratio.

d. reduce the current ratio.

08. Birch Products Inc. has the following current assets.

Cash	$250,000
Marketable securities	100,000
Accounts receivable	800,000
Inventories	1,450,000
Total current assets	$2,600,000

If Birch's current liabilities are $1,300,000, the firm's (CMA)

a. current ratio will decrease if a payment of $100,000 cash is used to pay $100,000 of accounts payable.

b. current ratio will not change if a payment of $100,000 cash is used to pay $100,000 of accounts payable.

c. quick ratio will decrease if a payment of $100,000 cash is used to purchase inventory.

d. quick ratio will not change if a payment of $100,000 cash is used to purchase inventory.

09. Garstka Auto Parts must increase its acid test ratio above the current 0.9 level in order to comply with the terms of a loan agreement. Which one of the following actions is most likely to produce the desired results? (CMA)

a. Expediting collection of accounts receivable.

b. Selling auto parts on account.

c. Making a payment to trade accounts payable.

d. Purchasing marketable securities for cash.

10. The owner of a chain of grocery stores has bought a large supply of mangoes and paid for the fruit with cash. This purchase will adversely impact which one of the following? (CMA)

a. Working capital   b. Current ratio

c. Quick or acid test ratio   d. Price earnings ratio

11. Both the current ratio and the quick ratio for Spartan Corporation have been slowly decreasing. For the past two years, the current ratio has been 2.3 to 1 and 2.0 to 1. During the same time period, the quick ratio has decreased from 1.2 to 1 to 1.0 to 1. The disparity between the current and quick ratios can be explained by which one of the following? (CMA)

a. The current portion of long-term debt has been steadily increasing.

b. The cash balance is unusually low.

c. The accounts receivable balance has decreased.

d. The inventory balance is unusually high.

12. Globetrade is a retailer that buys virtually all of its merchandise from manufacturers in a country experiencing significant inflation. Globetrade is considering changing its method of inventory costing from first-in, first-out (FIFO) to last-in, first-out (LIFO). What effect would the change from FIFO to LIFO have on Globetrade's current ratio and inventory turnover ratio? (CMA)

a. Both the current ratio and the inventory turnover ratio would increase.

b. The current ratio would increase but the inventory turnover ratio would decrease.

c. The current ratio would decrease but the inventory turnover ratio would increase.

d. Both the current ratio and the inventory turnover ratio would decrease.

13. Which one of the following is the best indicator of long-term debt paying ability? (CMA)

a. Working capital turnover   b. Asset turnover

c. Current ratio   d. Debt-to-total assets ratio

14. The interest expense for a company is equal to its earnings before interest and taxes (EBIT). The company's tax rate is 40%. The company's times-interest earned ratio is equal to (CMA)

a. 2.0   b. 1.0

c. 0.6   d. 1.2

Items through 15 and 16

> Bull & Bear Investment Banking is working with the management of Clark Inc. in order to take the company public in an initial public offering. Selected financial information for Clark is as follows.
>
> | | |
> |---|---:|
> | Long-term debt (8% interest rate) | $10,000,000 |
> | Common equity : Par value ($1 per share) | 3,000,000 |
> | Additional paid-in-capital | 24,000,000 |
> | Retained earnings | 6,000,000 |
> | Total assets | 55,000,000 |
> | Net income | 3,750,000 |
> | Dividend (annual) | 1,500,000 |

15. If public companies in Clark's industry are trading at twelve times earnings, what is the estimated value per share of Clark? (CMA)

a. $9.00   b. $12.00

c. $15.00   d. $24.00.

16. If public companies in Clark's industry are trading at a market to book ratio of 1.5, what is the estimated value per share of Clark? (CMA)

a. $13.50   b. $16.50

c. $21.50   d. $27.50.

Solution

1	2	3	4	5	6	7	8	9	10
C	A	B	B	C	C	D	C	B	C

11	12	13	14	15	16
D	C	D	B	C	B

1. ROE = Profit margin × asset turnover × financial leverage
   a. 부채비율의 감소 → financial leverage의 감소 → ROE의 감소
   b. 매출원가율의 감소 → Profit margin의 증가 → ROE의 증가
   c. 자산의 증가 → asset turnover의 감소 → ROE의 감소
   d. 자본의 증가 → financial leverage의 감소 → ROE의 감소

2. Quick assets = 10,000 + 18,000 + 120,000 = 148,000
   Current liabilities = 75,000 + 20,000 = 95,000
   Quick ratio = 148,000 ÷ 95,000 = 1.56

3. 채권자가 관심을 가지는 재무비율은 레버리지 (장기 안정성) 비율이다.

4. ROE = ROA × equity multipliers
   D/A = 0.4 → equity multipliers = A ÷ E = 10 ÷ 6 = 1.67
   ROA = 12% ÷ 1.67 = 7.2%

5. 외상매출과 현금매출이 구분되는 경우 매출채권회전율은 외상매출 기준으로 측정한다.
   Average AR = (2,140 + 3,060) ÷ 2 = 2,600
   AR turnover = 62,400 ÷ 2,600 = 24

6. 재고자산 증가, 매입채무 증가
   Current ratio 〉 1 → Current ratio 감소

7. 대손충당금 증가, net A/R 감소
   → 순운전자본, Current ratio, Quick ratio 모두 감소
   → 부채 변동없음, 부채비율 증가

8. Current ratio 〉 1, Quick ratio 〈 1
   매입채무 감소, 현금 감소 → Current ratio 증가, Quick ratio 감소
   재고자산 증가, 현금 감소 → Current ratio 변동없음, Quick ratio 감소

9. Quick ratio 〈 1

    a : 당좌자산 변동없음, Quick ratio 변동없음

    b : 재고자산 감소, 매출채권 증가, 당좌자산 증가, Quick ratio 증가

    c : 당좌자산 감소, 유동부채 감소, Quick ratio 감소

    d : 당좌자산 변동없음, Quick ratio 변동없음

10. 재고자산 증가, 현금 감소

   → 유동자산 변동없음, 당좌자산 감소,

     Current ratio 변동없음. Quick ratio 감소

11. 유동비율과 당좌비율의 차이가 큰 원인은 재고자산의 많기 때문이다.

12. 물가상승시 : FIFO → LIFO

    재고자산 감소, 매출원가 증가, 매출총이익 감소 .

13. 장기 지급능력은 레버리지 비율로 측정한다.

14. TIE = EBIT ÷ Interest = 1

15. EPS = \$3,750,000 ÷ 3,000,000 shares = \$1.25

    Price = P/E × EPS = 12 × 1.25 = \$15

16. BPS = (3,000,000 + 24,000,000 + 6,000,000) ÷ 3,000,000 = \$11

    Price = P/B × BPS = 1.5 × \$11 = \$16.5

04 ▶ Task-Based Simulation

Problem-1

Financial data (Calculation is based on a 365-day year) :

Debt ratio : 50%

Current ratio : 1.8

Total assets turnover : 1.5

Days sales outstanding : 36.5 days

Gross profit margin on sales : 25%

Inventory turnover ratio : 5

Balance Sheet

Accounts	Amount	Accounts	Amount
Cash		Accounts payable	
Accounts receivable		Long-term debt	60,000
Inventories		Common stock	
Fixed assets		Retained earnings	97,500
Total assets	$300,000	Total liabilities and equity	

Income statement

Accounts	Amount
Sales	
Cost of goods sold	

Required

Complete the balance sheet and sales information using the above financial data.

Problem-2

Data for KIM Co. follow.

Balance Sheet as of December 31, 20X1 (In Thousands)

Accounts	Amount	Accounts	Amount
Cash	$ 77,500	Accounts payable	$129,000
Accounts receivable	336,000	Notes payable	84,000
Inventories	241,500	Other current liabilities	117,000
Total current assets	$655,000	Total current liabilities	$330,000
Net fixed assets	292,500	Long-term debt	256,500
		Common equity	361,000
Total assets	$947,500	Total liabilities and equity	$947,500

Income Statement for Year Ended December 31, 20X1 (In Thousands)

Accounts	Amount
Sales	$1,607,500
Cost of goods sold	1,392,500
Gross profit	$ 215,000
Selling expenses	115,000
General and administrative expenses	30,000
Earnings before interest and taxes (EBIT)	$ 70,000
Interest expense	24,500
Earnings before taxes (EBT)	$ 45,500
Federal and state income taxes (40%)	18,200
Net income	$ 27,300

1. Calculate the indicated ratios for KIM. Calculation is based on a 365−day year.

   (1) Current

   (2) Quick

   (3) Days sales outstanding

   (4) Inventory turnover

   (5) Total assets turnover

   (6) Net profit margin

   (7) ROA

   (8) ROE

   (9) Total debt/total assets

2. Construct the Du Pont equation for Barry.

Problem-3

At the end of last year, KIM reported the following income statement
(in millions of dollars):

Accounts	Amount
Sales	$3,000
Operating costs excluding depreciation	2,450
EBITDA	$ 550
Depreciation	250
Earnings before interest and taxes (EBIT)	$ 300
Interest expense	125
Earnings before taxes (EBT)	$ 175
Income taxes (40%)	70
Net income	$ 105

Looking ahead to the following year, the company's CFO has assembled the following
information:

- Year-end sales are expected to be 10 percent higher than the $3 billion in sales generated last year.
- Year-end operating costs, excluding depreciation, are expected to equal 80 percent of year-end sales.
- Depreciation is expected to increase at the same rate as sales.
- Interest costs are expected to remain unchanged.
- The tax rate is expected to remain at 40 percent.

Required

On the basis of this information, what will be the forecast for KIM's year-end net income?

Government & Not-For-Profit Accounting For the **US CPA** Exam

부록

STATE OF CALIFORNIA

ANNUAL COMPREHENSIVE FINANCIAL REPORT

For the Fiscal Year Ended
June 30, 2021

Prepared by the office of

MALIA M. COHEN
California State Controller

Contents

UNITED STATES
SECURITIES AND EXCHANGE COMMISSION
Washington, DC 20549

FORM 10-K

☑ Annual report pursuant to Section 13 or 15(d) of the Securities Exchange Act of 1934
For the fiscal year ended December 31, 2022

or

☐ Transition report pursuant to Section 13 or 15(d) of the Securities Exchange Act of 1934
For the transition period from _____ to _____
Commission file number 1-3950

Ford Motor Company

(Exact name of Registrant as specified in its charter)

Delaware	**38-0549190**
(State of incorporation)	*(I.R.S. Employer Identification No.)*

One American Road	
Dearborn, Michigan	**48126**
(Address of principal executive offices)	*(Zip Code)*

313-322-3000
(Registrant's telephone number, including area code)

Securities registered pursuant to Section 12(b) of the Act:

Title of each class	Trading symbols	Name of each exchange on which registered
Common Stock, par value $.01 per share	F	New York Stock Exchange
6.200% Notes due June 1, 2059	FPRB	New York Stock Exchange
6.000% Notes due December 1, 2059	FPRC	New York Stock Exchange
6.500% Notes due August 15, 2062	FPRD	New York Stock Exchange

Securities registered pursuant to Section 12(g) of the Act: None.

Indicate by check mark if the registrant is a well-known seasoned issuer, as defined in Rule 405 of the Securities Act. Yes ☑ No ☐

Indicate by check mark if the registrant is not required to file reports pursuant to Section 13 or Section 15(d) of the Act. Yes ☐ No ☑

Indicate by check mark whether the registrant (1) has filed all reports required to be filed by Section 13 or 15(d) of the Securities Exchange Act of 1934 during the preceding 12 months (or for such shorter period that the registrant was required to file such reports), and (2) has been subject to such filing requirements for the past 90 days. Yes ☑ No ☐

Indicate by check mark whether the registrant has submitted electronically every Interactive Data File required to be submitted pursuant to Rule 405 of Regulation S-T (§ 232.405 of this chapter) during the preceding 12 months (or for such shorter period that the registrant was required to submit such files). Yes ☑ No ☐

FORD MOTOR COMPANY AND SUBSIDIARIES
CONSOLIDATED BALANCE SHEETS
(in millions)

	December 31, 2021	December 31, 2022
ASSETS		
Cash and cash equivalents (Note 9)	$ 20,540	$ 25,134
Marketable securities (Note 9)	29,053	18,936
Ford Credit finance receivables, net of allowance for credit losses of $282 and $255 (Note 10)	32,543	38,720
Trade and other receivables, less allowances of $48 and $105	11,370	15,729
Inventories (Note 11)	12,065	14,080
Assets held for sale (Note 22)	9	97
Other assets	3,416	3,780
Total current assets	108,996	116,476
Ford Credit finance receivables, net of allowance for credit losses of $643 and $590 (Note 10)	51,256	49,903
Net investment in operating leases (Note 12)	26,361	22,772
Net property (Note 13)	37,139	37,265
Equity in net assets of affiliated companies (Note 14)	4,545	2,798
Deferred income taxes (Note 7)	13,796	15,552
Other assets	14,942	11,118
Total assets	$ 257,035	$ 255,884
LIABILITIES		
Payables	$ 22,349	$ 25,605
Other liabilities and deferred revenue (Note 16 and Note 25)	18,686	21,097
Debt payable within one year (Note 19)		
Company excluding Ford Credit	3,175	730
Ford Credit	46,517	49,434
Total current liabilities	90,727	96,866
Other liabilities and deferred revenue (Note 16 and Note 25)	27,705	25,497
Long-term debt (Note 19)		
Company excluding Ford Credit	17,200	19,200
Ford Credit	71,200	69,605
Deferred income taxes (Note 7)	1,581	1,549
Total liabilities	208,413	212,717
EQUITY		
Common Stock, par value $0.01 per share (4,068 million shares issued of 6 billion authorized)	40	41
Class B Stock, par value $0.01 per share (71 million shares issued of 530 million authorized)	1	1
Capital in excess of par value of stock	22,611	22,832
Retained earnings	35,769	31,754
Accumulated other comprehensive income/(loss) (Note 23)	(8,339)	(9,339)
Treasury stock	(1,563)	(2,047)
Total equity attributable to Ford Motor Company	48,519	43,242
Equity attributable to noncontrolling interests	103	(75)
Total equity	48,622	43,167
Total liabilities and equity	$ 257,035	$ 255,884

The following table includes assets to be used to settle liabilities of the consolidated variable interest entities ("VIEs"). These assets and liabilities are included in the consolidated balance sheets above. See Note 24 for additional information on our VIEs.

	December 31, 2021	December 31, 2022
ASSETS		
Cash and cash equivalents	$ 3,407	$ 2,274
Ford Credit finance receivables, net	43,001	49,142
Net investment in operating leases	7,540	12,545
Other assets	39	264
LIABILITIES		
Other liabilities and deferred revenue	$ 6	$ 2
Debt	38,274	45,451

FORD MOTOR COMPANY AND SUBSIDIARIES
CONSOLIDATED INCOME STATEMENTS
(in millions, except per share amounts)

	For the years ended December 31,		
	2020	2021	2022
Revenues			
Automotive	$ 115,894	$ 126,150	$ 148,980
Ford Credit	11,203	10,073	8,978
Mobility	47	118	99
Total revenues (Note 4)	127,144	136,341	158,057
Costs and expenses			
Cost of sales	112,752	114,651	134,397
Selling, administrative, and other expenses	10,193	11,915	10,888
Ford Credit interest, operating, and other expenses	8,607	5,252	6,496
Total costs and expenses	131,552	131,818	151,781
Operating income/(loss)	(4,408)	4,523	6,276
Interest expense on Company debt excluding Ford Credit	1,649	1,803	1,259
Other income/(loss), net (Note 5)	4,899	14,733	(5,150)
Equity in net income/(loss) of affiliated companies (Note 14)	42	327	(2,883)
Income/(Loss) before income taxes	(1,116)	17,780	(3,016)
Provision for/(Benefit from) income taxes (Note 7)	160	(130)	(864)
Net income/(loss)	(1,276)	17,910	(2,152)
Less: Income/(Loss) attributable to noncontrolling interests	3	(27)	(171)
Net income/(loss) attributable to Ford Motor Company	$ (1,279)	$ 17,937	$ (1,981)
EARNINGS/(LOSS) PER SHARE ATTRIBUTABLE TO FORD MOTOR COMPANY COMMON AND CLASS B STOCK (Note 8)			
Basic income/(loss)	$ (0.32)	$ 4.49	$ (0.49)
Diluted income/(loss)	(0.32)	4.45	(0.49)
Weighted-average shares used in computation of earnings/(loss) per share			
Basic shares	3,973	3,991	4,014
Diluted shares	3,973	4,034	4,014

CONSOLIDATED STATEMENTS OF COMPREHENSIVE INCOME
(in millions)

	For the years ended December 31,		
	2020	2021	2022
Net income/(loss)	$ (1,276)	$ 17,910	$ (2,152)
Other comprehensive income/(loss), net of tax (Note 23)			
Foreign currency translation	(901)	43	(933)
Marketable securities	85	(175)	(423)
Derivative instruments	222	73	322
Pension and other postretirement benefits	27	18	30
Total other comprehensive income/(loss), net of tax	(567)	(41)	(1,004)
Comprehensive income/(loss)	(1,843)	17,869	(3,156)
Less: Comprehensive income/(loss) attributable to noncontrolling interests	2	(23)	(175)
Comprehensive income/(loss) attributable to Ford Motor Company	$ (1,845)	$ 17,892	$ (2,981)

FORD MOTOR COMPANY AND SUBSIDIARIES
CONSOLIDATED STATEMENTS OF EQUITY
(in millions)

	Capital Stock	Cap. in Excess of Par Value of Stock	Retained Earnings/ (Accumulated Deficit)	Accumulated Other Comprehensive Income/(Loss) (Note 23)	Treasury Stock	Total	Equity Attributable to Non-controlling Interests	Total Equity
			Equity Attributable to Ford Motor Company					
Balance at December 31, 2019	$ 41	$ 22,165	$ 20,320	$ (7,728)	$ (1,613)	$ 33,185	$ 45	$ 33,230
Adoption of accounting standards	—	—	(202)	—	—	(202)	—	(202)
Net income/(loss)	—	—	(1,279)	—	—	(1,279)	3	(1,276)
Other comprehensive income/(loss), net of tax	—	—	—	(566)	—	(566)	(1)	(567)
Common stock issued (a)	—	125	—	—	—	125	—	125
Treasury stock/other	—	—	—	—	23	23	86	109
Dividend and dividend equivalents declared (b)	—	—	(596)	—	—	(596)	(12)	(608)
Balance at December 31, 2020	$ 41	$ 22,290	$ 18,243	$ (8,294)	$ (1,590)	$ 30,690	$ 121	$ 30,811
Balance at December 31, 2020	$ 41	$ 22,290	$ 18,243	$ (8,294)	$ (1,590)	$ 30,690	$ 121	$ 30,811
Net income/(loss)	—	—	17,937	—	—	17,937	(27)	17,910
Other comprehensive income/(loss), net of tax	—	—	—	(45)	—	(45)	4	(41)
Common stock issued (a)	—	321	—	—	—	321	—	321
Treasury stock/other	—	—	—	—	27	27	5	32
Dividend and dividend equivalents declared (b)	—	—	(411)	—	—	(411)	—	(411)
Balance at December 31, 2021	$ 41	$ 22,611	$ 35,769	$ (8,339)	$ (1,563)	$ 48,519	$ 103	$ 48,622
Balance at December 31, 2021	$ 41	$ 22,611	$ 35,769	$ (8,339)	$ (1,563)	$ 48,519	$ 103	$ 48,622
Net income/(loss)	—	—	(1,981)	—	—	(1,981)	(171)	(2,152)
Other comprehensive income/(loss), net of tax	—	—	—	(1,000)	—	(1,000)	(4)	(1,004)
Common stock issued (a)	1	221	—	—	—	222	—	222
Treasury stock/other	—	—	—	—	(484)	(484)	7	(477)
Dividend and dividend equivalents declared (b)	—	—	(2,034)	—	—	(2,034)	(10)	(2,044)
Balance at December 31, 2022	$ 42	$ 22,832	$ 31,754	$ (9,339)	$ (2,047)	$ 43,242	$ (75)	$ 43,167

(a) Includes impacts of share-based compensation.
(b) We declared dividends per share of Common and Class B Stock of $0.15 and $0.10 in 2020 and 2021, respectively, and in 2022, $0.10 per share in the first and second quarter and $0.15 per share in the third and fourth quarter. On February 2, 2023, we declared a regular dividend of $0.15 per share and a supplemental dividend of $0.65 per share.

FORD MOTOR COMPANY AND SUBSIDIARIES
CONSOLIDATED STATEMENTS OF CASH FLOWS
(in millions)

	For the years ended December 31,		
	2020	2021	2022
Cash flows from operating activities			
Net income/(loss)	$ (1,276)	$ 17,910	$ (2,152)
Depreciation and tooling amortization (Note 12 and Note 13)	8,751	7,318	7,642
Other amortization	(1,294)	(1,358)	(1,149)
Held-for-sale impairment charges (Note 22)	23	—	32
Brazil manufacturing exit non-cash charges (excluding accelerated depreciation of $145, $322, and $17) (Note 21)	1,159	48	(82)
(Gains)/Losses on extinguishment of debt (Note 5 and Note 19)	1	1,702	121
Provision for/(Benefit from) credit and insurance losses	929	(298)	46
Pension and other postretirement employee benefits ("OPEB") expense/(income) (Note 17)	1,027	(4,865)	(378)
Equity method investment dividends received in excess of (earnings)/losses and impairments	130	116	3,324
Foreign currency adjustments	(420)	532	(27)
Net realized and unrealized (gains)/losses on cash equivalents, marketable securities, and other investments (Note 5)	(315)	(9,159)	7,518
Net (gain)/loss on changes in investments in affiliates (Note 5)	(3,446)	(368)	147
Stock compensation (Note 6)	199	305	336
Provision for deferred income taxes	(269)	(563)	(1,910)
Decrease/(Increase) in finance receivables (wholesale and other)	12,104	7,656	(10,560)
Decrease/(Increase) in accounts receivable and other assets	(63)	(1,141)	(1,183)
Decrease/(Increase) in inventory	148	(1,778)	(2,576)
Increase/(Decrease) in accounts payable and accrued and other liabilities	6,809	(36)	7,268
Other	72	(234)	436
Net cash provided by/(used in) operating activities	24,269	15,787	6,853
Cash flows from investing activities			
Capital spending	(5,742)	(6,227)	(6,866)
Acquisitions of finance receivables and operating leases	(55,901)	(48,379)	(45,533)
Collections of finance receivables and operating leases	48,746	52,094	46,276
Proceeds from sale of business (Note 22)	1,340	145	449
Purchases of marketable securities and other investments	(39,624)	(27,491)	(17,458)
Sales and maturities of marketable securities and other investments	32,395	33,229	19,117
Settlements of derivatives	(323)	(272)	94
Capital contributions to equity method investments (Note 24)	(4)	(57)	(738)
Other	498	(297)	312
Net cash provided by/(used in) investing activities	(18,615)	2,745	(4,347)
Cash flows from financing activities			
Cash payments for dividends and dividend equivalents	(596)	(403)	(2,009)
Purchases of common stock	—	—	(484)
Net changes in short-term debt	(2,291)	3,273	5,460
Proceeds from issuance of long-term debt	65,900	27,901	45,470
Payments of long-term debt	(60,514)	(54,164)	(45,655)
Other	(184)	(105)	(271)
Net cash provided by/(used in) financing activities	2,315	(23,498)	2,511
Effect of exchange rate changes on cash, cash equivalents, and restricted cash	225	(232)	(414)
Net increase/(decrease) in cash, cash equivalents, and restricted cash	$ 8,194	$ (5,198)	$ 4,603
Cash, cash equivalents, and restricted cash at beginning of period (Note 9)	$ 17,741	$ 25,935	$ 20,737
Net increase/(decrease) in cash, cash equivalents, and restricted cash	8,194	(5,198)	4,603
Cash, cash equivalents, and restricted cash at end of period (Note 9)	$ 25,935	$ 20,737	$ 25,340

Not-for-Profit Entity A
Statements of Financial Position
June 30. 20X1 and 20X0(in thousands)

	20X1	20X0
Assets		
Current assets		
Cash and cash equivalents	$ 4,575	$ 4,960
Accounts and interest receivable	2,130	1,670
Inventories and prepaid expenses	610	1,000
Contributions receivable	1,825	1,200
Short-term investments	1,400	1,000
Long-term investments appropriated for current use	10,804	10,075
Total current assets	21,344	19,905
Noncurrent assets		
Contributions receivable	1,200	1,500
Assets restricted to investment in land, buildings, and equipment	5,210	4,560
Land, buildings, and equipment	61,700	63,590
Long-term investments, net of amounts appropriated	207,266	193,425
Total noncurrent assets	275,376	263,075
Total assets	$ 296,720	$ 282,980
Liabilities and net assets:		
Current liabilities		
Accounts payable	$ 2,570	$ 1,050
Refundable advance		550
Grants payable	550	600
Notes payable		140
Annuity trust obligations	985	1,050
Total current liabilities	4,105	3,390
Noncurrent liabilities		
Refundable advance		100
Grants payable	325	700
Notes payable		1,000
Annuity obligations	700	650
Long-term debt	5,500	6,500
Total noncurrent liabilities	6,525	8,950
Total liabilities	10,630	12,340
Net assets:		
Without donor restrictions	92,677	73,619
With donor restrictions	193,413	197,021
Total net assets	286,090	270,640
Total liabilities and net assets	$ 296,720	$ 282,980

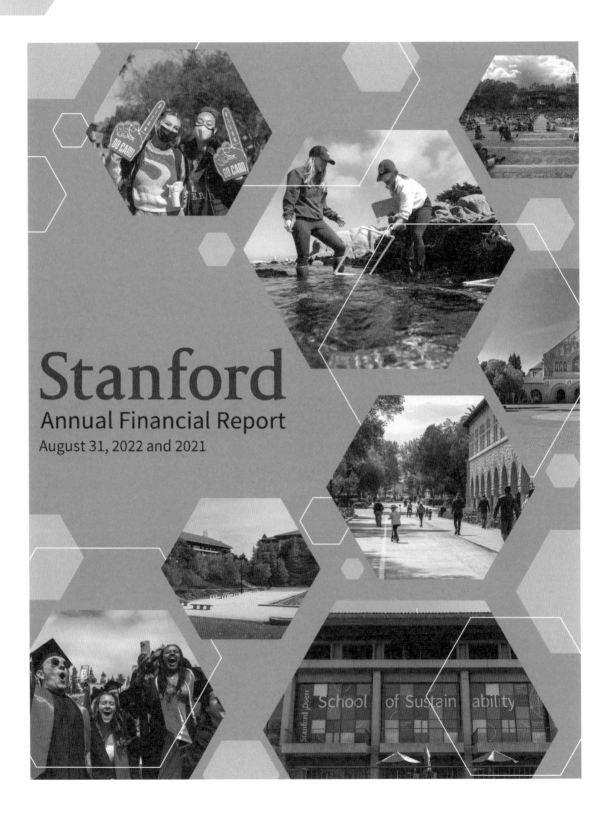

Stanford
Annual Financial Report
August 31, 2022 and 2021

Table of Contents

CONSOLIDATED STATEMENTS OF FINANCIAL POSITION

At August 31, 2022 and 2021 (in thousands of dollars)

	2022	2021
ASSETS		
Cash and cash equivalents	$ 2,346,372	$ 1,672,789
Accounts receivable, net	2,007,638	1,754,010
Prepaid expenses and other assets	512,188	510,490
Pledges receivable, net	2,201,736	1,700,525
Student loans receivable, net	37,524	42,699
Faculty and staff mortgages and other loans receivable, net	984,106	892,098
Assets limited as to use	397,926	453,452
Investments at fair value	52,180,412	54,039,545
Right-of-use assets	1,038,384	999,513
Plant facilities, net of accumulated depreciation	13,377,434	13,078,630
Works of art and special collections	—	—
TOTAL ASSETS	**$ 75,083,720**	**$ 75,143,751**
LIABILITIES AND NET ASSETS		
LIABILITIES:		
Accounts payable and accrued expenses	$ 2,805,757	$ 2,806,361
Liabilities associated with investments	863,746	974,756
Lease liabilities	1,093,986	1,047,618
Deferred income and other obligations	1,991,260	1,988,117
Accrued pension and postretirement benefit obligations	562,496	629,851
Notes and bonds payable	8,271,006	8,302,590
TOTAL LIABILITIES	**15,588,251**	**15,749,293**
NET ASSETS:		
Without donor restrictions	35,519,294	35,452,324
With donor restrictions	23,976,175	23,942,134
TOTAL NET ASSETS	**59,495,469**	**59,394,458**
TOTAL LIABILITIES AND NET ASSETS	**$ 75,083,720**	**$ 75,143,751**

The accompanying notes are an integral part of these consolidated financial statements.

CONSOLIDATED STATEMENTS OF ACTIVITIES

For the years ended August 31, 2022 and 2021 (in thousands of dollars)

	2022	2021
NET ASSETS WITHOUT DONOR RESTRICTIONS		
OPERATING REVENUES:		
TOTAL STUDENT INCOME, NET	$ 715,465	$ 507,923
Sponsored support:		
Direct costs - University	971,253	900,635
Direct costs - SLAC National Accelerator Laboratory	524,943	489,872
Indirect costs	315,562	297,514
TOTAL SPONSORED SUPPORT	**1,811,758**	**1,688,021**
TOTAL HEALTH CARE SERVICES, primarily net patient service revenue	**9,232,029**	**8,301,556**
TOTAL CURRENT YEAR GIFTS IN SUPPORT OF OPERATIONS	**278,501**	**293,715**
Net assets released from restrictions:		
Payments received on pledges	224,177	245,873
Prior year gifts released from donor restrictions	81,402	99,352
TOTAL NET ASSETS RELEASED FROM RESTRICTIONS	**305,579**	**345,225**
Investment income distributed for operations:		
Endowment	1,475,411	1,349,444
Expendable funds pools and other investment income	276,740	401,838
TOTAL INVESTMENT INCOME DISTRIBUTED FOR OPERATIONS	**1,752,151**	**1,751,282**
TOTAL SPECIAL PROGRAM FEES AND OTHER INCOME	**1,036,678**	**1,051,292**
TOTAL OPERATING REVENUES	**15,132,161**	**13,939,014**
OPERATING EXPENSES:		
Salaries and benefits	8,881,869	7,877,461
Depreciation	851,818	866,675
Other operating expenses	4,863,755	4,349,432
TOTAL OPERATING EXPENSES	**14,597,442**	**13,093,568**
CHANGE IN NET ASSETS FROM OPERATING ACTIVITIES	$ 534,719	$ 845,446

CONSOLIDATED STATEMENTS OF ACTIVITIES, Continued

For the years ended August 31, 2022 and 2021 (in thousands of dollars)

	2022	2021
NET ASSETS WITHOUT DONOR RESTRICTIONS (continued)		
CHANGE IN NET ASSETS FROM OPERATING ACTIVITIES	$ 534,719	$ 845,446
NON-OPERATING ACTIVITIES:		
Increase (decrease) in reinvested gains	(743,938)	5,548,668
Donor advised funds, net	34,611	3,395
Current year gifts not included in operations	5,053	408
Capital and other gifts released from restrictions	71,100	71,698
Pension and other postemployment benefit related changes other than service cost	89,504	107,179
Transfer to net assets with donor restrictions, net	(70,233)	(75,080)
Swap interest and change in value of swap agreements	138,866	53,351
Gain (loss) on extinguishment of debt	6,947	(2,558)
Non-controlling interest	2,207	—
Other	(1,866)	(6,958)
NET CHANGE IN NET ASSETS WITHOUT DONOR RESTRICTIONS	**66,970**	**6,545,549**
NET ASSETS WITH DONOR RESTRICTIONS		
Gifts and pledges, net	1,679,138	1,104,077
Increase (decrease) in reinvested gains	(1,255,771)	4,817,896
Change in value of split-interest agreements, net	(63,311)	122,553
Net assets released to operations	(321,244)	(370,724)
Capital and other gifts released to net assets without donor restrictions	(71,100)	(71,698)
Transfer from net assets without donor restrictions, net	70,233	75,080
Other	(3,904)	(1,134)
NET CHANGE IN NET ASSETS WITH DONOR RESTRICTIONS	**34,041**	**5,676,050**
NET CHANGE IN TOTAL NET ASSETS	**101,011**	**12,221,599**
Total net assets, beginning of year	59,394,458	47,172,859
TOTAL NET ASSETS, END OF YEAR	**$59,495,469**	**$59,394,458**

CONSOLIDATED STATEMENTS OF CASH FLOWS

For the years ended August 31, 2022 and 2021 (in thousands of dollars)

	2022	2021
CASH FLOW FROM OPERATING ACTIVITIES		
Change in net assets	$ 101,011	$ 12,221,599
Adjustments to reconcile change in net assets to net cash provided by operating activities:		
Depreciation	852,123	866,675
Amortization of bond premiums, discounts and other	28,637	19,569
Net losses (gains) on investments	884,229	(12,230,714)
Change in fair value of interest rate swaps	(161,455)	(78,195)
Change in split-interest agreements	(28,173)	158,814
Change in deferred tax asset and liability	(23,182)	129,127
Investment income (expense) for restricted purposes	(48,573)	99,098
Gifts restricted for long-term investments	(756,085)	(863,431)
Gifts of securities and properties	(22,698)	(30,509)
Gain on extinguishment of debt	(6,947)	—
Other	31,040	33,740
Premiums received from bond issuance	—	96,831
Changes in operating assets and liabilities:		
Accounts receivable	(242,890)	(245,004)
Pledges receivable, net	(345,886)	(15,298)
Prepaid expenses and other assets	(88,117)	(63,056)
Accounts payable and accrued expenses	213,018	(98,896)
Accrued pension and postretirement benefit obligations	(67,355)	(90,028)
Lease liabilities	(43,160)	(38,247)
Deferred income and other obligations	(33,402)	259,373
NET CASH PROVIDED BY OPERATING ACTIVITIES	**242,135**	**131,448**
CASH FLOW FROM INVESTING ACTIVITIES		
Additions to plant facilities, net	(925,020)	(790,859)
Student, faculty and other loans:		
New loans made	(179,632)	(178,342)
Principal collected	77,393	105,835
Purchases of investments	(17,466,423)	(20,316,653)
Sales and maturities of investments	18,336,816	18,387,854
Change associated with short term investments	111,202	437,983
Swap settlement payments, net	(19,811)	(21,420)
NET CASH USED FOR INVESTING ACTIVITIES	**(65,475)**	**(2,375,602)**
CASH FLOW FROM FINANCING ACTIVITIES		
Gifts and reinvested income for restricted purposes	627,369	548,843
Proceeds from borrowing	268,547	1,027,471
Repayment of notes and bonds payable	(263,377)	(1,012,887)
Bond issuance costs and interest rate swaps	(2,225)	(5,412)
Contributions received for split-interest agreements	17,676	19,709
Payments made under split-interest agreements	(57,515)	(51,186)
Securities lending collateral sold, net	(7,696)	9,393
Other	(5,269)	(4,907)
NET CASH PROVIDED BY FINANCING ACTIVITIES	**577,510**	**531,024**
INCREASE (DECREASE) IN CASH AND CASH EQUIVALENTS	**754,170**	**(1,713,130)**
Cash and cash equivalents, beginning of year	1,865,725	3,578,855
CASH AND CASH EQUIVALENTS, END OF YEAR	$ **2,619,895**	$ **1,865,725**
SUPPLEMENTAL DATA:		
Cash and cash equivalents as shown in the *Statements of Financial Position*	$ 2,346,372	$ 1,672,789
Restricted cash and cash equivalents included in assets limited as to use	81,946	117,179
Restricted cash included in other assets	12,382	28,432
Cash and restricted cash included in investments	179,195	47,325
TOTAL CASH AND CASH EQUIVALENTS AS SHOWN ON THE CONSOLIDATED STATEMENTS OF CASH FLOWS	$ **2,619,895**	$ **1,865,725**
Interest paid, net of capitalized interest	$ 286,217	$ 294,161
Change in payables for plant facilities	$ 25,300	$ (27,908)
Right-of-use assets obtained in exchange for lease liabilities	$ 172,836	$ 66,534

NOTES TO THE CONSOLIDATED FINANCIAL STATEMENTS

1. Basis of Presentation and Significant Accounting Policies

BASIS OF PRESENTATION

The *Consolidated Financial Statements* include the accounts of The Leland Stanford Junior University ("Stanford University" or the "University"), Stanford Health Care (SHC), Lucile Salter Packard Children's Hospital at Stanford (LPCH) and other majority-owned or controlled entities of the University, SHC and LPCH. Collectively, all of these entities are referred to as "Stanford". All significant inter-entity transactions and balances have been eliminated in consolidation. Certain prior year amounts have been reclassified to conform to the current year's presentation. These reclassifications had no impact on total net assets or the change in total net assets.

University

The University is a private, not-for-profit educational institution, founded in 1885 by Senator Leland and Mrs. Jane Stanford in memory of their son, Leland Stanford Jr. A Board of Trustees (the "Board") governs the University. The University information presented in the *Consolidated Financial Statements* comprises all of the accounts of the University, including its institutes and research centers, and the Stanford Management Company.

SLAC National Accelerator Laboratory (SLAC) is a federally funded research and development center owned by the U.S. Department of Energy (DOE). The University manages and operates SLAC for the DOE under a management and operating contract; accordingly, the revenues and expenditures of SLAC are included in the *Consolidated Statements of Activities*, but SLAC's DOE funded assets and liabilities are not included in the *Consolidated Statements of Financial Position*. SLAC employees are University employees and participate in the University's employee benefit programs. The University holds some receivables from the DOE substantially related to reimbursement for employee compensation and benefits.

Hospitals

SHC and LPCH (the "Hospitals") are California not-for-profit public benefit corporations, each governed by a separate Board of Directors. The University is the sole member of each of these entities. SHC and LPCH support the mission of medical education and clinical research of the University's School of Medicine (SOM). Collectively, the SOM and Hospitals comprise Stanford Medicine. SHC and LPCH operate two licensed acute care and specialty hospitals on the Stanford campus, a leading community acute care hospital, and numerous physician clinics on the campus, in community settings and in association with regional hospitals in the San Francisco Bay Area and elsewhere in California. The University has partnered with SHC and LPCH, respectively, to establish physician medical foundations to support Stanford Medicine's mission of delivering quality care to the community and conducting research and education.

TAX STATUS

The University, SHC and LPCH are exempt from federal and state income taxes to the extent provided by Section 501(c)(3) of the Internal Revenue Code and equivalent state provisions, except with regard to unrelated business income which is taxable at corporate income tax rates.

In accordance with the guidance on accounting for uncertainty in income taxes, management regularly evaluates its tax positions and does not believe the University, SHC or LPCH have any uncertain tax positions that require disclosure in or adjustment to the *Consolidated Financial Statements*. The University, SHC and LPCH are subject to routine audits by taxing jurisdictions. Management of each of the consolidated entities believes they are no longer subject to income tax examinations for fiscal years prior to August 31, 2018.

BASIS OF ACCOUNTING

The *Consolidated Financial Statements* are prepared in accordance with accounting principles generally accepted in the United States of America ("U.S. GAAP"). These principles require management to make estimates and assumptions that affect the reported amounts of assets and liabilities, the disclosure of contingent assets and liabilities at the date of the *Consolidated Financial Statements* and the reported amounts of revenues and expenses during the reporting period. Actual results could differ from those estimates.

For financial reporting purposes, net assets and revenues, expenses, gains and losses are classified into one of two categories - net assets without donor restrictions and net assets with donor restrictions based on the existence or absence of legal or donor-imposed restrictions (see *Note 10*).

Net assets without donor restrictions are expendable resources which are not subject to donor-imposed restrictions. These net assets may be designated by Stanford for specific purposes under internal operating and administrative arrangements or be subject to contractual agreements with external parties (see *Note 10*).

Net assets with donor restrictions include gifts, pledges and split-interest agreements (a) which by donor stipulation must be made available in perpetuity for investment or specific purposes, or (b) for which legal or donor-imposed restrictions have not yet been met. Such restrictions include purpose restrictions where donors have specified the purpose for which the net assets are to be spent, or time restrictions imposed by donors, or appreciation and income on certain donor-restricted endowment funds that have not yet been appropriated for spending (see Note 11).

Gifts and pledges subject to donor-imposed restrictions for specific purposes are recorded as net assets with donor restrictions and reclassified to net assets without donor restrictions upon expiration of time and purpose restrictions. Donor-restricted resources intended for capital projects are initially recorded as "Net assets with donor restrictions" and then released and reclassified as "Net assets without donor restrictions" when the asset is placed in service. Contributions with donor restrictions that are received and expended or deemed expended, based on the nature of donors' restrictions, in the same fiscal year are recorded as "Net assets without donor restrictions".

Transfers from net assets without donor restrictions to net assets with donor restrictions are primarily the result of donor redesignations or matching funds that are added to donor gift funds which then take on the same restrictions as the donor gift.

The operating activities of Stanford include the revenues earned and expenses incurred in the current year to support education, research, and health care. The non-operating activities of Stanford include increases in reinvested gains, current year gifts not included in operations, capital and other gifts released from restrictions, pension and other postemployment benefit related changes other than service cost, and certain other non-operating activities. All expenses are recorded as a reduction of net assets without donor restrictions with the exception of investment expenses that are required to be netted against investment returns.

CASH AND CASH EQUIVALENTS

"Cash and cash equivalents" included in the *Consolidated Statements of Financial Position* primarily consist of U.S. Treasury bills, certificates of deposit, repurchase agreements, money market funds and all other short-term investments available for current operations with original maturities of 90 days or less at the time of purchase. These amounts are carried at amortized cost, which approximates fair value. Cash and cash equivalents that are held for investment purposes are classified as investments (see *Note 6*). The University has elected the policy to treat cash equivalents held for investment as short-term investments, and are therefore excluded from "Cash and cash equivalents" on the *Consolidated Statements of Cash Flows.*

ASSETS LIMITED AS TO USE

Assets limited as to use consist of deferred compensation plan assets and tax-exempt bond proceeds as described below:

Deferred compensation plan assets

The University's custodians hold 457(b) non-qualified deferred compensation plan assets under a grantor trust which requires that they be used to satisfy plan obligations to participants and beneficiaries unless the University becomes insolvent. The funds are primarily invested in mutual funds, at the participants' discretion, which are valued based on quoted market prices (and exchange rates, if applicable) on the last trading date of the principal market on or before August 31.

4. Pledges Receivable

Pledges are recorded at discounted rates ranging from 0.6% to 5.7%. At August 31, 2022 and 2021, pledges receivable, net of discounts and allowances, in thousands of dollars, are as follows:

	UNIVERSITY	SHC	LPCH	ELIMINATIONS	CONSOLIDATED
2022					
One year or less	$ 652,373 $	29,346 $	138,364 $	(54,141) $	765,942
Between one year and five years	1,180,469	13,695	94,257	(18,653)	1,269,768
More than five years	325,449	2,250	25,020	(200)	352,519
	2,158,291	45,291	257,641	(72,994)	2,388,229
Less discounts and allowances	(171,411)	(3,414)	(11,668)	—	(186,493)
PLEDGES RECEIVABLE, NET	**$ 1,986,880 $**	**41,877 $**	**245,973 $**	**(72,994) $**	**2,201,736**
2021					
One year or less	$ 281,562 $	29,398 $	79,879 $	(19,030) $	371,809
Between one year and five years	1,121,211	19,755	58,269	(27,688)	1,171,547
More than five years	272,670	4,000	25,237	(5,027)	296,880
	1,675,443	53,153	163,385	(51,745)	1,840,236
Less discounts and allowances	(125,129)	(4,293)	(10,289)	—	(139,711)
PLEDGES RECEIVABLE, NET	**$ 1,550,314 $**	**48,860 $**	**153,096 $**	**(51,745) $**	**1,700,525**

During fiscal year 2022, John and Ann Doerr pledged $1.1 billion to support the new Stanford Doerr School of Sustainability. The gift will be recorded in the financial statements as milestones in establishing the school are completed. In fiscal year 2022, $99.6 million of the gift was recorded. The University had total conditional pledges of approximately $1.0 billion and $7.8 million at August 31, 2022 and 2021, respectively, which are subject to specified future events. SHC and LPCH had no conditional pledges at August 31, 2022 and 2021.

Lucile Packard Foundation for Children's Health (LPFCH) is the primary community fundraising agent for LPCH and the pediatric faculty and programs at the University's SOM. Pledges received by LPFCH on behalf of the University are recorded by the University as beneficial interest in LPFCH. At August 31, 2022 and 2021 the University held $73.0 million and $51.7 million, respectively, of beneficial interest in LPFCH, which is included in "Pledges receivable, net", and eliminated in consolidation.

10. Net Assets

Net assets without donor restrictions include Board-designated funds functioning as endowment (see Note 11), net investment in plant facilities and other operating funds.

Net assets with donor restrictions consist primarily of endowment gifts that are limited for long-term investment, and accumulated appreciation that may be appropriated for expenditure by the University (see Note 11). Net assets with donor restrictions also include gifts and pledges that are subject to donor-imposed restrictions that expire with the passage of time, payment of pledges, and/or actions of the University, and other funds including Stanford's net equity in split-interest agreements and student loans.

Net assets at August 31, 2022 and 2021, in thousands of dollars, are as follows:

	UNIVERSITY	SHC	LPCH	ELIMINATIONS	CONSOLIDATED
2022					
NET ASSETS WITHOUT DONOR RESTRICTIONS					
Board designated endowment - Funds functioning as endowment	$ 16,915,950	$ —	$ 144,650	$ —	$ 17,060,600
Net investment in plant facilities and other plant funds	4,742,628	2,216,499	926,193	—	7,885,320
Operating funds	5,719,867	3,756,261	1,268,887	(171,641)	10,573,374
Total net assets without donor restrictions	27,378,445	5,972,760	2,339,730	(171,641)	35,519,294
NET ASSETS WITH DONOR RESTRICTIONS					
Subject to expenditure for specified purpose:					
Unspent gifts and gifts with undecided purpose restrictions	864,997	—	—	—	864,997
Plant facilities	298,676	13,390	87,629	—	399,695
Total	1,163,673	13,390	87,629	—	1,264,692
Subject to passage of time:					
Pledges receivable	1,182,846	41,877	268,983	(46,254)	1,447,452
Other funds	329,483	48,550	30,276	—	408,309
Total	1,512,329	90,427	299,259	(46,254)	1,855,761
Subject to University's spending policy:					
Accumulated appreciation	10,808,455	25,737	198,821	—	11,033,013
Subject to restrictions in perpetuity:					
Endowment funds	8,454,185	15,544	260,854	—	8,730,583
Pledges receivable	804,034	—	2,376	—	806,410
Other funds	285,716	—	—	—	285,716
Total	9,543,935	15,544	263,230	—	9,822,709
Total net assets with donor restrictions	23,028,392	145,098	848,939	(46,254)	23,976,175
TOTAL NET ASSETS	**$50,406,837**	**$6,117,858**	**$3,188,669**	**$ (217,895)**	**$ 59,495,469**

11. Endowments

The University classifies a substantial portion of its financial resources as endowment, which is invested to generate income to support operating and strategic initiatives. The endowment, which includes endowed lands, is comprised of pure endowment funds, term endowment funds, and funds functioning as endowment (FFE). Depending on the nature of the donor's stipulation, these resources are recorded as net assets with donor restrictions or net assets without donor restrictions. Term endowments are similar to other endowment funds except that, upon the passage of a stated period of time or the occurrence of a particular event, all or part of the principal may be expended. Accordingly, term endowments are classified as net assets with donor restrictions until expiration of the term. FFE are University resources designated by the Board as endowment and are invested for long-term appreciation and current income. These assets, however, remain available and may be spent at the Board's discretion. Accordingly, FFE are recorded as net assets without donor restrictions.

Stanford classifies as net assets with donor restrictions (a) the original value of gifts donated to the endowment with donor restrictions and (b) accumulations to the endowment with donor restrictions made in accordance with the direction of the applicable donor gift instrument at the time the accumulation is added to the fund. The remaining accumulation to the endowment funds that are required to be maintained in perpetuity in accordance with the direction of the applicable donor gift instrument, is classified as net assets with donor restrictions until those amounts are authorized for expenditure. The aggregate amount by which fair value was below historic value was $15.5 million and $2.8 million at August 31, 2022 and 2021, respectively.

Endowment funds by net asset classification at August 31, 2022 and 2021, in thousands of dollars, are as follows:

	2022	2021
University endowment		
Endowment funds without donor restrictions:		
Funds functioning as endowment	$ 16,915,950	$ 17,556,924
Endowment funds with donor restrictions:		
Original donor-restricted gift amount and gains maintained in perpetuity	8,454,185	7,959,566
Term endowment and related gains	259,640	264,314
Additional accumulated gains available for expenditure, subject to spending policy	10,709,019	12,007,383
Total endowment funds with donor restrictions	19,422,844	20,231,263
University endowment	36,338,794	37,788,187
LPCH endowment		
Endowment funds without donor restrictions:		
Funds functioning as endowment	144,650	162,832
Endowment funds with donor restrictions	477,209	509,796
LPCH endowment	621,859	672,628
SHC endowment funds with donor restrictions	41,281	31,249
TOTAL ENDOWMENT FUNDS	**$ 37,001,934**	**$ 38,492,064**

Most of Stanford's endowment is invested in the MP. The return objective for the MP is to generate optimal long-term total return while maintaining an appropriate level of risk. Investment returns are achieved through both capital appreciation (realized and unrealized gains) and current yield (interest and dividends). Portfolio asset allocation targets as well as expected risk, return and correlation among the asset classes are reevaluated regularly by Stanford Management Company.

The Museum of Modern Art
Consolidated Statements of Financial Position
June 30, 2022 and 2021

(in thousands of dollars)		2022		2021
Assets				
Cash and cash equivalents	$	192,559	$	137,279
Receivables				
Accounts receivable and other		7,024		5,451
Contributions receivable, net		90,147		144,605
The Trust for Cultural Resources		28,342		29,542
Inventories		14,148		12,569
Prepaid expenses and other assets		11,069		12,811
Investments				
Accrued investment income and other receivables		677		688
Investments, at fair value		1,489,905		1,645,810
Interest in net assets of International Council		8,998		9,328
Right of use assets		23,863		23,071
Property, plant and equipment, net		671,532		710,435
Museum collections (Note 1)		-		-
Total assets	$	2,538,264	$	2,731,589
Liabilities and Net Assets				
Accounts payable, accrued expenses and other liabilities	$	44,621	$	38,297
Lease liability		24,961		23,772
Loans payable, bond premium and deferred financing costs, net of accumulated amortization		358,307		363,172
Pension and postretirement benefit obligations		46,575		74,339
Total liabilities		474,464		499,580
Net assets				
Without donor restrictions		1,199,098		1,308,974
With donor restrictions		864,702		923,035
Total net assets		2,063,800		2,232,009
Total liabilities and net assets	$	2,538,264	$	2,731,589

The Museum of Modern Art
Consolidated Statements of Activities
Years Ended June 30, 2022 and 2021

	2022					2021				
	Without Donor Restrictions					Without Donor Restrictions				
(in thousands of dollars)	Museum Operations	Plant and Equipment Funded by Designated Gifts	Total Without Donor Restrictions	With Donor Restrictions	Total	Museum Operations	Plant and Equipment Funded by Designated Gifts	Total Without Donor Restrictions	With Donor Restrictions	Total
Operating revenues and other support										
Admissions	$ 22,473	$ -	$ 22,473	$ -	$ 22,473	$ 6,654	$ -	$ 6,654	$ -	$ 6,654
Membership	13,164	-	13,164	-	13,164	12,218	-	12,218	-	12,218
Investment income-spending policy	58,581	-	58,581	-	58,581	51,827	-	51,827	-	51,827
Annual fund contributions	12,331	-	12,331	-	12,331	14,106	-	14,106	-	14,106
Other grants and contributions	19,573	-	19,573	26,752	46,325	14,924	-	14,924	13,321	28,245
Other	4,070	-	4,070	-	4,070	2,291	-	2,291	-	2,291
Revenue of auxiliary activities	71,192	-	71,192	-	71,192	51,887	-	51,887	-	51,887
Net assets released from restrictions	31,163	-	31,163	(31,163)	-	23,992	-	23,992	(23,992)	-
Total operating revenues and other support	232,547	-	232,547	(4,411)	228,136	177,899	-	177,899	(10,671)	167,228
Operating expenses										
Curatorial and related support services	43,509	-	43,509	-	43,509	38,867	-	38,867	-	38,867
Exhibitions	11,482	-	11,482	-	11,482	6,371	-	6,371	-	6,371
Other museum programs	4,616	-	4,616	-	4,616	3,925	-	3,925	-	3,925
Cost of sales/auxiliary activities	69,204	-	69,204	-	69,204	55,618	-	55,618	-	55,618
Depreciation (nonauxiliary)	5,315	38,115	43,430	-	43,430	5,551	37,805	43,356	-	43,356
Public services	4,287	-	4,287	-	4,287	3,773	-	3,773	-	3,773
Membership, development and cultivation	11,447	-	11,447	-	11,447	9,588	-	9,588	-	9,588
Facilities, security and other	36,418	-	36,418	-	36,418	32,029	-	32,029	-	32,029
Public information	7,099	-	7,099	-	7,099	5,970	-	5,970	-	5,970
Administration and other	28,147	-	28,147	-	28,147	23,806	-	23,806	-	23,806
Total operating expenses	221,524	38,115	259,639	-	259,639	185,498	37,805	223,303	-	223,303
Excess/(Deficit) of operating revenues and support over operating expenses	11,023	(38,115)	(27,092)	(4,411)	(31,503)	(7,599)	(37,805)	(45,404)	(10,671)	(56,075)
Nonoperating revenues, expenses and other support										
Sales of works of art	-	-	-	9,902	9,902	-	-	-	5,620	5,620
Acquisition of works of art	(16,694)	-	(16,694)	-	(16,694)	(8,568)	-	(8,568)	-	(8,568)
Net assets released from restrictions for art acquisitions	16,694	-	16,694	(16,694)	-	8,568	-	8,568	(8,568)	-
Net assets released from restrictions for renovation, expansion and specific purpose	2,877	-	2,877	(2,877)	-	19,198	11,724	30,922	(30,922)	-
Investment return in excess of (less than) amounts designated for operations and specific purposes	(103,985)	-	(103,985)	(74,499)	(178,484)	185,606	-	185,606	156,989	342,595
Contributions restricted for art acquisitions	-	-	-	12,086	12,086	-	-	-	10,220	10,220
Contributions restricted for capital acquisition and permanent endowment	-	-	-	18,160	18,160	-	-	-	42,843	42,843
Board-designated and other contributions	17	-	17	-	17	7	-	7	-	7
Defined benefit plan changes other than net periodic benefit cost	24,010	-	24,010	-	24,010	33,205	-	33,205	-	33,205
Other pension and voluntary transition plan costs	2,293	-	2,293	-	2,293	(8,559)	-	(8,559)	-	(8,559)
Interest expense, change in fair value of interest rate swap agreements and other financing costs	(7,996)	-	(7,996)	-	(7,996)	(6,925)	-	(6,925)	-	(6,925)
Total nonoperating revenues, expenses and other support	(82,784)	-	(82,784)	(53,922)	(136,706)	222,532	11,724	234,256	176,182	410,438
Change in net assets	(71,761)	(38,115)	(109,876)	(58,333)	(168,209)	214,933	(26,081)	188,852	165,511	354,363
Net Assets										
Beginning of year	832,920	476,054	1,308,974	923,035	2,232,009	617,987	502,135	1,120,122	757,524	1,877,646
End of year	$ 761,159	$ 437,939	$ 1,199,098	$ 864,702	$ 2,063,800	$ 832,920	$ 476,054	$ 1,308,974	$ 923,035	$ 2,232,009

The accompanying notes are an integral part of these consolidated financial statements.

4

The Museum of Modern Art
Consolidated Statements of Cash Flows
Years Ended June 30, 2022 and 2021

(in thousands of dollars)		2022		2021
Cash flows from operating activities				
Change in net assets	$	(168,209)	$	354,363
Adjustments to reconcile change in net assets to net cash				
used in operating activities				
Depreciation and amortization		41,534		37,968
Debt extinguishment costs		-		2,716
Defined benefit plan changes other than net periodic benefit cost		(24,010)		(33,205)
Change in interest in net assets of International Council		330		(2,382)
Net realized (gain) loss and unrealized appreciation on investments		121,963		(398,911)
Contributions restricted for capital acquisition and permanent endowment		(64,556)		(84,043)
Contributed securities		(4,223)		(14,691)
Proceeds from sales of contributed securities		4,123		3,331
Change in fair value of interest rate swap agreement		(807)		(672)
Sales of works of art		(9,902)		(5,620)
Acquisition of works of art		16,694		8,568
Change in right of use assets		333		-
Changes in assets and liabilities				
Accounts receivable and other		(1,573)		427
Contributions receivable		45,391		51,942
Accrued investment income and other investment receivables		11		571
Inventories		(1,579)		3,049
Prepaid expenses and other assets		1,742		(4,286)
Accounts payable, accrued expenses and other liabilities		7,130		3,216
Pension and postretirement benefit obligations		(3,754)		1,152
Lease liability		(2,353)		(1,770)
Net cash used in operating activities		(41,715)		(78,277)
Cash flows from investing activities				
Purchases of property, plant and equipment		(5,078)		(11,046)
Proceeds from disposition of investments		189,244		340,955
Purchase of investments		(155,488)		(337,493)
Distributions from Trust for Cultural Resources		1,200		640
Proceeds from sales of works of art		9,902		5,620
Acquisition of works of art		(16,694)		(8,568)
Net cash provided by (used in) investing activities		23,086		(9,892)
Cash flows from financing activities				
Contributions restricted for capital acquisition and permanent endowment		64,556		84,043
Proceeds from sales of contributed securities restricted for capital and permanent endowment		9,167		22,540
Proceeds from taxable bond Series 2021 issuance		-		100,000
Partial defeasance of Series 2016 One E Bonds		-		(35,000)
Payments for Series 2021 financing costs and Series 2016 One E debt defeasance		-		(3,440)
Repayment of line of credit and revolvers borrowing		-		(33,800)
Net cash provided by financing activities		73,723		134,343
Net increase in cash, cash equivalents, and restricted cash		55,094		46,174
Cash, cash equivalents, and restricted cash				
Beginning of year		146,192		100,018
End of year	$	201,286	$	146,192

The Museum of Modern Art
Notes to Consolidated Financial Statements
June 30, 2022 and 2021

(in thousands of dollars)

1.   Organization and Summary of Significant Accounting Policies

The accompanying consolidated financial statements have been prepared on the accrual basis of accounting in conformity with accounting principles generally accepted in the United States of America and reflect the consolidation of the following entities:

- The Museum of Modern Art (the "Museum");

- P.S. 1 Contemporary Art Center ("MoMA PS1");

- Modern and Contemporary Art Support Corp. (the "Support Corp"); and

- AFE, LLC.

Intercompany transactions have been eliminated in consolidation. The Museum is the sole member of MoMA PS1, the Support Corp, and AFE, LLC. In addition, the International Council of The Museum of Modern Art (the "Council") provides exhibition and programming support to the Museum. The Council exclusively supports the Museum in its international programs and activities. The Museum has recorded its interest in 100% of the Council's net assets of $8,998 and $9,328 in the consolidated statements of financial position as of June 30, 2022 and 2021, respectively. These net assets are classified as net assets with donor restrictions. The Council's net assets consist primarily of cash and cash equivalents and investments which were $1,429 and $7,570 respectively, at June 30, 2022 and $1,189 and $8,395, respectively, at June 30, 2021. All of the Council's investments (as of June 30, 2022 and 2021) are maintained within the Museum's investment portfolio (Notes 3 and 4).

The Museum, MoMA PS1, the Support Corp and the Council are not-for-profit organizations exempt from tax under Section 501(c)(3) of the Internal Revenue Code; AFE, LLC is a limited liability corporation.

The Museum's significant accounting policies are described below:

Collections
The Museum is chartered as an educational institution whose collection of modern and contemporary art is made available to its members and the public to encourage an ever-deeper understanding and enjoyment of such art by the diverse local, national, and international audiences that it serves. Through the leadership of its Board of Trustees (the "Board") and staff, the Museum strives to establish, preserve, and document a permanent collection of the highest order that reflects the vitality, complexity and unfolding patterns of modern and contemporary art; present exhibitions and educational programs of unparalleled significance; sustain a library, archives, and conservation laboratory that are recognized as international centers of research; and support scholarship and publications of preeminent intellectual merit. The Museum's mission is to connect people from around the world to the art of our time.

The Museum's collections, acquired through purchase and contributions, are not recognized as assets on the consolidated statements of financial position. Purchases of collection items are recorded in the year in which the items were acquired as decreases in net assets without donor restrictions. Contributed collection items are not reflected in the consolidated financial statements. Proceeds from sales of works of art, which are reflected as increases in net assets with donor restrictions, are used primarily to acquire other items for the collection.

The Museum of Modern Art
Notes to Consolidated Financial Statements
June 30, 2022 and 2021

(in thousands of dollars)

Endowment net asset composition by type of fund as of June 30, 2022 and 2021:

	With Restrictions	Without Restrictions	Total 2022
Donor-restricted endowment funds	$ 649,549	$ -	$ 649,549
Board-designated endowment funds	-	159,438	159,438
Total endowment funds	$ 649,549	$ 159,438	$ 808,987

	With Restrictions	Without Restrictions	Total 2021
Donor-restricted endowment funds	$ 717,494	$ -	$ 717,494
Board-designated endowment funds	-	177,765	177,765
Total endowment funds	$ 717,494	$ 177,765	$ 895,259

The composition of the Museum's endowment by net asset class and purpose at the end of the period is:

	2022	2021
Net assets with restrictions		
Museum programs	$ 211,676	$ 231,504
Acquisition of works of art	84,003	90,598
Museum operations and other activities	310,021	357,848
Support of exhibitions	43,849	37,544
Total endowment funds classified as net assets with restrictions	649,549	717,494
Net assets without restrictions		
Total endowment funds classified as net assets without restrictions	159,438	177,765
Total endowment funds	$ 808,987	$ 895,259

As a result of unfavorable market fluctuations, the fair market value of assets associated with some individual donor-restricted endowment funds are below historic dollar value. The aggregate amount by which fair value was below historic dollar value at June 30, 2022 was $554 and included 5 funds with original donor contributions totaling $5,692. As of June 30, 2021 there were no assets associated with individual donor-restricted endowment funds where fair market value was below historic dollar value. When donor-restricted endowment fund deficits exist, they are classified as a reduction of net assets with donor restrictions. The Museum has interpreted NYPMIFA to permit spending from endowments with a deficit in accordance with prudent measures required under law. Continued future appropriations from underwater endowment funds will be considered based on current facts and circumstances on the next appropriation decision date.

The Museum of Modern Art
Notes to Consolidated Financial Statements
June 30, 2022 and 2021

(in thousands of dollars)

In accordance with the New York State legislation pertaining to the Trust, the Museum Tower is exempt from real property taxation, but the Trust collects the equivalent of real property taxes from the owners of individual condominium units in the Museum Tower. These tax-equivalency payments ("TEPs") are based on the real property tax assessment of the Museum Tower.

In connection with the 1980 expansion, the Museum agreed to advance funds to the Trust to the extent that TEPs and the proceeds of the Serial Bonds are not sufficient to pay debt service due from time to time from the Trust to the holders of the Serial Bonds and to complete the 1980 expansion project. Such advances totaled $28,342 and $29,542, respectively, at June 30, 2022 and 2021.

The advances bore interest at a rate of 9% annually through June 30, 2004. Pursuant to an agreement in January 2006 between the Museum and the Trust, the interest rate on the outstanding advances from the Museum was converted to a market-based floating rate. The Museum also agreed that no additional interest would accrue on the advances for a five-year period beginning July 1, 2004 through June 30, 2009. Cumulative interest totaled $150,041 and $149,191 at June 30, 2022 and 2021, respectively.

Commencing on July 1, 2009 and thereafter, the unpaid balance of any outstanding advances will accrue interest at a floating rate equal to the 3-year Treasury rate in effect on July 1 of that year. The rate was 0.47% and 0.19% for fiscal years 2022 and 2021, respectively. This agreement provided for the issuance of new instruments to the Museum to evidence the obligations of the Trust, which required the authorization of the Comptroller of the State of New York and of the Comptroller of the City of New York. These authorizations were obtained in August 2006 and the new instruments evidencing the Trust's obligations have now been issued.

Pursuant to the New York Arts and Cultural Affairs Law, the Trust uses TEPs to pay administrative expenses, the portion of the TEPs due to the City of New York, and debt service on the Serial Bonds. Any TEPs that remain after such payments have been made are applied to repay the Museum advances made to the Trust described above and interest earned thereon.

In the event that the Museum is required to make further advances to cover debt service on the Serial Bonds described above, the Trust has agreed to issue to the Museum instruments for the amount of each such advance, which will be subject to the same terms and conditions as the instruments currently outstanding with respect to the previous advances from the Museum.

Statutory law limits the Museum's right to collect unpaid interest and principal with respect to any advance not paid within 57 years from the date of the original advance. Accordingly, to the extent that any advance and all accrued interest are not repaid in full within 57 years, the obligation of the Trust to the Museum will be extinguished and the Museum will thereafter have no right to collect from the Trust with respect to such obligations. The earliest expiration date for any advance will occur in 2039.

TEPs available in accordance with the Arts and Cultural Affairs Law described above to reimburse the Museum for its advances were $1,200 and $640 in 2022 and 2021, respectively. The amounts were paid to the Museum, decreasing the receivable from the Trust. The Museum receives annual audited financial statements of the Trust. In addition, the Museum reviews the tax equivalency billings, subsequent collection and allocation of proceeds.

THE AMERICAN NATIONAL RED CROSS

Consolidated Statement of Financial Position

June 30, 2022
(With comparative information as of June 30, 2021)

(In thousands)

Assets		2022	2021
Current assets:			
Cash and cash equivalents	$	292,369	205,148
Investments (note 4)		470,946	562,450
Trade receivables, including grants, net of allowance for doubtful accounts of $1,792 in 2022 and $2,155 in 2021 (note 11)		244,559	226,657
Contributions receivable (note 2)		30,724	26,089
Inventories, net of allowance for obsolescence of $250 in 2022 and $87 in 2021		59,996	47,394
Other current assets		48,518	50,231
Total current assets		1,147,112	1,117,969
Noncurrent assets:			
Investments (note 4)		1,515,968	1,329,448
Contributions receivable (note 2)		24,936	13,939
Right-of-use assets-operating leases (note 6)		123,213	121,765
Land, buildings, and other property, net (note 3)		700,114	728,858
Assets held for sale, net (note 3)		27,985	33,602
Prepaid pension assets (note 10)		66,975	—
Other assets (note 9)		265,879	322,919
Total noncurrent assets		2,725,070	2,550,531
Total assets	$	3,872,182	3,668,500
Liabilities and Net Assets			
Current liabilities:			
Accounts payable and accrued expenses	$	354,043	299,798
Current portion of debt (note 5)		8,331	19,169
Current portion of lease obligation-operating (note 6)		25,530	25,214
Postretirement benefits (note 10)		3,745	3,731
Other current liabilities (notes 9 and 11)		135,141	146,439
Total current liabilities		526,790	494,351
Noncurrent liabilities:			
Debt (note 5)		373,103	383,420
Long-term lease obligation-operating (note 6)		110,686	109,971
Pension and postretirement benefits (note 10)		39,047	167,317
Other liabilities (notes 5 and 9)		122,266	145,054
Total noncurrent liabilities		645,102	805,762
Total liabilities		1,171,892	1,300,113
Net assets (notes 7 and 8):			
Without donor restrictions net assets		1,016,509	710,028
With donor restrictions net assets		1,683,781	1,658,359
Total net assets		2,700,290	2,368,387
Commitments and contingencies (notes 4, 5, 6, 10, 11)			
Total liabilities and net assets	$	3,872,182	3,668,500

THE AMERICAN NATIONAL RED CROSS

Consolidated Statement of Activities

Year ended June 30, 2022

(With summarized information for the year ended June 30, 2021)

(In thousands)

	Without donor restrictions	With donor restrictions	Totals 2022	2021
Operating revenues and gains:				
Contributions:				
Corporate, foundation and individual giving	$ 254,678	577,434	832,112	529,405
United Way and other federated	5,292	16,857	22,149	23,719
Contracts, including federal government	5,687	52,957	58,644	180,817
Legacies and bequests	89,593	25,457	115,050	100,912
Services and materials	16,637	36,981	53,618	55,096
Products and services:				
Biomedical Services	1,883,092	—	1,883,092	1,883,815
Program materials	135,663	—	135,663	115,800
Investment return, net (note 4)	1,729	46,976	48,705	63,924
Other revenues	69,422	69	69,491	177,156
Net assets released from restrictions	634,694	(634,694)	—	—
Total operating revenues and gains	3,096,487	122,037	3,218,524	3,130,644
Operating expenses:				
Program services:				
Services to the Armed Forces	69,074	—	69,074	55,201
Biomedical Services	2,022,534	—	2,022,534	1,834,750
Community Services	28,383	—	28,383	22,995
Domestic Disaster Services	443,229	—	443,229	503,552
Training Services	118,082	—	118,082	102,394
International Relief and Development Services	116,434	—	116,434	69,105
Total program services	2,797,736	—	2,797,736	2,587,997
Supporting services:				
Fundraising	188,885	—	188,885	165,392
Management and general	97,856	—	97,856	83,097
Total supporting services	286,741	—	286,741	248,489
Total operating expenses	3,084,477	—	3,084,477	2,836,486
Change in net assets from operations	12,010	122,037	134,047	294,158
Nonoperating investment return, net (note 4)	(14,508)	(96,615)	(111,123)	277,710
Pension-related changes other than net periodic benefit cost (note 10)	308,979	—	308,979	(15,696)
Change in net assets	306,481	25,422	331,903	556,172
Net assets, beginning of year	710,028	1,658,359	2,368,387	1,812,215
Net assets, end of year	$ 1,016,509	1,683,781	2,700,290	2,368,387

See accompanying notes to consolidated financial statements.

THE AMERICAN NATIONAL RED CROSS

Consolidated Statement of Functional Expenses

Year ended June 30, 2022
(With summarized information for the year ended June 30, 2021)

(In thousands)

	Program services						
	Service to Armed Forces	Biomedical Services	Community Services	Domestic Disaster Services	Training Services	International Relief and Development Services	Total program services
Salaries and wages	$ 30,656	772,611	11,782	120,538	46,855	13,135	995,577
Employee benefits	15,929	401,446	6,122	62,632	24,345	6,825	517,299
Subtotal	46,585	1,174,057	17,904	183,170	71,200	19,960	1,512,876
Travel and maintenance	843	18,708	88	22,735	1,332	795	44,501
Equipment maintenance and rental	413	43,660	456	9,533	178	251	54,491
Supplies and materials	1,304	277,178	1,106	3,697	15,624	236	299,145
Contractual services	6,951	446,097	3,791	58,673	26,435	3,961	545,908
Financial and material assistance	11,412	2,416	3,825	153,592	932	91,203	263,380
Depreciation and amortization	1,566	60,418	1,213	11,829	2,381	28	77,435
Total expenses	$ 69,074	2,022,534	28,383	443,229	118,082	116,434	2,797,736

	Supporting services			Total expenses	
	Fundraising	Management and general	Total supporting services	2022	2021
Salaries and wages	$ 84,248	44,998	129,246	1,124,823	1,077,306
Employee benefits	43,775	23,381	67,156	584,455	274,742
Subtotal	128,023	68,379	196,402	1,709,278	1,352,048
Travel and maintenance	1,332	434	1,766	46,267	35,114
Equipment maintenance and rental	971	921	1,892	56,383	61,023
Supplies and materials	1,888	421	2,309	301,454	279,184
Contractual services	51,284	25,919	77,203	623,111	719,709
Financial and material assistance	370	783	1,153	264,533	307,336
Depreciation and amortization	5,017	999	6,016	83,451	82,072
Total expenses	$ 188,885	97,856	286,741	3,084,477	2,836,486

See accompanying notes to the consolidated financial statements.

THE AMERICAN NATIONAL RED CROSS

Notes to Consolidated Financial Statements

June 30, 2022

(With summarized information for the year ended June 30, 2021)

The Organization reports contributions in the donor restricted net asset class if they are received with donor stipulations as to their use and/or time. When a donor restriction expires, that is, when a stipulated time restriction ends or purpose restriction is accomplished, net assets with donor restriction are released and reclassified to net assets without donor restriction in the consolidated statement of activities.

Donor-restricted contributions are initially reported as net assets with donor restrictions, even if it is anticipated such restrictions will be met in the current reporting period, except for conditional grants discussed in note (1)(n)(v).

(ii) *Revenue from Contracts with Customers*

Revenue is recognized when control of the promised goods or services is transferred to customers, in an amount that reflects the consideration the Organization expects to be entitled to in exchange for those goods or services. Revenue from contracts with customers is disaggregated between Biomedical and Program Materials on the consolidated statement of activities.

(iii) *Biomedical Revenues*

Biomedical provides goods (blood products for hospitals) and related services under single contracts with customers with multiple performance obligations. Blood products sold fall under two main categories – Whole Blood Derived Products, which include red cells, plasma, and cryoprecipitate; and Plateletpheresis Products, which include single donor platelets and plasma. Testing services are performed over all products prior to the sale and delivery of the products. Because the blood products and related blood testing services are not capable of being distinct, the products and services are treated as a bundled performance obligation.

For products, the performance obligation is satisfied when the customer gains control over the promised asset, which is generally at the time of shipment based on the contractual terms with the customers. Blood products have a limited shelf life, therefore, any associated refunds or discounts, which historically have not been material, are generally recognized in the same accounting period in which the initial revenue is recognized.

For services, the service has been substantially performed and the obligation met at the point in time at which the service is completed. Services are invoiced once the regulated process is complete and documentation is sent to the customer.

Performance obligations for blood products and blood testing services are generally satisfied within 30 days, and therefore, there is no substantial difference in revenue recognition based on bundled performance obligations.

The expected length of time between when Organization transfers the promised goods or services to the customer and when the customer pays for those goods or services is 30 days. Generally, there is no difference between the amount of consideration promised and the cash selling price of the blood products and services.

8th
Government
&
Not-For-Profit
Accounting

2025년 3월 7일 8판 1쇄 발행

저 자 | 김용석
편집·디자인 | (주) 이러닝코리아
인쇄·제본 | 천광인쇄

펴낸이 | 김용석
펴낸곳 | (주) 이러닝코리아
출판등록 | 제 2016-000021
주 소 | 서울시 금천구 가산동 60-5번지 갑을그레이트밸리 A동 503호
전 화 | 02)2106-8992
팩 스 | 02)2106-8990

ISBN 979-11-89168-44-5   93320